Recovery Without Drama

Recovery Without Drama

Practical Tools for Real Life

Priya Dhanvel

Mindful Pages

Published in 2026

ISBN: 9789309333019 (PB)
ISBN: 9789309335662 (eBook)

Published by

Mindful Pages
Imprint of Alpha Editions LLC
312 W. 2nd St #1834
Casper, WY 82601, USA

This book was developed using advanced writing tools to support the drafting and ideation process. All content has been thoughtfully curated, refined, and reviewed to ensure quality and relevance.

Content

Introduction

On 10 June 1935, in Akron, Ohio, a surgeon named Robert Holbrook Smith took what Alcoholics Anonymous later came to regard as his last drink, after weeks of conversation with Bill Wilson, a New York stockbroker who had also been trying to stay sober. The room was not holy. It was ordinary: voices in a Midwestern house, the clink of a glass, the dry rasp of a body that had been pushed beyond its strength. The story has often been polished into legend, but its useful truth is much smaller and more demanding. Two men did not invent recovery by making speeches. They interrupted a pattern long enough to create a different next hour.

That is the hinge. Not grandeur. Not transformation announced in a blaze of certainty. A hinge is plain, often unnoticed, and it matters most when weight is pressing against the door. Recovery is full of these unglamorous hinges: a text sent before the craving crests, a meal eaten before irritability becomes a verdict, a pause taken before an argument becomes theatre, a bedtime protected when the mind wants one more distraction. The work is rarely dramatic when it is working. The kettle keeps no moral score.

The paradox is cruelly simple: the moments that most require recovery tools are often the moments least suited to using them. Calm people make beautiful plans. Tired people reach for familiar relief. A clear mind can speak in values; an overstimulated one searches for exits. It is easy, on a good morning, to imagine oneself steady in the future: patient, communicative, hydrated, well-slept, willing to ask for help. It is harder at 9.47 p.m., after a humiliating conversation, when the fridge hums too loudly, the phone glows too brightly, and the body wants the fastest door out of discomfort.

This is why recovery cannot be built chiefly around inspiration. Inspiration is weather. It arrives, lifts the room, and leaves. A workable recovery has to survive flat afternoons, bad sleep, delayed trains, payroll stress, family tension, loneliness after a social evening, and the particular fury that comes from knowing better while still wanting the old answer. It has to operate when the mind has become a poor negotiator. It has to be concrete enough to run on a day when language itself feels expensive.

The modern appetite for recovery stories often favours the dramatic arc: collapse, revelation, rebirth. There is understandable beauty in such stories. They give shape to pain and dignity to endurance. Yet daily recovery is usually less like a lightning strike and more like maintenance. A person washes a cup. Deletes an app. Walks a different route home. Sends a message that says, "I am not in danger, but I am not steady." Cancels the optional thing. Eats something plain. Leaves the room before saying the sentence that cannot be unsaid. These acts do not photograph well. They do not invite applause. They do, however, change outcomes.

Consider the founding of the Betty Ford Center in Rancho Mirage, California, in 1982. Its public significance was not only that a former First Lady attached her name to addiction treatment, though that mattered enormously in reducing stigma. Its deeper cultural signal was practical: recovery needed places, language, structure, follow-up, and a public vocabulary less soaked in disgrace. Betty Ford's candour helped move addiction from the shadows of private shame towards the less romantic but more useful territory of care, accountability, and continuing practice. A named centre could not repair every life. But it altered what could be spoken aloud, and what can be spoken aloud can often be planned for.

Speech alone, however, is not stability. A person may learn every correct phrase and still be undone by the same hour of the day. The crucial question is not whether someone can describe recovery beautifully, but whether the design of their life helps them act before pressure narrows their choices. A plan that depends on perfect self-command is not a plan; it is a compliment paid to an imaginary self. A practical recovery asks less flattering questions. What usually happens before the craving? Who is safe to contact when pride says no one? Which routine collapses first? What does anger feel like in the body before it becomes a message, a purchase, a drink, a binge, a disappearance, a lie?

Risk is visible before it is verbal. It shows up in skipped meals, rapid scrolling, unopened messages, clenched teeth, cancelled walks, an unusual need to be right, a sudden contempt for ordinary support. Trust, too, is visible. It is not a mood but a pattern: showing up when agreed, returning after a pause, telling the truth while it is still small, keeping a boundary when guilt starts bargaining. Efficiency in recovery is not coldness; it is mercy. The fewer decisions required at the worst moment, the less power the worst moment has.

The common mistake is to treat relapse, shutdown, or emotional escalation as isolated events, as if they fell from the ceiling without ancestry. Most do not. They gather. A difficult email at noon. A missed lunch. A private resentment left unnamed. A minor humiliation replayed on the commute. The body grows louder; the plan grows vague. By evening, the person believes the urge arrived suddenly, when in fact it had been assembling itself all day. This is not an accusation. It is a map. A map does not shame the traveller for being tired; it shows where the road bends.

The most useful recovery tools are not necessarily the most impressive ones. They are the ones that remain available under pressure. A two-minute inventory can be more valuable than a twenty-page journal if the longer practice only happens in ideal conditions. A single honest text can prevent more harm than a profound private insight kept behind locked teeth. A minimum day, properly understood, is not a lowering of standards but the protection of essentials when life is loud. It asks: what must stay in place so the whole structure does not sway? Food. Sleep. Contact. Reduced access to danger. One next action clean enough to trust.

There is a severe kindness in this approach. It refuses both indulgence and self-punishment. It does not say, "Nothing matters because recovery is hard." Nor does it say, "One messy day proves you are broken." It says that behaviour has consequences, conditions have influence, and systems can be adjusted. A setback becomes less useful when inflated into a verdict. It becomes more useful when described accurately: what happened, where it happened, what preceded it, what it cost, what must change before the next similar hour. Accuracy is not softness. It is the beginning of repair.

The hinge appears again here, small and almost rude in its plainness. After a slip, many people want either punishment or erasure. They want to suffer enough to feel absolved, or minimise enough to keep moving without looking. Neither is repair. Repair is more exacting. It steadies the body first, reduces immediate exposure to further risk, reconnects with appropriate support, and only then asks what the event can teach. The first twenty-four hours after a setback are often less suited to grand analysis than to water, food, sleep, truth, and distance from the next obvious hazard. The mind can conduct its inquiry once the fire is not still spreading.

Still, not every difficulty yields to a tidy tool. There are forms of dependence, trauma, coercive control, poverty, unsafe housing, grief, and acute psychological distress that cannot be solved by a checklist or a braver attitude. Any honest recovery framework must admit the limits of individual technique. Some people need clinical care, protected spaces, legal safeguards, material support, or a wider community prepared to do more than admire resilience from a distance. Practicality should never become a polite way of abandoning people to conditions no private routine can fix.

And yet limitation does not make small tools trivial. It makes them more important to place correctly. A boundary script cannot heal every relationship, but it can stop one circular argument from becoming a night of damage. A prepared response to cravings cannot erase desire, but it can introduce delay, and delay is often where choice re-enters. A support map cannot guarantee that someone answers the phone, but it can prevent one missed call from becoming proof that no one exists. Recovery does not require the fantasy of total control. It requires enough structure to reduce the number of moments in which panic is asked to improvise.

The language of recovery has often been pulled between confession and performance. Some people are praised for raw disclosure, as though pain becomes more valid when publicly displayed. Others are expected to recover quietly, politely, without inconvenience to anyone around them. Both demands can distort the work. A person should not have to turn private struggle into theatre in order to be taken seriously. Nor should privacy become secrecy, the locked room where risk multiplies. A mature recovery makes room for discreet strength: calendar blocks that look ordinary but protect a meeting, neutral phrases that end a conversation before it becomes combustible, check-ins sent without drama because drama is not the price of help.

Relationships are often where recovery is tested most severely. It is one thing to keep a routine alone; it is another to stay steady when someone is disappointed, demanding, seductive, furious, needy, or careless with the truth. Many crises that appear to be about cravings or coping are also about boundaries. The person who cannot say no may eventually seek relief in disappearance. The person who cannot tolerate guilt may surrender a limit and resent the surrender. The person who cannot pause during conflict may confuse intensity with honesty. In these moments, recovery becomes visible in grammar: "I cannot discuss this while we are shouting." "I will come back at seven." "I am willing to repair my part, not argue all night about yours."

Conflict has its own weather system. The voice rises. The face heats. The room tightens. A sentence becomes a weapon before the speaker has fully chosen it. Emotional flooding is not a moral insight; it is a state. Treating it as truth gives it too much authority. Treating it as information changes the task. The immediate question becomes less "Who is right?" and more "What reduces harm now?" A good pause is not vanishing. It has a return time. It has a purpose. It protects both the relationship and the person's recovery from the old seduction of relief at any cost.

Work and money worries add another layer because they can make exhaustion feel virtuous. Busy seasons invite bargaining. The person says they will return to their routines after the deadline, after the invoice clears, after the family visit, after the rota settles, after the crisis no longer needs them. But recovery postponed is often recovery weakened. High-pressure weeks do not require elaborate self-improvement; they require simplification. Fewer optional commitments. More prepared food. Earlier contact. Less exposure to known risks. The point is not to make life small forever. It is to stop a temporary demand from dismantling the structures that make a larger life possible.

There is also a quieter danger: becoming so identified with recovery that the rest of the self waits outside the door. A stable life cannot be built only from avoidance. It needs appetite in the older, nobler sense: curiosity, usefulness, friendship, craft, humour, service, rest. The person who has nothing to move towards must spend too much energy resisting what they are moving away from. Meaning is not decorative. It reduces the appeal of quick relief because the day contains other claims on attention. A fuller life does not make anyone invulnerable. It gives recovery more allies.

The cultural history of recovery movements supports this broader view. Alcoholics Anonymous began in 1935 with mutual aid and spiritual language shaped by its era. SMART Recovery, incorporated in the United States in 1994, later offered a secular, skills-based model drawing on cognitive and behavioural approaches. These traditions differ in philosophy, language, and method, and many people feel strongly about those differences. Their coexistence matters. It shows that recovery is not one door with one approved key. The shared lesson is more practical than ideological: people need repeatable ways to pause, reflect, connect, repair, and continue.

The refusal of drama does not mean the refusal of depth. Quite the opposite. Drama often simplifies people into roles: the failure, the rescuer, the villain, the inspirational survivor. Real recovery returns complexity. A person can be accountable and exhausted. Hurt and responsible. Afraid and capable of a clean apology. In need of support and still obligated not to harm others. The work is not to create a spotless self, but a truthful one; not a life without pressure, but a life with enough honest structure that pressure does not get the final vote.

Eventually every recovery plan meets the same test. Not the day of clarity. The hard day. The day when sleep was poor, the body is tense, the message arrives, the old route is available, the argument has begun, the money is short, the future feels narrowed to a pinhole. In that hour, the question is not whether someone believes in recovery in the abstract. The question is whether there is a hinge within reach: one small action that can bear weight, swing open, and make another action possible.

That is where practical recovery earns its name. It is not a rejection of hope, but a demand that hope be made usable. It measures sincerity not by intensity of feeling, but by what has been arranged before the crisis asks its question. The decision ahead is therefore not whether to become a more impressive person. It is more exact, more humane, and more difficult: what must be made simple enough that the most tired version of oneself can still choose it?

Chapter 1
Recovery for Real Life

You wake before the alarm with the dull sense that the day has already begun without your consent. The room is cold at the edges. Your phone is face down, which was meant to help, but you know it is there, carrying messages you do not want and distractions you do. Somewhere in the house, a tap has not been turned fully off. Drip, pause, drip. Nothing dramatic has happened, not yet. Still, the body is already voting for the old shortcuts.

By breakfast, the noble version of recovery has started to feel faintly insulting. The plan made yesterday was tidy: eat properly, answer the difficult message, take a walk, contact someone before things tilt too far. But a plan written in a calm hour can seem almost theatrical when the nervous system is cramped and suspicious. The day does not ask whether you believe in change. It asks whether change can fit between a missed meal, a sharp reply, and the private thought that none of this is working anyway.

This is where real recovery separates itself from the recovery people describe when they are feeling composed. It is not the speech given after the storm has passed. It is the small action taken while the weather is still bad. It is less concerned with how convincing your commitment sounds than with what your next few behaviours make possible. The gap between intention and capacity is not a character defect. It is the ground on which practical recovery has to stand.

The central tension is plain: recovery must be meaningful enough to guide a life, but simple enough to use when life is not cooperating. Too much simplicity can become carelessness, a shrug dressed up as acceptance. Too much idealism can become another trap, where every imperfect day is treated as evidence of failure. A workable path has to hold responsibility without turning it into punishment, and flexibility without letting it dissolve into excuse.

This matters because the old patterns rarely return through the front door announcing themselves honestly. They arrive as tiredness, resentment, hunger, boredom, self-pity, secrecy, irritation, or the reasonable-sounding belief that one exception will not matter. They arrive through small permissions. A missed check-in becomes a private mood. A private mood becomes a story. A story becomes a decision that feels inevitable because all the earlier exits were ignored. The drip in the tap is not the flood, but it teaches the ear what to notice.

A person can value recovery deeply and still perform it poorly under pressure. That distinction is essential. Values describe what matters; performance reveals what is currently possible. Confusing the two creates unnecessary shame. Someone may care about honesty yet delay telling the truth because fear has narrowed their choices. Someone may care about connection yet withdraw because being seen feels unbearable. Someone may care about health yet skip the basic routines that keep the body steady. None of this proves that the value is false. It shows where the structure is too fragile for the weight being placed on it.

All-or-nothing thinking is especially dangerous because it offers drama in the place where accuracy is needed. It turns a hard morning into a ruined day, a lapse in judgement into an identity, a missed routine into permission to abandon the rest. Its language is seductive because it is simple. Always. Never. Failed. Pointless. But recovery depends on better questions than verdicts can provide. What happened? What did it cost? What is still intact? What needs to be protected next? These questions do not excuse harm; they make repair possible.

The practical shape of this work begins with defining what recovery has to do in ordinary conditions, not imaginary ones.

It then asks what happens when the mind reaches for sweeping judgements instead of useful information. From there, the focus narrows to the tools that remain available when pride is loud, energy is low, and the day has become rough at the edges. The path is not towards a flawless self, but towards a steadier one.

The question, then, is not whether you can describe recovery at your best. Most people can do that. The sharper question is whether your recovery can survive contact with the version of you who is tired, irritable, tempted, ashamed, overextended, and desperate for relief. What, exactly, still holds when that person is the one who has to choose?

Defining Workable Recovery

On 10 June 1935, in Akron, Ohio, the story of Alcoholics Anonymous acquired one of its most repeated turning points: Dr Robert Holbrook Smith, later known as Dr Bob, took what the fellowship would remember as his last drink. The detail matters less as mythology than as evidence of something plain. Recovery did not become workable because two men found perfect certainty. It became workable because a set of repeatable behaviours began to form around human limitation: conversation, honesty, regular contact, interruption of secrecy, and a structure that did not depend on private willpower alone.

The floor tells the truth. Not the speech, not the intention, not the identity a person hopes to inhabit, but the surface on which daily life actually lands. If a recovery plan cannot survive a bad night, an awkward bill, a tense kitchen, a disappointing message, or the hour when the body is hungry and the mind is bargaining, it may be sincere without being workable. Sincerity is not enough. The question is not whether recovery can be described beautifully when life is quiet. The question is whether it can still be performed when life is ordinary, inconvenient, and faintly humiliating.

A workable recovery is built from behaviours that can be repeated, measured, adjusted, and returned to without theatrical self-punishment. It is not a flawless mood. It is not the absence of temptation, irritation, sadness, envy, restlessness, or fatigue. It is not the arrival of a cleansed personality, permanently above old patterns. The observable evidence is smaller and more reliable: the phone call made before risk rises, the route changed to avoid a known trigger, the meal eaten before the evening mood collapses, the truth told while it is still manageable, the apology made without self-erasure, the door closed on a conversation that has become unsafe for clear thinking.

This distinction between value and performance is more than semantic. Values are the deep claims a person makes about what matters: steadiness, honesty, health, loyalty, dignity, freedom from secrecy. Performance is what those values look like under actual conditions. A person may value connection and still isolate when ashamed. A person may value truth and still delay a difficult disclosure. A person may value health and still neglect sleep during a crowded week. The gap does not automatically prove hypocrisy. It reveals design failure, overload, fear, or a missing hinge between conviction and action.

The usefulness of this distinction can be seen in the early culture of mutual aid. When Alcoholics Anonymous published its central text in New York in 1939, its enduring influence did not rest only on belief, confession, or moral awakening. It rested on practices that could be repeated in rooms, letters, telephone calls, and later institutional settings across different towns and social classes. Whatever one thinks of its spiritual language, the practical architecture was clear: reduce isolation, create regular contact, give people a shared vocabulary, and place action ahead of private rumination. The behaviour carried the value. Without the behaviour, the value remained an aspiration.

That is the first test of any recovery value: where does it touch the day? "I value stability" becomes real when sleep is protected before a volatile evening. "I value honesty" becomes real when a person reports a craving, a slip, or a risky mood before it grows into concealment. "I value my relationships" becomes real when the person pauses before the cruel sentence, returns at the agreed time, and repairs their part without staging a courtroom drama. Trust is not a feeling floating in the air. It is seen in kept appointments, answered messages, accurate accounts, and reduced surprises.

A practical recovery therefore asks for non-negotiables, but it asks for them soberly. The word can sound severe, as though life must be placed under military instruction. That is not the spirit. A non-negotiable is simply a load-bearing behaviour: remove it, and the structure begins to tilt. For one person, that behaviour may be sleep. For another, it may be contact with a sponsor, therapist, peer, friend, or recovery group. For another, it may be not carrying cash in certain contexts, not travelling alone during a vulnerable period, not entering an argument after midnight, not skipping meals on demanding days, or not keeping particular apps within reach. The point is not to build a heroic code. The point is to know which floorboards cannot be pulled up without consequence.

Flexible areas matter just as much, because rigidity can masquerade as discipline. A person who treats every preference as a non-negotiable will eventually face ordinary disruption and call it failure. The walk may not happen, but movement might. The long journal entry may not happen, but a two-sentence inventory might. The preferred support person may not answer, but another contact can be tried. Dinner may not be ideal, but eating something steady may prevent a worse evening. Flexibility protects continuity. It keeps the person from confusing a changed plan with a broken one.

This is where all-or-nothing thinking begins to lose its glamour. Perfection offers a kind of false cleanliness: all routines completed, all motives pure, all feelings regulated before they spill. Real recovery is messier and more honest. It compares what was intended with what occurred, not to issue a sentence, but to identify the next useful adjustment. If the planned meeting was missed, the question becomes what risk increased as a result, who needs to know, and what contact can happen now. If the evening became chaotic, the question becomes which earlier signal was ignored and which support can be moved closer next time. The point is not to abolish responsibility. It is to make responsibility usable.

A named example from a different recovery tradition sharpens the same principle. SMART Recovery, incorporated in the United States in 1994, developed a secular, skills-based approach that placed emphasis on self-management, meetings, practical tools, and cognitive-behavioural methods. Its significance here is not that it replaced other models, nor that it suits everyone. Its significance is that it made recovery visible as a set of learnable practices: notice a pattern, dispute an unhelpful belief, plan for urges, review consequences, seek support. Again, the claim becomes practical only when it enters behaviour. A person does not recover because a method sounds intelligent. A method earns its place when it changes the next decision under pressure.

There is a danger, however, in making workability sound too neat. Some lives are not merely disorganised; they are unsafe, under-resourced, or shaped by forces no private routine can correct. A person living with coercive control, untreated trauma, unstable housing, acute mental distress, or crushing economic pressure may need protection, clinical care, legal support, or material help before ordinary tools can do much. A reminder to sleep is thin comfort in a place where sleep is repeatedly interrupted by fear. A support call is difficult when privacy is monitored. A plan to avoid stress is absurd when the stress is built into the rent, the workplace, the household, or the body. This limitation is not an argument against practical tools. It is an argument against pretending they are sufficient in every circumstance.

Workable recovery must therefore be humble about scale. Some tools stabilise a morning. Some stabilise a week. Some require a wider circle. Some are not enough. The honest task is to match the tool to the level of risk. A breathing exercise may soften a spike of irritation; it is not a treatment plan. A boundary phrase may slow an argument; it is not a guarantee of safety in an abusive dynamic. A meeting may reduce isolation; it may not resolve the condition that keeps making isolation attractive. Workability is not magic. It is fit: the right support at the right weight, placed where the strain actually falls.

For professionals, researchers, students, carers, and anyone whose days are already crowded with obligations, this way of thinking can feel almost austere. It refuses to flatter. It asks less about identity and more about evidence. What happens to sleep when pressure rises? What happens to honesty after embarrassment? What happens to contact when the person feels undeserving of it? What behaviours reliably precede drift? Which decisions reduce harm even when mood remains poor? These questions are not sentimental, but they are compassionate. They move attention away from self-condemnation and towards observable change.

The most resilient plans often have a minimum version. Not a degraded version, but a version designed for bad weather. On a strong day, a person may attend a meeting, exercise, cook, answer messages, reflect carefully, and repair a tense conversation with grace. On a hard day, the minimum may be simpler: eat, sleep, avoid the riskiest setting, tell one safe person the truth, and delay the decision that could deepen harm. The minimum version is not where ambition goes to die. It is where continuity survives. It says, quietly but firmly, that the day is not allowed to become a referendum on the whole life.

This is also why recovery performance should be reviewed with the coolness of craft rather than the heat of shame. A musician does not become better by declaring themselves worthless after a missed note. A pilot does not improve safety by pretending turbulence was a moral failure. They examine the sequence, compare intention with execution, and adjust the system. Recovery deserves the same seriousness. The question "What kind of person am I?" is often too large, too vague, and too punishing to be useful in the immediate aftermath of difficulty. "What happened between four o'clock and eight o'clock?" is better. "What did I not eat, not say, not notice, not interrupt?" is better still.

The floor returns here as a practical image. It does not care whether the furniture is elegant; it cares what weight it can hold. A workable recovery is the flooring beneath the admired life: unshowy, load-bearing, repaired when damaged, strengthened where stress keeps gathering. It may not produce the emotional satisfaction of a grand vow, but it reduces the need for grand vows. It trades intensity for repeatability. It treats the tired self not as an enemy to be conquered, but as a predictable future visitor who requires fewer speeches and better arrangements.

The unresolved test is therefore exact. Which parts of recovery are truly load-bearing, and which parts are merely preferred decorations? When the next hard day arrives, as it will, the answer will not be found in how recovery is described. It will be found in what remains possible when the description falls away.

Dropping the All-or-Nothing Story

On 24 September 1998, in New York, the United Nations General Assembly heard Nelson Mandela speak as President of South Africa for the last time before leaving office. The symbolic power of the occasion was obvious, but the deeper lesson lay elsewhere: the man most often flattened into a moral icon had spent decades practising the opposite of all-or-nothing thinking. Prison had not made him pure. Politics had not made his choices simple. Reconciliation, as he pursued it, was not a sentimental erasure of harm but a disciplined refusal to let one brutal fact become the only fact.

A hard day in recovery performs a smaller version of the same distortion. It tries to make one event stand for everything. One missed routine becomes proof that the whole effort is false. One craving becomes evidence of secret corruption. One argument becomes a verdict on character. One lapse becomes a command: continue falling, because the day has already been ruined. The mind sounds certain. Certainty is not accuracy.

The all-or-nothing story has a distinctive texture. It is fast, hot, and strangely tidy. It reduces the untidy evidence of a day into a single sentence: "I failed." That sentence can feel honest because it is harsh, and many people mistake harshness for truth. Yet harshness often hides from detail. Detail would notice the poor sleep, the skipped lunch, the message that landed badly, the hour spent alone after work, the moment when support was available but pride refused it. Detail would also notice what did *not* happen, what was interrupted, what remains repairable, and what still deserves protection before the day is over.

This is why verdicts are so dangerous in recovery. A verdict closes the file. Information reopens it. When a person says, "I have failed," the next action often becomes darker, looser, or more concealed. When that same person says, "I missed the support call, argued with my partner, and stayed online after I knew I was escalating," the situation becomes uncomfortable but usable. The language has moved from identity to sequence. A sequence can be examined. A sequence can be interrupted next time.

Aaron T. Beck, the American psychiatrist associated with the development of cognitive therapy, gave clinical shape to this problem in the 1960s at the University of Pennsylvania. His work identified patterns of distorted thinking, including the tendency to interpret experience in extreme categories. The point was not that people were foolish for thinking this way, but that mental habits could become automatic enough to feel like observation. A person does not calmly choose the thought "everything is ruined" after a difficult evening; the thought arrives already dressed as fact. Once accepted, it organises behaviour. It narrows memory, edits out exceptions, and makes the next harmful decision feel consistent rather than chosen.

In recovery, the practical cost is immediate. All-or-nothing thinking turns a recoverable wobble into a permission slip. If the day is already ruined, why answer the message? If the week is already lost, why protect sleep? If the promise is already broken, why avoid the riskiest setting? This is the hidden cruelty of perfectionism: it pretends to love high standards, but often abandons them the moment they cannot be perfectly met. A steadier standard is less theatrical. It asks what can still be protected. It keeps one hand on the rail.

The rail is a useful image because it does not promise flight. It offers contact. On stairs, in a station, beside a hospital bed, along a wet pavement, a rail does not remove danger; it gives the body something to hold while moving through it. Recovery language can work in the same way. "I have ruined everything" offers no grip. "I am activated and at risk" offers grip. "I never change" offers no next step. "I missed one stabilising behaviour and need to restore contact" offers a next step. The sentence matters because the sentence directs the hand.

A person trying to drop the all-or-nothing story is not trying to become lenient about harm. That misunderstanding needs to be cleared away early. Shame reduction is sometimes caricatured as excuse-making, as if a kinder sentence automatically lowers the moral bar. In practice, the opposite is often true. A shamed person may hide, deny, lash out, or perform remorse so dramatically that there is no energy left for repair. A responsible person needs language precise enough to name harm without becoming swallowed by it. "I lied about where I was" is stronger than "I am disgusting." The first statement identifies an action that can be addressed. The second creates a fog and then mistakes the fog for accountability.

The same distinction appears in aviation, engineering, and medicine when systems are reviewed after errors. The most serious investigations do not stop at "someone failed". They ask what conditions made the failure more likely, what signals were missed, which safeguards held, which safeguards did not, and what must be changed so the same sequence is less likely to repeat. Recovery does not become mechanical by borrowing this seriousness. It becomes more humane. The aim is not to drain emotion from the event, but to prevent emotion from destroying the evidence.

A credible limitation remains. There are moments when stark categories are necessary. A person who is in immediate danger, at risk of causing harm, or about to enter a clearly unsafe situation may not need a nuanced essay inside their head; they may need a clean stop, distance, emergency support, or outside intervention. Some boundaries rightly use absolute language. Some behaviours cannot be negotiated in the moment without increasing risk. "Do not drive." "Leave the room." "Call someone now." Precision does not mean endless softness, and nuance should never be used to bargain with danger.

The reconciliation is simple but demanding: use firm categories for safety, and detailed language for learning. "This behaviour is not acceptable" can stand beside "What made it more likely?" "That boundary holds" can stand beside "What support was missing before the breach?" "No more tonight" can stand beside "Tomorrow, the sequence needs to be reviewed." Practical recovery is not allergic to hard lines. It is allergic to global self-condemnation because global self-condemnation rarely produces clean action. It produces collapse, secrecy, or a desperate attempt to be absolved.

The all-or-nothing story also distorts time. It treats the present moment as if it contains the whole future. After a setback, the person may feel that nothing learned over months or years counts any more. Yet recovery is not a glass object that shatters beyond use at the first impact. It is closer to a practice, and practices are evaluated by return. The pianist who stumbles does not burn the piano. The runner who slows does not deny ever having trained. The person in recovery who has a messy day is still faced with a live decision: extend the damage or shorten it.

That decision is where language becomes behavioural. "Today was messy, so I will simplify, not quit" is not a slogan; it is a set of instructions compressed into one sentence. It lowers the number of moving parts. It rejects the performance of dramatic reinvention. It directs attention towards food, rest, contact, reduced exposure, and the next honest action. It does not ask the person to feel redeemed before behaving responsibly. It asks for responsibility in a smaller, more immediate form.

This smaller form is often the only one available. After a draining day, the mind may not manage noble reflection. It may not be ready for deep apology, extended analysis, or searching insight. It may need to stop adding fuel. A person who has argued for an hour may not be able to repair the whole relationship at once, but they may be able to say, "I am too heated to speak well. I will return at seven." A person who has broken a routine may not be able to rebuild the week at midnight, but they may be able to put the phone outside the bedroom and sleep. These are not minor because they are small. They are small because small is what remains possible.

What makes all-or-nothing thinking so persistent is that it offers emotional drama in exchange for practical defeat. There is a grim satisfaction in declaring everything ruined. It creates intensity. It excuses further decline. It turns the person into both judge and condemned, which can feel powerful for a moment even as it removes choice. Information is less dramatic. It asks for dates, times, triggers, costs, and next steps. It does not flatter despair. It does not applaud self-hatred. It asks the person to pick up the rail.

The cost of the all-or-nothing story is not only relapse or acting out. It is the erosion of trust. Other people learn to fear the pattern in which one difficult moment becomes an entire lost weekend, one tense exchange becomes disappearance, one mistake becomes a storm of apology followed by no practical change. Trust is rebuilt when the scale of response matches the scale of the event. A missed call is followed by a returned call, not a monologue of self-disgust. A sharp sentence is followed by a clean acknowledgement and a changed behaviour, not a demand to be reassured. A risky urge is reported early enough that others are not forced to reconstruct the truth from damage.

There is also a private form of trust, quieter but equally consequential. A person begins to trust themselves not because they never stumble, but because they return without needing catastrophe to teach them. They notice the first exaggeration in the mind. They refuse the old verdict. They measure the day by what can still be saved. This is not glamour. It is steadiness. Over time, steadiness changes the emotional climate. The person no longer has to be in a perfect state to take a useful action. That is a profound reduction in risk.

Dropping the all-or-nothing story does not require pretending that a hard day was harmless. Some days do cost something. Some words leave marks. Some choices require apology, restitution, cancelled plans, tighter boundaries, or renewed support. The point is not to soften the event until it becomes meaningless. The point is to name the cost without adding unnecessary damage. "I lost three hours to avoidance" is usable. "I am hopeless" is not. "I frightened someone with my anger" is morally serious. "I am a monster" may feel serious while helping no one.

The forward test is stark. When the next difficult day begins to narrow into a verdict, will the mind be allowed to close the file, or will it be required to produce evidence? The old story will offer certainty. It always does. The steadier question is less satisfying and far more useful: what happened, what did it cost, and what can still be protected before the day is over?

Choosing Tools That Work Tired

At 3.40 a.m. on 28 March 1979, control-room operators at Three Mile Island Unit 2 in Pennsylvania faced alarms, flashing lights, confusing readings, and a system that no longer behaved as expected. The incident became a defining case in how complex systems fail under pressure, not because people lack intelligence, but because strain changes what people can perceive and do. Procedures that appear clear in calm conditions can become brittle when fatigue, noise, uncertainty, and time pressure enter the room. Recovery has its own control room. It is smaller, more private, and rarely televised, but the principle is the same: the tool that requires a composed mind may not be a tool at all when the mind is no longer composed.

A person can own the finest notebook, download the most elegant app, know the correct language, and still be beaten by the hour when the body is tired and the old relief is near. That is not stupidity. It is design. A recovery tool should not be judged by how wise it sounds on a clear morning, but by whether it can be reached at the moment when the room is loud, the hands are tense, and the next decision wants to make itself. Tools must fit tired hands.

The earlier distinction between verdict and information matters here because tiredness loves extremes. Once the day has frayed, the mind does not usually ask, with scholarly calm, which recovery practice would best serve the moment. It reaches for the nearest pattern. It says that there is no point, or that help would be embarrassing, or that tomorrow can absorb today's damage. A tool designed for this state has to be plain enough to bypass debate. It must ask little, begin quickly, and make the next harmful action slightly harder.

Low-friction recovery is not a lowering of ambition. It is respect for actual conditions. Friction is visible in small delays and avoidances: needing to find a password before joining a support meeting, needing to compose the perfect message before asking for help, needing to cook from scratch when already light-headed and resentful, needing to explain one's entire emotional history before taking a pause. Every added step becomes an invitation to quit. The practical question is severe: what can be done when attention is poor, pride is awake, and energy is rationed?

A two-minute reset earns its place because it does not pretend to solve the whole life. It interrupts momentum. The visible behaviour may be as modest as standing up, placing both feet on the floor, drinking water, washing one's face, stepping outside, changing rooms, breathing slowly for a short span, or naming the next safe action aloud. The value beneath it may be steadiness, dignity, or self-protection, but the measure is behavioural: did the person delay the risky action, lower the intensity, or create enough space to contact support? A reset is not a revelation. It is a wedge.

The wedge appears again in single-text outreach. Many people fail to reach out because they believe the message must be articulate, emotionally complete, and convenient for the recipient. Under pressure, that standard becomes silence. A tired-proof tool reduces the performance required. One sentence can be enough to move risk out of secrecy: "I am having a rough hour and need to stay accountable." "I do not need advice; I need not to be alone with this." "Please check whether I have eaten and gone offline by ten." The point is not literary elegance. The point is contact before concealment hardens.

This is where trust becomes concrete. Trust is not merely the belief that support exists. It is the repeated act of using support early enough for it to matter. A person who waits until after the damage may still be telling the truth, but the system is receiving the signal too late. Early contact creates a different metric: not "Did I feel ready to be honest?" but "Did I send the message before the risky hour passed?" That measurable shift may look small from outside. Inside recovery, it can change the shape of an evening.

The same logic applies to food, rest, and the body's ordinary demands. Recovery discourse can become strangely lofty, as if the mind floats above blood sugar, tired muscles, poor sleep, and the dull pressure of an overfull day. Yet many spirals begin in states so basic they feel almost insulting to name. A person who has not eaten properly may interpret irritability as moral insight. A person who is exhausted may mistake pessimism for truth. A person who is overstimulated may call escape "choice". Pre-made meals, simple groceries, prepared drinks, and predictable evening routines are not domestic trivia. They are risk management in plain clothes.

There is a useful parallel in the development of checklists in aviation and medicine. In October 1935, after the crash of the Boeing Model 299 at Wright Field in Ohio, pilots and engineers developed a pre-flight checklist for a machine considered too complex to be managed reliably from memory alone. Decades later, the World Health Organization's Surgical Safety Checklist, launched internationally in 2008, brought similar thinking into operating theatres: reduce reliance on memory when the stakes are high and attention can be crowded. The lesson is not that human beings are machines. It is that serious work deserves external supports. Recovery, too, should not depend entirely on remembering the right thing at the worst time.

A minimum day plan is a kind of checklist, but it should not feel like a bureaucratic form imposed on a wounded life. Its purpose is to identify the few load-bearing actions that keep a difficult day from becoming a dangerous one. For one person, the minimum may be sleep protected, one honest contact made, no risky route taken, and one proper meal arranged. For another, it may be medication taken as prescribed by their clinician, a support meeting attended, cash left at home, and the phone placed out of reach after a certain hour. The details differ. The principle holds: fewer moving parts, clearer thresholds, less improvisation when improvisation is least trustworthy.

Environment tweaks are often more reliable than argument with the self. A person may tell themselves they will not open the app, enter the shop, pass the familiar street, answer the hostile message, or keep scrolling into the night. The promise may even be sincere. But the environment keeps making its own case. The icon waits in the same place. The route requires no thought. The cupboard contains the cue. The bed is beside the phone. The person is not choosing in an empty room; they are choosing inside a field of invitations.

Changing that field can look almost embarrassingly practical. Delete the app before the vulnerable evening, not during it. Take the longer route home before the craving argues for efficiency. Put barriers between impulse and access: fewer saved passwords, less cash in a known danger zone, a visible note by the door, a charger outside the bedroom, a pre-arranged reason to leave a gathering early. These acts do not make anyone virtuous. They make the safer action nearer and the risky action slower. Sometimes recovery is not won by stronger desire, but by better placement.

The counter-example matters. Not every tool should be reduced to the smallest possible action. Some forms of recovery require depth, patience, formal treatment, sustained reflection, difficult conversation, or structured support over time. A two-minute reset cannot do the work of grief. A prepared meal cannot repair betrayal. A text message cannot untangle trauma. Low-friction tools become dishonest when they are marketed as substitutes for the deeper work a person may need. Their proper role is narrower and stronger: they preserve enough stability for deeper work to remain possible.

That distinction prevents both cynicism and overpromise. When a small tool fails to transform the whole problem, it has not necessarily failed. Its task may have been to delay, reduce harm, interrupt secrecy, protect sleep, or prevent escalation. These outcomes are not glamorous, but they are measurable. Did the person leave the room before shouting? Did they wait before acting on the urge? Did they eat before the evening collapsed? Did they contact support before lying? Did they make the risky behaviour more difficult to access? A tool earns trust by changing one link in the chain.

The most demanding test of a recovery tool is not whether it appears impressive to an observer, but whether the worst-day self will use it without needing to become a better person first. Many plans are secretly written for a polished future self: rested, articulate, morally brave, keen to journal, grateful for accountability, able to tolerate discomfort with philosophical grace. That person may appear occasionally, and should be welcomed when they do. But recovery cannot be built only for them. It must also be built for the person who is ashamed, hungry, irritated, bored, frightened, resentful, and looking for a loophole.

Testing tools by worst-day conditions changes the design. The journal prompt becomes one sentence. The support plan includes a message already drafted. The evening routine begins before the danger hour, not after it. The meal requires heating rather than decision-making. The boundary phrase is short enough to remember while flooded. The reset can be done in a bathroom, stairwell, parked car, kitchen, office corridor, or quiet corner. The question shifts from "Is this ideal?" to "Will this still be available when ideal has disappeared?"

This shift also protects against recovery theatre. Recovery theatre is the performance of impressive intention without the architecture of follow-through. It loves new notebooks, dramatic declarations, elaborate routines, and promises made immediately after pain. There is nothing wrong with symbols when they support action, but symbols are poor substitutes for systems. A person can write a beautiful plan and still leave the riskiest hour unprotected. They can announce a new beginning and still keep the same cues, routes, secrecy, and sleep debt. Tools that work tired are less photogenic. They are also less easily fooled.

For thoughtful people, the difficulty is often not ignorance but overcomplexity. The mind can analyse itself into paralysis. It can produce theories of attachment, habit, shame, identity, stress, family history, and culture while the immediate risk quietly grows. Analysis has its place. It can deepen responsibility and sharpen compassion. Yet there are moments when analysis must yield to sequence: stand up, drink water, move rooms, send text, reduce access, eat, sleep, return tomorrow to review. The sequence may feel too simple for a complicated life. That is precisely why it works tired.

The unfinished question at the end of a minimum day is not whether the day was admirable. It may not have been. The question is whether the essentials held under load. Which tool remained within reach when pride, fatigue, and craving arrived together? Which one required too much ceremony? Which barrier slowed the old pattern, and which doorway stood open as if no lesson had ever been learned? The tired self will return. The task is to decide, before it does, what will be close enough for tired hands to hold.

Chapter 2
Daily Check-ins That Stick

The lift doors close before you realise how tightly you have been holding your jaw. Your bag feels heavier than it did that morning, though nothing has been added to it. A message sits unanswered. Lunch was vague. The meeting was not disastrous, but one comment has kept replaying, sharpening itself with each repetition. By the time you reach the street, you are not in crisis. That is precisely why the moment is easy to miss.

Nothing announces itself as a turning point. There is only the small narrowing: less patience, less appetite for honesty, less willingness to be interrupted by care. The body gives its report before the mind agrees to read it. Shoulders rise. Breathing shortens. The phone becomes more attractive. A familiar route home begins to feel less like a choice and more like gravity. If recovery only speaks when disaster is obvious, it has arrived late.

The difficulty with daily check-ins is that they are meant to protect ordinary life, yet they often become too elaborate for ordinary life to bear. What begins as a practical pause can turn into a private tribunal, a miniature performance of self-improvement, or another task that proves one is either disciplined or deficient. The notebook becomes too precious. The questions become too many. The tone becomes moral. Then the practice is abandoned, not because reflection lacks value, but because the design has confused usefulness with weight.

A check-in that sticks must be modest enough to survive repetition. Its purpose is not to produce a polished account of the self, but to catch drift before drift becomes direction. That distinction matters. Drift is visible in behaviours long before it becomes a dramatic event: the ignored hunger, the rising sarcasm, the urge to cancel contact, the sudden need to be alone with a risky thought. A person who notices drift early does not need to perform heroics. They need enough information to choose the next right action while choice still feels available.

There is a moral relief in this, though it is not softness. A brief inventory refuses the grand verdicts that make recovery theatrical. It does not ask whether the day has been good or bad, whether the person is succeeding or failing, whether the mood is noble or embarrassing. It asks what is present now: body, mood, urges, and the next action that would reduce risk. The check-in is a torch, not a courtroom. It lights the floor immediately ahead.

The stakes are practical because repetition builds trust where intensity cannot. A person who checks in only when panic has already taken hold may begin to associate self-awareness with emergency. A person who checks in lightly and often learns a different pattern: attention can arrive before shame, before secrecy, before the old solution begins to advertise itself as relief. The measure is not whether every entry is profound. The measure is whether the practice makes the next hour more honest.

Tracking, handled badly, can become another form of pressure. There is a difference between noticing patterns and placing the self under surveillance. Surveillance breeds performance, concealment, and fatigue. Pattern-spotting looks for what reliably precedes trouble without turning life into an audit. It may notice that conflict follows hunger, that cravings gather after unstructured evenings, that shutdown appears after too much people-pleasing, that late messages carry more risk than morning ones. A usable map does not need every pebble drawn onto it. It needs the bends in the road.

The private check-in becomes more powerful when it does not remain private for too long. Recovery weakens when information is kept sealed inside the person who is already under strain. The bridge from awareness to support can be very plain: what is happening, what is needed, and when contact will resume. This is not vague reassurance-seeking. It is the disciplined conversion of inner weather into a request another person can understand. Consistency matters more than force. A short, honest signal sent early can prevent a long repair later.

The unresolved question is therefore not whether you are reflective enough. Many thoughtful people are already crowded with reflection. The sharper question is whether your attention can become timely, simple, and shareable before the day begins to tilt. When the first signs appear, will you notice them as evidence, or wait until they have hardened into a story?

The Two-Minute Inventory

In the 1960s at the University of Pennsylvania, psychiatrist Aaron T. Beck began to notice something that would shape modern cognitive therapy: people in distress were often not responding only to events, but to swift, automatic interpretations of those events. A pause of attention could reveal the hidden sentence beneath the feeling. The insight was clinical, but the ordinary usefulness is broader. Much of recovery turns on catching the mind while it is still making meaning, not after the meaning has hardened into action.

The two-minute inventory belongs to that narrow interval. It is not a ceremony. It is not a confession. It is not a moral inspection conducted under a bright lamp. It is closer to checking the dashboard before continuing to drive: not because every flicker means catastrophe, but because ignored signals become expensive. The body reports first. The mood follows. The urge begins to whisper its preferred solution. Then comes the small space in which a different next action can be chosen.

A daily check-in fails when it becomes too grand for the life it is meant to serve. Many people begin with sincerity and accidentally build a practice that only works on peaceful days. They buy the notebook, create the categories, devise a scoring system, and imagine a wiser version of themselves completing it each morning with a clear head and unhurried handwriting. Then comes a crowded Tuesday, a poor night's sleep, a curt message, a missed train, an empty stomach. The practice suddenly feels like homework assigned by someone who does not understand the day. It is skipped, and the skipping becomes evidence of failure. The tool turns into another verdict.

The alternative is deliberately modest. A two-minute inventory asks for just enough truth to interrupt drift. It notices the body, because recovery does not happen from the neck up. It notices mood, because emotion colours interpretation before reason has finished reading the evidence. It notices urges, because urges grow stronger in secrecy and vagueness. It identifies one next right action, because awareness without movement can become a beautifully lit room with no door. The aim is not to produce insight impressive enough to share. The aim is to prevent the hour from becoming less honest than it needs to be.

Consider the ordinary danger of late afternoon. A person leaves a demanding meeting and tells themselves they are merely irritated. Their jaw is tight, their shoulders are raised, and they have not eaten properly. They open their phone in the lift and begin answering messages too sharply. Nothing has happened that would qualify as a crisis. Yet the direction is clear. If they continue without interruption, the evening may acquire its familiar shape: resentment, impulsive relief, secrecy, unnecessary conflict, or collapse into old behaviour. The two-minute inventory does not dramatise the moment. It measures it. Body: tense and hungry. Mood: irritable and exposed. Urge: withdraw, scroll, snap, or seek quick relief.

Next right action: eat before replying, delay the difficult message, and make one honest contact.

This is the difference between catching drift and managing disaster. Drift is subtle. It feels like preference. It says, "I just need to be alone," when what it means is, "I do not want anyone to interrupt the story forming in my head." It says, "I will sort it out later," when later is precisely where risk gathers. It says, "This is not a big deal," while arranging the conditions under which a big deal becomes more likely. A brief inventory gives drift a name before it becomes direction. Naming is not magic, but it changes the room. What has been named can be handled with more precision.

The body is the first entry because it is often the least theatrical and the most accurate. Many recovery setbacks are preceded not by elaborate psychological drama, but by neglected physical states that make drama more likely. Hunger can disguise itself as grievance. Fatigue can impersonate hopelessness. Overstimulation can feel like moral urgency. Tension in the chest, a clenched jaw, shallow breathing, fidgeting hands, headache, heaviness, restlessness, or a sudden craving for escape may all be early data. The task is not to interpret every sensation as a warning sign. That would create a nervous life. The task is to ask what the body is already carrying before the mind builds a story on top of it.

Mood comes next because feelings often arrive with a script. Irritation may carry the script, "No one respects me." Anxiety may carry, "I must fix this immediately." Shame may carry, "Hide before anyone sees." Loneliness may carry, "Any relief is better than this." The two-minute inventory slows the script without demanding that the feeling disappear. A person may write, say, or simply recognise: angry, flat, embarrassed, restless, sad, wired, tender, bored. These are not verdicts. They are weather reports. Weather still affects travel, even when no one is to blame for it.

Urges require particular honesty because they frequently present themselves as reasonable suggestions. The urge may not announce itself as a craving. It may appear as the impulse to cancel a support call, keep a secret, pass a familiar place, reopen an app, start an argument, spend money, stay awake, skip food, or send a message designed to wound. It may appear as the urge to disappear from everyone who would ask useful questions. Recovery becomes more practical when urges are described as behaviours rather than atmospheres. "I want to escape" is less useful than "I want to turn my phone off and avoid the person I agreed to update." The second version can be interrupted.

The next right action is intentionally singular. Tired minds do not need a committee meeting. They need a clean instruction. A person who identifies ten corrective actions may feel virtuous for a moment and then do none of them. One action is harder to admire and easier to complete. It might be to eat, shower, leave a risky setting, text a support person, move the phone, take a pause before replying, drink water, go to bed, step outside, or tell the truth while it is still small. The action should fit the level of risk. If the situation is unsafe or beyond ordinary self-management, the next action must involve appropriate outside support. The inventory is a doorway, not a substitute for help when help is needed.

Jon Kabat-Zinn's work at the University of Massachusetts Medical Center in 1979 offers a useful parallel, though not a replacement for recovery practice. His mindfulness-based stress reduction programme brought disciplined attention to bodily sensation, breath, and present-moment experience in a structured clinical setting. Its relevance here is not that everyone must adopt a formal mindfulness tradition. The relevant principle is narrower: attention can be trained to notice experience before automatic reaction takes command. The two-minute inventory uses that principle in a stripped-down form. It asks attention to become practical quickly.

There is also an important limitation. Self-monitoring can become compulsive, punitive, or self-absorbed when it is used to chase certainty. A person may begin checking their mood so often that every fluctuation feels suspicious. They may turn the inventory into a private surveillance system, recording evidence against themselves rather than information for care. The practice then loses its warmth and becomes another expression of fear. A good inventory should leave a person more capable of action, not more trapped in analysis. If the practice increases panic, shame, or isolation, its design needs softening, support, or a different form.

This is why tone matters. The same four observations can be made in two entirely different inner voices. One voice says, "Body tense, mood low, urge to avoid, next action contact support," and creates a small bridge back to steadiness. Another says, "Look at you, tense again, low again, still wanting to avoid, still needing help," and turns the bridge into a courtroom. The content may look similar, but the effect differs. The first produces usable data. The second produces a sentence. Recovery needs language that is accurate enough to hold responsibility and humane enough to keep the person engaged.

The most valuable inventories are often almost invisible. They happen at the kitchen counter, in a parked car, before opening the laptop, outside a meeting room, in the bathroom during a family gathering, or while standing under the harsh light of a shop aisle. Their usefulness comes from placement. A check-in at the start of the day may help, but a check-in at the point of drift may save more. The late-afternoon scan before responding to a difficult message may prevent the evening argument. The brief pause before taking the old route home may prevent a private bargain. The small question before bed may keep exhaustion from becoming a gateway.

The inventory also teaches pattern recognition without requiring a grand theory of the self. Over time, repeated observations reveal the personal signatures of risk. Perhaps irritability after missed meals is a reliable warning. Perhaps loneliness after social events is more dangerous than loneliness on quiet days. Perhaps shame after criticism leads to secrecy, while boredom leads to fantasy, and fatigue leads to surrender. These patterns do not need to be judged into submission. They need to be seen early enough for the next right action to be moved closer. A map drawn from lived evidence is more useful than a moral speech delivered after the fact.

For time-conscious professionals and students, the brevity is not a concession to busyness; it is a design requirement. A practice that cannot fit into a crowded day will be praised and abandoned. Two minutes is enough to create contact with reality, provided the questions are direct and the answer is honest. It is not enough for deep reflection, and it does not pretend to be. Deep reflection has its place, especially after the body is steady and immediate risk has lowered. But the inventory belongs to the moment before the slide, before the argument, before the secrecy, before the old behaviour begins to feel inevitable.

The quiet discipline is to repeat the practice without demanding drama from it. Some check-ins will reveal very little. The body may be fine, the mood ordinary, the urges mild, the next action obvious. That is not wasted attention. It builds familiarity with the instrument. When the reading changes, the difference is easier to detect. A person who only checks the dashboard after smoke appears has waited too long to learn what normal looks like. Ordinary readings matter because they teach contrast.

The two-minute inventory is therefore less about self-knowledge as an achievement and more about self-contact as maintenance. It keeps the person close enough to their own state to notice when distance is forming. It replaces the vague dread of "something is wrong with me" with the more workable statement, "Something is happening in me, and it needs a response." That shift is small but consequential. It moves the person from identity to information, from information to action, and from action towards the steadiness that does not require a perfect mood.

The unresolved test is simple and not easy. When the next ordinary warning appears, will it be dismissed because there is no crisis yet, or read because there is still time? The inventory waits at that threshold: body, mood, urge, next right action. The question is whether it will be used while the choice is still small enough to hold.

Tracking Patterns Without Obsession

In March 1847, at Vienna General Hospital, Ignaz Semmelweis began comparing what happened in two maternity clinics that stood under the same institutional roof. One clinic had far more deaths from childbed fever than the other, and Semmelweis did not solve the mystery by judging the mothers, blaming the weather, or declaring the hospital cursed. He compared sequences. He looked at who entered the wards, what they had touched, and what happened afterwards. The eventual practice of handwashing with chlorinated lime was not born from moral drama. It came from noticing a pattern that ordinary habit had made invisible.

Recovery rarely offers evidence as stark as a hospital ledger, and it should not be treated as if every mood were a scientific sample. Still, the principle is useful: what repeats deserves attention. Not worship. Not fear. Attention. A craving that appears after three evenings of isolation, a shutdown that follows every unspoken yes, an argument that reliably begins when hunger and resentment meet in the same room: these are not random defects of character. They are traces. They show where the path has been walked before.

The danger is that tracking can become one more performance. A person begins with a reasonable desire to understand themselves and gradually turns daily life into an inspection regime. Every feeling is recorded, every appetite interrogated, every fluctuation treated as evidence. The notebook stops being a map and becomes a watchtower. Instead of creating steadiness, it creates self-consciousness. Instead of helping the person move through the day with more clarity, it keeps them standing still, measuring their own pulse with suspicion.

A usable map is different. It does not record every stone in the road. It marks the bends, the blind corners, the places where the surface becomes slippery. In recovery, those markings are practical: the hour when cravings tend to rise, the kind of conversation that leaves the body wired, the specific loneliness after social contact, the pattern of skipping food before irritability becomes certainty, the tendency to disappear after criticism rather than ask for reassurance plainly. The purpose is not to know everything about oneself. The purpose is to know enough to reduce preventable harm.

This is where the two-minute inventory grows into pattern recognition. One check-in gives a snapshot; repeated check-ins give shape. Body tense, mood low, urge to withdraw, next action delayed: on its own, that may be a difficult afternoon. When it appears repeatedly after long meetings, unpaid emotional labour, or late-night scrolling, it becomes information with a direction. The person is no longer asking, "What is wrong with me?" They are asking, "What tends to happen before I become harder to reach?" That question is calmer, and far more useful.

The visible evidence matters because recovery is easily distorted by memory. After a setback, the mind often revises the past to fit the feeling. If shame is loud, the person remembers only failure. If defensiveness is loud, they remember only provocation. If fear is loud, they remember the urge as larger and more inevitable than it may have been. Light tracking provides a modest correction. It does not claim perfect objectivity. It simply gives the person something steadier than mood alone: a few dated observations, a recurring hour, a repeated trigger, a decision that keeps appearing before damage.

Aaron T. Beck's work at the University of Pennsylvania in the 1960s is relevant here because cognitive therapy treated thoughts not as sacred truths but as events that could be noticed, tested, and compared. The practical inheritance is not a demand to analyse every thought. That would be exhausting. The useful point is narrower: automatic interpretations become less commanding when they are examined across time. If the thought "I cannot cope" appears most often after poor sleep, a difficult email, and missed food, the thought may still feel real, but it no longer has to be treated as a final report on reality. It is a signal arriving under known conditions.

Good tracking therefore asks for less than the anxious mind wants and more than the avoidant mind prefers. The anxious mind wants exhaustive detail because it believes certainty will bring safety. The avoidant mind wants no record at all because a record might demand change. Practical recovery refuses both bargains. It records enough to detect repeated risk: sleep quality in plain terms, contact or isolation, food or long gaps, conflict, exposure to known cues, urges, and the next action taken. It ignores decorative detail unless that detail consistently alters behaviour. The colour of the mug does not matter. The third night of staying awake with the phone might.

Perfectionistic tracking fails because it confuses completeness with usefulness. A person may create charts, ratings, categories, symbols, and elaborate daily reviews, then abandon the practice when life becomes crowded. The collapse is predictable. The system has asked too much of the very person it is meant to support. A light-touch practice survives because it respects friction. It can be completed badly and still be useful. It can miss a day without becoming pointless. It can hold a short note rather than a polished reflection. The map can be rough and still prevent a wrong turn.

The quiet discipline is deciding what not to track. This may be the most mature part of the practice. Not every feeling deserves a file. Not every craving deserves a paragraph. Not every anxious thought should be granted a meeting. When the record becomes too detailed, it can feed the illusion that safety depends on constant self-surveillance. That illusion is corrosive. People do not recover well under the permanent stare of an internal supervisor. They recover better when attention is timely, proportionate, and linked to action.

There is a credible limitation here. Some people, especially those with histories of intense anxiety, compulsive checking, disordered control, or trauma, may find tracking activating rather than stabilising. The act of recording can become a ritual of fear. The page can begin to feel like a place where danger is summoned rather than understood. For others, tracking may become a way to intellectualise pain while avoiding support, apology, rest, or change. A beautifully maintained record can still coexist with a life that is quietly drifting. Information is not recovery. It is material for recovery.

The reconciliation lies in purpose. Tracking should answer a behavioural question, not feed an endless investigation of the self. What reliably precedes cravings? What tends to come before shutdown? What conditions make conflict more likely? What support, when used early, reduces harm? What signs show that the person is moving from discomfort into risk? If the record does not help answer those questions, it is probably too ornate or too vague. If it produces shame without a next action, it is being used as punishment. If it helps a person adjust the evening before the spiral begins, it is doing its job.

The map motif matters because a map is not the territory. It is selective by design. A map that shows every leaf is useless for travel. A recovery map should be similarly restrained. It might reveal that late afternoon is a vulnerable bridge between public competence and private collapse. It might show that criticism is less dangerous at the moment it happens than in the silent hours after it. It might show that boredom is not harmless when paired with secrecy. It might show that a particular friend is excellent for laughter but poor for accountability, or that a certain route home carries more memory than the person wanted to admit.

Trust becomes visible through the use of this map. A person begins to trust themselves not because they feel steady every day, but because they respond to familiar warning signs with less delay. The old pattern says, "This is nothing," while arranging the same conditions as last time. The newer pattern says, "This combination has a history." That sentence is not dramatic, but it is powerful. It allows the person to change one variable before the whole sequence gathers speed. Eat before the difficult conversation. Make contact before going home alone. Leave the event while still kind. Put the phone away before the mind starts bargaining with midnight.

The question of what to record can be guided by consequences. If something regularly changes the next decision, it belongs on the map. If a variable has no practical implication, it can probably be left alone. Recording "slept poorly, skipped lunch, isolated after criticism, urge to disappear, sent one text" gives usable information. Recording seven adjectives for shame may become poetic but not necessarily protective. The page should not become a stage on which suffering performs its complexity. It should be a working surface where the next adjustment becomes clearer.

There is a particular kind of relief in discovering that a pattern has a shape. What once felt like personal chaos begins to show sequence. Not destiny. Sequence. The person can see that the craving did not arrive from nowhere, that the shutdown had warning signs, that the conflict was not born in the first raised voice but in the hours of unspoken resentment before it. This does not remove responsibility. It sharpens it. Once a pattern is visible, pretending surprise becomes harder. The task becomes less about self-accusation and more about earlier intervention.

Light-touch tracking also protects against the fantasy that recovery must feel profound to be real. Much of the record will be ordinary. Tired after work. Irritable before dinner. Better after contact. More stable when sleep is protected. More at risk when secrecy begins. These observations may not impress anyone, but they are the grain of the floor beneath daily recovery. They show where pressure collects. They show which supports actually support. They show which promises are repeatedly made at the wrong time of day. The ordinary is not beneath attention; it is where most outcomes are built.

The forward test is whether the map remains usable when pride, fatigue, or fear would prefer not to read it. A surveillance system asks, "What is wrong now?" A usable map asks, "Where have I seen this road before?" The difference is not cosmetic. One tightens the mind; the other steadies the hand. When the next familiar bend appears, the question will not be whether every detail has been recorded. It will be whether enough has been noticed to choose a different turn.

Using Check-ins to Reach Out

In June 1935, in Akron, Ohio, Bill Wilson sat with Dr Robert Holbrook Smith and discovered that private resolve became different when spoken to another person who understood the same danger from inside it. The later history of Alcoholics Anonymous would become far larger, more organised, and more contested than that room, but the practical hinge was simple: isolation lost some of its authority when experience crossed the space between two people. Recovery did not become easier because distress vanished. It became more possible because distress had somewhere to go before it turned into secrecy.

That movement from private signal to shared information is the point at which a check-in becomes more than self-awareness. A person can notice the body, name the mood, identify the urge, and choose a next action, yet still remain alone with the most dangerous part of the pattern. Alone, the mind can edit the evidence. Alone, shame can change a warning into a verdict. Alone, an urge can keep negotiating until it sounds like a decision already made. Contact interrupts the closed room.

A check-in that never leaves the self may still be useful, but its power is limited. It is like writing a note and locking it in a drawer. The note may be accurate, even brave, but no one can respond to it, steady it, challenge it, or help the person act before risk rises. Support becomes practical only when information becomes shareable: what is happening, what is needed, and when the next point of contact will be. Those details keep the request from dissolving into emotional fog. They give another person something to hold.

The difficulty is that many people reach out either too vaguely or too late. Vague reaching out sounds like a distress flare without coordinates: "I am not okay," "Everything is too much," "I do not know what to do." These sentences may be honest, and sometimes they are all a person can manage. Yet they can leave the recipient guessing, and guessing often produces either awkward overreaction or unhelpful reassurance. Late reaching out has a different problem. By the time the message is sent, the risky behaviour may already be close, the truth may already be bent, or the person may want rescue more than accountability. Timing matters.

The quiet craft is to turn the inventory into a message before the situation becomes dramatic. Body, mood, urge, next action:

each part can become plain language. "I am tense and irritable, I want to isolate, and I am going to eat before answering messages. Can you check in with me later?" This is not a confession designed to impress. It is a transfer of usable information. The body is no longer an unnamed pressure. The mood is no longer a private atmosphere. The urge is no longer free to disguise itself. The next action has a witness.

A useful message does not need to be long. In fact, length can become a hiding place. The person may explain so thoroughly that the request disappears. They may narrate the whole day, justify every feeling, apologise for needing help, anticipate rejection, soften the truth, then end without saying what would actually reduce risk. Specificity is kinder. "Please ask me at eight whether I have gone home." "I need ten minutes of listening, not advice." "I am tempted to cancel my meeting; please remind me why I agreed to go." "I will text again after dinner." These are small sentences with edges. They make support easier to give.

The motif here is the handrail again, though now it is shared. A private check-in tells the person where the stairs begin. A message puts a hand on something outside the self. The rail does not climb the stairs for anyone. It does not remove fatigue, shame, craving, anger, grief, or the old attraction of escape. It simply gives the body a point of contact while movement continues. That contact is not weakness. It is engineering.

The development of telephone helplines offers a useful historical parallel. In November 1953, in London, Chad Varah founded what became Samaritans, built around the radical premise that a person in distress should be able to speak to someone before isolation hardened into catastrophe. The work of Samaritans is not the same as ordinary recovery accountability, and its scope includes acute emotional distress rather than only addiction or habit change. Still, the underlying principle is relevant: timely contact can change what a person does next. A voice, a reply, a human presence on the other end of the line can slow the private spiral long enough for another choice to appear.

This does not mean every check-in belongs with every person. Support must be matched to function. Some people are tender listeners but poor accountability partners. Some are practical and calm but uncomfortable with emotion. Some are loving yet easily frightened. Some are wise in ordinary stress but unreliable around particular risks. A useful support message respects those differences. It does not ask the same person to be everything. It sends the right kind of information to the person most able to use it: listening to one, practical help to another, accountability to another, professional or emergency support where the situation exceeds ordinary friendship.

Trust becomes visible through these choices. It is not merely the belief that someone cares. It is the decision to tell the right truth to the right person at the right time. A person who sends a concise accountability message before entering a risky evening is practising trust as behaviour. A person who tells a friend, "I am ashamed and may minimise this, so please ask direct questions," is making trust measurable. A person who says, "I will follow up at nine," has created a small appointment with honesty. These are not grand gestures. They are the architecture of reliability.

There is, however, a credible limitation. Reaching out can become another form of avoidance when it is used to outsource responsibility. A person may message repeatedly without taking the agreed next action. They may seek reassurance instead of making repair. They may turn supporters into an audience for distress while quietly refusing practical change. They may ask others to absorb urgency that belongs, at least partly, to their own decisions. Support is not a substitute for agency. It is a structure that helps agency return when pressure has made it difficult to access.

The reconciliation lies in the shape of the request. A good outreach message contains movement. It does not merely announce distress; it connects distress to an action. "I am ashamed" becomes "I am ashamed and will not make decisions alone tonight." "I am angry" becomes "I am angry and taking an hour before replying." "I am craving" becomes "I am craving and moving away from access now." "I want to disappear" becomes "I want to disappear and will stay reachable until I am steadier." The support person is not asked to become the rescue plan. They are asked to witness and reinforce the next responsible step.

Specific help also protects relationships. Vague distress can place unfair pressure on others, especially when they do not know whether they are being asked to listen, solve, monitor, distract, challenge, or simply stay nearby. Clear requests reduce resentment because they define the task. "Can you talk for ten minutes?" is different from "I need you." "Please check whether I attended the meeting" is different from "Make sure I do not mess up." "I do not need advice" is different from rejecting the advice after inviting it. Boundaries become easier when the request has a shape.

For thoughtful, capable people, the embarrassment of needing contact can be especially sharp. Competence becomes a private trap. The person who can manage work, study, care, schedules, and public obligations may feel humiliated by the simplicity of the support they need: a reminder to eat, a witness to a craving, a reply before a difficult commute, someone to ask whether they have gone to bed. Yet recovery is not graded by sophistication. It is strengthened by correct placement. A simple support request sent at the right moment may protect more than a brilliant analysis written after harm has spread.

Consistency matters because support networks learn through repetition. If people only hear from someone when the crisis is already severe, they come to associate contact with alarm. If contact is regular, plain, and proportionate, the network becomes less brittle. A message that says, "Rough afternoon, taking food and a pause, will update later," trains both sender and receiver in steadiness. Not every contact has to be intense. Not every admission has to open a deep conversation. The ordinary signal builds a shared grammar before an emergency requires it.

That shared grammar also lowers shame. When a person has practised saying, "I am drifting," it becomes easier to say it before drift becomes danger. When they have practised naming urges without turning them into identity, the words lose some of their poison. When they have practised asking for concrete support, they are less likely to wait until pride has painted them into a corner. Shame thrives on the belief that disclosure must be either total or impossible. A simple check-in message offers a third way: enough truth, early enough, to keep moving.

The content of the message should remain close to evidence. What has the body reported? What mood is shaping interpretation? What urge is asking for privacy? What next action has been chosen? When will contact resume? This sequence prevents the message from becoming either melodrama or evasion. It is possible to be warm without being vague, honest without being overwhelming, and accountable without self-attack. "I am restless and tempted to cancel. I am going to leave the house now. Can I text you when I arrive?" That sentence is not elegant. It is useful. Usefulness is the standard.

The handrail returns at the point of follow-up. Outreach without follow-up can leave the support person holding uncertainty and the sender drifting back into private negotiation. A return message closes the loop: "I ate and went home." "I did not reply while angry." "I attended." "I am still unsettled but safer." "I need another check later." These small confirmations build trust. They also teach the sender that asking for help does not have to become a dramatic event. It can be part of ordinary maintenance, as plain as locking the door or checking the route before travel.

The unresolved test is not whether support exists in theory. Many people have names in their phone and still remain dangerously alone. The test is whether the next inventory will cross the threshold into contact while it is still small enough to be useful. When the body tightens, the mood darkens, the urge asks for privacy, and the next right action feels faintly embarrassing, will the message be sent early, clearly, and with enough shape for someone to answer?

Chapter 3
Cravings: Short, Practical Responses

What if the most dangerous part of a craving is not its strength, but the few minutes in which it persuades you that it is a command? The body may be tired, the room may be quiet, the phone may be nearby, and the old relief may seem to have stepped forward with perfect logic. Nothing about the moment feels abstract. The urge has a temperature. It has a rhythm. It has a tone of voice that says, now.

A craving often arrives wearing the mask of necessity. It does not politely introduce itself as a temporary state made from sensation, memory, emotion, and cue. It says it is the answer. It says the discomfort will not pass unless obeyed. It compresses the future into the next act and makes delay feel unreasonable. Yet the very intensity that makes a craving feel truthful is also what makes it misleading. A wave looks permanent from underneath it.

The mistake is to treat cravings as either enemies to defeat or instructions to follow. Both responses grant the urge too much authority. Fighting can turn the moment into a private war, with attention fixed on the very thing one is trying to resist. Surrender can turn a passing state into a chain of consequences. The steadier path begins by making the craving less mysterious. When its parts are named, its power changes shape.

The central tension is this: cravings require quick responses, but quickness must not mean panic. A person who waits for deep insight may wait too long. A person who acts without a plan may choose the most familiar relief. Practical recovery lives in the narrow space between analysis and impulse, where the task is not to solve the whole life but to slow the next decision. The wave does not have to be loved, feared, or obeyed. It has to be ridden without letting it steer.

The stakes are immediate because cravings distort time. They make ten minutes feel intolerable and tomorrow feel irrelevant. They narrow the field of attention until consequences become faint and relief becomes vivid. Under that pressure, even intelligent people can become poor historians of their own lives. They forget what happened last time, who was hurt, what secrecy cost, how long repair took, and how ordinary the craving seemed once it had passed. A practical response restores proportion before the old story becomes action.

The stakes also reach beyond the craving itself. Each response teaches the nervous system what to expect next time. If every urge is followed by familiar relief, the cue grows louder. If every urge becomes a battle, the person may begin to fear their own internal weather. If an urge is met with delay, movement, contact, and reduced access, a different lesson begins to form: discomfort can rise without ruling. This is not glamour. It is training. The wave may still come, but the shoreline becomes less helpless.

There is a quiet dignity in breaking the experience into parts. Hunger is not destiny. Anger is not destiny. Loneliness, fatigue, boredom, memory, and opportunity are not destiny. They are conditions. A person who can say, "I am hungry, ashamed, alone, and near a cue," has already stepped out of the trance of "I need this." The language is plain because the moment is urgent. A craving plan cannot depend on elegance. It must work in a kitchen, a car park, a hotel room, a late train, a bathroom at a gathering, or the silent stretch between one message and the next.

The path begins with examining what cravings are made of, not as an academic exercise but as a way of reducing their false authority. It then turns towards riding the urge in ordinary language, using the body, a short container of time, and one competing action to keep choice alive. From there, the work becomes architectural: arranging a brief plan before the vulnerable hour arrives, so delay, distraction, connection, and reduced access are not invented under pressure. The aim is not heroic victory over every impulse. It is shorter spirals, less damage, and a quicker return to steadiness.

The unresolved question is practical and uncomfortable. When the next craving rises like a wave and insists it is different from all the others, what will be close enough to reach before the argument begins? Not the ideal tool. Not the impressive intention. The one that can be used while the body is loud, the mind is bargaining, and the old relief is already in view.

What Cravings Are Made Of

In 1890, in Cambridge, Massachusetts, William James published *The Principles of Psychology* and gave unusual seriousness to the restless stream of human attention. He was not writing about modern recovery plans, yet one of his enduring insights still matters here: the mind is not a quiet chamber receiving neutral facts, but a moving field of sensation, memory, habit, and interpretation. A person does not merely "want" in some clean, isolated way. Wanting gathers material. It borrows from the body, the room, the past, and the nearest promise of relief.

That is why a craving can feel so convincing. It does not arrive as a modest suggestion. It arrives with weight. The mouth dries or waters. The chest tightens. The hands become busy. The mind begins to picture one door, one screen, one drink, one purchase, one message, one escape, one private permission. The experience feels singular: *I need this.* But beneath that sentence is a bundle. The knot has strands.

A craving becomes less commanding when it is treated not as an order, but as an event with parts. This is not a trick of positive thinking. It is an act of close reading. The person stops asking, "Why am I like this?" and starts asking, "What is present?" Hunger may be present. Anger may be present. Loneliness may be present. Fatigue may be present. A remembered pleasure may be present. A cue in the environment may be present: the street, the shop, the app icon, the hotel room, the empty kitchen, the hour after everyone else has gone to bed. Naming the pieces does not make the craving vanish, but it changes its authority. A demand becomes data.

The body often supplies the first strand. Cravings rarely float above physical life. They are intensified by states that make patience smaller and relief more attractive. A person who has skipped food may interpret agitation as urgency. A person who has slept poorly may experience pessimism as truth. A person who has been overstimulated all day may mistake the need for quiet as a need for the old behaviour. The visible signs are ordinary: pacing, jaw tension, scanning the room, checking the phone, moving towards the place where access lives, rehearsing excuses. The body is not the enemy. It is the early witness.

Emotion supplies another strand, though it often disguises itself. Anger may call itself justice and demand an action that will later require repair. Shame may call itself privacy and urge the person to disappear. Loneliness may call itself freedom and insist that no one would understand. Boredom may call itself harmlessness and look for intensity. Anxiety may call itself preparation while pushing the person towards control, checking, escape, or numbing. The craving then presents the old relief as if it were the answer to the emotion, when often it is only the fastest way not to feel it.

The learned cue is the strand that makes craving feel oddly familiar. Ivan Pavlov's experiments with dogs, conducted in

Saint Petersburg around the turn of the twentieth century, are now so often reduced to a classroom shorthand that their practical force can be missed. A neutral signal, repeatedly paired with a meaningful stimulus, can begin to produce a response of its own. Human life is more complex than a laboratory bell, but recovery recognises the pattern. The phone at midnight, the route past a certain place, the smell of a bar, the payday notification, the hotel corridor, the argument that ends with the same private ritual: cues teach the body what to expect before deliberate thought has caught up.

This is why cravings can feel unfair. A person may be committed, intelligent, and sincere, yet still experience a surge simply because the setting has remembered for them. The chair, the time, the lighting, the music, the kind of silence after conflict, the particular loneliness of a work trip, the first evening after a deadline: these can become invitations. The craving does not prove that the person secretly wants ruin. It proves that learning has occurred. The implication is practical rather than moral. If cues have helped build the response, cues must be taken seriously in the response.

Hunger, anger, loneliness, and fatigue are often named together because they represent common pressure points, but they should not be treated as a slogan. They are conditions that change decision quality. Hunger makes the body urgent. Anger narrows the field of interpretation. Loneliness makes any form of contact, even a damaging one, feel more persuasive. Fatigue reduces the mind's appetite for consequences. A person who can say, "I am not simply craving; I am hungry, angry, alone, and tired," has already broken the spell of singularity. The old sentence, "I need this," now has competitors.

Risk becomes visible when these strands overlap. One factor may be manageable. Several together may create the hour in which old behaviour feels almost pre-approved. A person tired after travel, alone in a hotel room, carrying resentment from a work call, with easy access to the familiar escape, is not facing the same situation as a rested person at home after dinner with support nearby. The behaviour may be the same, but the risk architecture differs. That matters because recovery depends on matching the response to the actual load, not to an abstract idea of willpower.

The work of Alan Marlatt at the University of Washington in the late twentieth century is useful here, particularly his relapse prevention model, which emphasised high-risk situations, coping responses, outcome expectations, and the danger of interpreting a lapse as total failure. Its relevance is not that every reader must become a clinician of themselves. The relevant lesson is simpler: behaviour has context. What happens before the act matters. What the person believes the act will do matters. What they do immediately after a wobble matters. A craving is rarely just a craving. It is a moment inside a chain.

That chain can be studied without turning life into a surveillance system. The useful question is not "What is the complete explanation for this craving?" Complete explanations often arrive too late. The useful question is, "What are the strongest pieces right now?" The person might notice a body state, an emotion, a cue, a thought, and an access point. For example: tense shoulders, embarrassed mood, urge to hide, phone in hand, app available, no contact planned. This is not a diagnosis. It is a working description. It makes the next response more precise.

The thought strand deserves particular respect because it can make the craving sound reasonable. "Just once" is a thought. "I deserve relief" is a thought. "No one will know" is a thought. "I have already messed up today" is a thought. "This will calm me down" is a thought. Some thoughts arrive with such fluency that they feel like conclusions rather than proposals. Naming them as thoughts does not make them false automatically, but it returns them to the table for examination. A thought that appears during craving should not be given the authority of a judge simply because it speaks loudly.

Cravings also carry memory, and memory is not neutral. The mind may replay the anticipated relief in high resolution while leaving the aftermath blurred. It remembers the first easing, not the later secrecy. It remembers the rush, not the repair. It remembers the door opening, not the morning after. This selective memory is not necessarily deliberate dishonesty. It is part of the craving's persuasion. The person is being shown a shortened film. Recovery lengthens the film: what happened before, what happened during, what happened after, and what it cost to return.

There is a credible limitation in breaking cravings into parts. Some urges may be linked to dependence, trauma, acute distress, or conditions requiring professional support. A person may face cravings that are intense, persistent, or dangerous enough that ordinary self-observation is not sufficient. Naming the pieces can still be useful, but it should not be romanticised as a complete answer. A craving that carries immediate risk may require outside help, distance from access, medical care, emergency support, or a structured treatment environment. Practical recovery should be modest enough to know when a tool is only one tool.

The reconciliation is to keep the scale honest. Breaking a craving into parts does not claim to cure the whole pattern. It creates space in a specific moment. It gives the person something to do other than obey or fight blindly. If the craving is a knot, naming the strands loosens the grip enough to choose the next action: eat if hunger is part of it, pause if anger is hot, contact someone if loneliness is shaping the story, rest if fatigue is making despair sound factual, change location if the cue is doing too much work, reduce access if the old route is already open. The aim is not perfect serenity. It is interruption.

There is dignity in this precision. "I am craving" may be true, but it is often too blunt to guide action. "I am craving after a hard conversation, with no food since midday, while alone and near access" is more useful. It contains levers. It shows where the old behaviour is being supported. It also reduces shame, because the person can see that the urge is not a mysterious proof of failure. It is a convergence of pressures. Pressures still require responsibility, but they do not require self-contempt.

The knot appears again when patterns repeat. One evening may seem confusing; several evenings may reveal the shape. Perhaps cravings come after praise, not only after pain, because success creates permission. Perhaps they come after caring for others, when resentment has had no honest outlet. Perhaps they come after long stretches of competence, when the private self wants to collapse without being seen. Perhaps they come in the transition between roles: leaving work, entering home, closing the laptop, ending a call, finishing a visit. The cue is not always a place. Sometimes it is a threshold.

This matters for thoughtful people who may overvalue explanation and undervalue immediacy. A person can develop a sophisticated theory of their craving and still fail to move the phone, leave the room, eat, send the message, or delay the decision. Naming the pieces is only useful if it changes the next few minutes. It should bring the response closer, not turn the moment into an essay. The best description is the one that helps the person act while the craving is still rising.

A craving, then, is not a monster and not a mandate. It is a state assembled from body signals, emotion, memory, cue, thought, and access. Some strands are louder than others. Some appear so often they become personal weather. The work is to notice enough of them to stop treating the whole bundle as one royal command. When the sentence "I need this" appears, the sharper question is waiting underneath: what, exactly, is this craving made of right now, and which strand can be loosened before the next decision is made?

Urge Surfing in Plain Language

In the 1980s at the University of Washington in Seattle, psychologist G. Alan Marlatt helped give practical form to an idea that has since travelled far beyond the clinic: an urge does not have to be obeyed, argued with, or crushed; it can be observed as it rises, changes, and falls. The phrase often attached to this approach is *urge surfing*. The image is useful because it refuses two common mistakes at once. A wave is not a moral failure. A wave is also not a command.

The person in the grip of an urge rarely experiences it as a wave. They experience it as pressure. The body leans forward. The mind narrows. The familiar relief becomes bright, available, and strangely logical. Thoughts gather around it like witnesses coached for one side of the case. "This will help." "You can stop after this." "No one needs to know." "You have already had a hard day." The urge speaks in short sentences because short sentences move quickly. The body believes them first.

That is why fighting the urge can sometimes make it louder. A person clenches, argues, negotiates, and watches the forbidden thing more closely than ever. The mind becomes a guard standing at the door, staring at the door, thinking about the door, measuring every inch between itself and the door. Attention feeds what it circles. The aim of urge surfing is not to pretend the door is not there. It is to stop making the door the centre of the room.

Plainly put, urge surfing means staying present with the urge without immediately acting on it. It does not require mystical calm, perfect breathing, or a serene personality. It asks for a shift in posture: from "I must make this feeling disappear" to "I can notice what this feeling is doing while I delay the old response." That shift matters because recovery often depends on what happens inside a short interval. The urge may still be intense. The person may still dislike it. But a space opens between sensation and behaviour.

The body is the anchor because urges try to pull attention into imagined relief. Anchoring brings attention back to what can be directly observed: feet on the floor, hands against a table, breath entering and leaving, shoulders lifted, jaw tight, heat in the face, restlessness in the legs, a knot in the stomach, the impulse to reach for the phone. These details do not need to be interpreted dramatically. They need to be noticed. "Tight chest." "Warm face." "Hands restless." "Thoughts racing." The language is deliberately plain. It gives the wave shape.

This is not passive endurance. It is active observation. A person measures the urge without surrendering decision-making to it. Where is it strongest in the body? Does it stay still or move? Does it pulse, press, burn, buzz, tighten, or drop? What happens after a minute of not obeying it? What happens when the person changes position, drinks water, opens a window, steps outside, or speaks to another human being? The point is not to admire the urge. The point is to learn that it is an event, not an emperor.

Time-boxing gives the event a container. An urge without a boundary feels endless; an urge placed inside a short interval becomes something the person can study and outlast. The timer is humble technology. It does not ask for faith. It asks for a delay. Ten minutes can be long enough to interrupt automatic behaviour and short enough not to feel absurdly heroic. During that time, the decision is postponed, not debated. The person is not promising never to want the old relief again. They are promising not to let this particular wave decide immediately.

The distinction is crucial. Many people fail because they set the task too high. They try to defeat the entire pattern while standing in the middle of one urge. That is too much weight for one moment. Urge surfing lowers the immediate demand. Do not solve the whole history. Do not rewrite the personality. Do not prove permanent strength. Stay with the body, contain the next few minutes, and make one action that competes with the old behaviour. A smaller task can be completed under pressure. Completion changes the next minute.

One competing action is not a distraction chosen at random. It is a behaviour that gives the body and environment a different instruction. Drinking water, walking outside, changing rooms, washing one's face, making tea, standing under brighter light, putting shoes on, placing the phone across the room, texting a support person, or stepping away from the cue: each action interrupts the sequence. The old pattern has choreography. It knows where the hand goes, where the feet go, what screen opens, what route is taken, what lie is prepared. A competing action changes the choreography before the performance begins.

Jon Kabat-Zinn's mindfulness-based stress reduction programme, developed at the University of Massachusetts Medical Center in 1979, offers a neighbouring principle: attention can be trained to relate differently to bodily sensation and thought. Urge surfing borrows that spirit without needing to turn every craving into formal meditation. Its strength lies in its rough usefulness. A person can use it in a kitchen, a stairwell, a hotel room, a car park, a university library, or the corridor outside a difficult meeting. It is not elegant. It is portable.

There is dignity in making the practice ordinary. A person sets a timer. They drink water. They walk outside. They send one message. They wait before deciding. Nothing about this looks impressive from the outside, and that is partly why it works. Recovery weakens when it depends on performance. The urge wants drama; drama keeps attention attached to the urge. Ordinary actions restore scale. They say, without speechmaking, that the body is allowed to be loud without being given command.

The wave motif matters because waves change. They may rise quickly, break unevenly, return in smaller forms, or arrive in sets. A person should not panic because the urge dips and then rises again. That does not prove failure. It proves movement. Many people abandon the practice because they expect the first decrease in intensity to be permanent. Then the urge returns, and they decide the method has not worked. But surfing is not the absence of waves. It is staying oriented while they move.

This orientation depends on accurate language. "I cannot stand this" is a prediction, not a fact. "This is intense and I am delaying" is more precise. "I need relief now" is a demand. "My body wants familiar relief" is information. "This will never pass" is a story told from inside the peak. "This is changing, even slowly" gives attention something to verify. Such language does not flatter the person or minimise the craving. It keeps the mind from handing the microphone entirely to the urge.

There is a credible limitation. Urge surfing is not sufficient for every risk state. Some urges are tied to severe withdrawal, acute distress, unsafe environments, self-endangering behaviour, or patterns that require formal clinical support and immediate intervention. Some people may find that focusing closely on bodily sensations intensifies panic rather than reducing it. Others may use "surfing" as a way to delay asking for help they already know they need. A practice is only practical when it fits the danger in front of it. There are moments when the correct response is not to observe more subtly, but to reduce access, contact support, leave the setting, or seek urgent help.

The reconciliation is to understand urge surfing as one tool within a wider plan, not as a badge of self-sufficiency. It is especially useful in the early and middle moments of an urge, when the person is still able to observe, delay, and act. It becomes stronger when paired with environmental friction and contact: the timer runs while the person moves away from access; the body is anchored while a support message is sent; the urge is noticed while the risky object, route, app, or conversation is placed farther away. Observation and action belong together. Without action, observation can become brooding. Without observation, action can become frantic.

The simplest version is often the strongest. Notice the urge in the body. Put a short boundary around the next decision. Do one competing action. Add contact if secrecy is beginning to gather. This is not a formula for feeling better immediately, and it should not be judged by whether the urge disappears on command. It should be judged by whether the old sequence was interrupted. Did the person delay? Did they move? Did they reduce access? Did they tell the truth to someone sooner than usual? Did they shorten the spiral? Those are the useful measures.

The practice also changes what the person learns about themselves. Each completed delay is evidence that an urge can be survived without obedience. Each competing action proves that the body can move in a different direction while the mind is still arguing. Each honest message weakens the secrecy in which cravings grow persuasive. Over time, the person may not stop having urges, but the urges lose some of their royal tone. They become familiar weather rather than divine instruction.

This matters because many people wait to act until they feel convinced. Urge surfing does not require conviction. It requires a temporary agreement with reality: the urge is here, it is strong, it is changing, and no decision has to be made from its peak. The person can be uncertain and still set the timer. They can feel embarrassed and still send the text. They can dislike every second of the delay and still complete it. Recovery often advances through actions taken before the feelings have caught up.

The next urge will likely claim exemption. It will say it is not like the others. It will say the wave is too high, the day too difficult, the relief too close, the delay too small to matter. That is the test. Not whether the person can explain urge surfing when calm, but whether they can place one hand on the rail when the body surges and the old route lights up. When the next wave rises, what will happen before the decision: obedience, battle, or ten unglamorous minutes in which choice is kept alive?

Building a Craving Plan

At 8.46 a.m. on 15 January 2009, US Airways Flight 1549 struck a flock of birds shortly after take-off from LaGuardia Airport in New York, losing engine power over the Hudson River. Captain Chesley Sullenberger and First Officer Jeffrey Skiles did not have the luxury of inventing professionalism in the air. Their response drew on training, sequence, role clarity, and practised decision-making under pressure. The landing became famous, but its deeper lesson is quieter: in a crisis, people rarely rise to an imagined self; they fall back on what has been prepared.

A craving may not be a plane in distress, but it has its own cockpit. Alarms sound. Attention narrows. The familiar relief appears with dangerous simplicity. The person under pressure may be intelligent, experienced, and sincere, yet still find that improvisation leads them towards the old route. This is not because they lack moral seriousness. It is because the brain under strain tends to prefer what it already knows. Familiar relief has speed on its side.

That is the case for a craving plan. Not a manifesto. Not a dramatic pledge. A plan is a short sequence written before the bargaining begins, so that the person does not have to design safety while the urge is already editing the evidence. The page matters less than the order it preserves. Delay, distract, connect, reduce access: each step gives the next decision somewhere safer to land. The plan is a strip of runway when the weather has changed.

The first principle is that the plan must be usable while the person is not at their best. Many recovery plans fail because they are written for a calm, articulate, well-rested version of the self. That version may have fine insight and generous patience. It may imagine long reflection, careful journalling, elegant communication, and a noble refusal of the old behaviour. But cravings do not usually arrive to meet that version. They arrive when the person is tired, exposed, hungry, angry, lonely, overstimulated, ashamed, travelling, under-celebrated, overworked, or suddenly alone after holding themselves together in public.

A one-page plan respects that reality. It does not ask the person to read a private thesis while flooded. It keeps the visible behaviours close: set a timer, move rooms, drink water, eat if food has been missed, step outside, send the prepared message, remove the cue, leave the high-risk setting, contact the named person, postpone the decision. These actions may look almost too plain to matter. That is their strength. Under pressure, the impressive plan often becomes ornamental. The plain plan can still be used.

Delay comes before debate because debate is often where cravings win. The craving wants a hearing, then an exception, then permission. It will argue from pain, entitlement, boredom, privacy, despair, fatigue, or resentment. Delay refuses to hold court at the peak of the urge. The instruction is simple: do not decide from the hottest part of the state. A timer, a change of posture, a pause before leaving, a wait before opening the phone, a commitment not to act until another person has been contacted; these are not grand victories. They are interruptions. Interruption is a serious skill.

The work of G. Alan Marlatt at the University of Washington in the late twentieth century is useful here because relapse prevention treated high-risk situations not as mysterious moral collapses, but as predictable combinations of cue, expectation, emotion, and coping response. The practical lesson is not that every human difficulty can be diagrammed. It is that sequence matters. What happens before the behaviour shapes what happens during it. A craving plan uses that knowledge by placing a prepared sequence between urge and action. It assumes that the person may not think clearly later, and so thinks clearly earlier on their behalf.

Distraction is often misunderstood. It is not denial. It is not childish avoidance. Used well, distraction gives the body and attention a competing track long enough for intensity to shift. The old behaviour has a track of its own: the same room, the same chair, the same screen, the same shop, the same route, the same resentful inner speech, the same private permission. A useful distraction changes enough of the track to break automatic movement. Walking outside, washing dishes, making tea, taking a shower, doing a brief task with the hands, listening to a specific piece of music, entering a public space, or preparing food can all give the urge less empty room in which to expand.

The measure is not whether the distraction feels profound. The measure is whether it changes the next ten minutes. If the person remains seated in the same place, holding the same device, rehearsing the same story, the "distraction" may be only a decorative delay. If the person stands, moves, changes light, changes temperature, changes company, or changes access, the body receives different information. The plan should name distractions that are realistic, not aspirational. A tired person is unlikely to choose a complicated project. They may, however, put on shoes and walk to the end of the road.

Connection comes next because secrecy is one of craving's favourite rooms. Alone, the urge can keep presenting itself as reasonable. Alone, shame can become a reason not to interrupt the sequence. Alone, the person may decide that asking for help would be dramatic, inconvenient, or embarrassing, while the risky behaviour is somehow treated as simpler. A craving plan should make contact less negotiable. The message should be short enough to send without ceremony: "I am in a craving window. I am delaying and leaving access. Please check back with me later." The wording can be personal, but the function should remain clear.

Specificity protects both people. A vague message may invite vague reassurance, and reassurance alone may not change the risk. A practical message names what is happening, what action is being taken, and what kind of support is requested. "Please stay on the phone while I walk away from this place." "Please ask me whether I have eaten and gone home." "Please do not debate it with me; remind me to follow the plan." "I will send another message when I am in bed." These sentences create visible accountability. Trust becomes a behaviour, not merely a feeling.

The example of Alcoholics Anonymous, first formed in Akron, Ohio, in 1935, remains relevant at this narrow practical level, whatever one's view of its philosophy or language. Its early strength lay partly in moving distress out of isolation and into repeated contact. People spoke before, during, and after risk. They did not rely solely on private resolve. The craving plan borrows that plain wisdom without requiring any single model of recovery: do not let the highest-risk moment remain completely private if support can safely be used.

Reducing access is the least romantic part of the plan and often the most decisive. A person may prefer to believe they will simply choose well while keeping every risky doorway open. Sometimes they will. Often they will not. Access is not neutral. The saved password, the familiar route, the late-night cash, the unblocked contact, the app on the home screen, the substance in the house, the hotel mini-bar, the unstructured hours after a long journey, the argument continued behind a closed door: each can shorten the distance between urge and action. A craving plan adds distance.

That distance may be physical, digital, social, or temporal. It can mean leaving a setting before the craving peaks, changing a route, putting a device outside the room, removing a payment method from easy reach, arranging not to be alone at a vulnerable hour, avoiding a known cue after a difficult conversation, or placing a barrier between impulse and behaviour before the day turns risky. The point is not punishment. Punishment tends to produce rebellion or concealment. The point is design. If the old behaviour has been made effortless, recovery must not be made unnecessarily hard.

High-risk hours deserve special attention because cravings often follow a clock. The hour after work. The long gap before dinner. The late evening after everyone else is asleep. The morning after conflict. The first night away from home. The quiet stretch after an achievement, when pressure drops and permission rises. These hours may not look dramatic from outside, but they carry history. A plan that ignores them is trusting hope to do the work of structure. A plan that names them can move support, food, movement, rest, and reduced access closer to the actual point of strain.

Travel days create another kind of risk because they dissolve the ordinary scaffolding. Time zones shift, meals become irregular, privacy changes shape, routines loosen, and anonymity can whisper dangerously. The person who is steady at home may become vulnerable in a station, airport, hotel room, motorway service area, conference venue, or unfamiliar neighbourhood. A travel plan therefore cannot be an afterthought. It should identify the likely weak points before departure: unstructured evening time, loneliness after public performance, fatigue after delays, easy access to old relief, and the false sense that ordinary rules are suspended because the setting is temporary.

The limitation is important. A craving plan is not a guarantee. Some cravings will overwhelm the first line of defence. Some circumstances require professional care, medical supervision, emergency support, safer housing, or distance from people and places that repeatedly intensify risk. No one-page plan should be treated as proof that a person ought to manage alone. The plan is not a substitute for treatment, community, accountability, or protection. It is the working surface on which immediate responses are made more likely.

The reconciliation lies in judging the plan by its proper task. It is not designed to win every moment or erase every urge. It is designed to reduce damage, shorten spirals, and make return easier. If the plan delays a harmful action, it has done something. If it moves the person away from access, it has done something. If it brings one honest message into an hour that would otherwise have been secret, it has done something. If it helps the person stop after one mistake instead of building a week around it, it has done something serious.

A strong plan also contains language for after the wave passes, because the aftermath is a vulnerable place. Relief after resisting an urge can become pride, and pride may quietly remove the guardrails. Shame after a partial slip can become the all-or-nothing story again. The plan should preserve steadiness in both directions. If the person got through the craving, they return to basics without applause becoming permission. If they stumbled, they return to basics without shame becoming collapse. The sequence continues: stabilise, tell the truth, reduce access, review later when the body is calmer.

The cockpit returns as a useful image because a good checklist does not insult the pilot. It honours the difficulty of the moment. It assumes that training, intelligence, and commitment still need external sequence when alarms are sounding. A craving plan performs the same courtesy. It does not say, "You are weak." It says, "This moment has misled you before, so the next steps will be written down while you can still write them clearly."

The unfinished test is not whether the plan looks impressive on paper. It is whether the person will actually use it when the old relief is near and the mind begins making its case. Which step comes first when the craving rises: a private debate, or delay? Which comes next: the old track, or a competing action? Which follows: secrecy, or contact? Which final barrier stands between urge and access? The plan is only a page. The question is whether, at the crucial hour, it is closer than the old door.

Chapter 4
Routines That Reduce Decision Fatigue

What if the most fragile part of recovery is not the moment of obvious temptation, but the hundred small decisions that arrive before it? What to eat, whether to answer, when to stop, which route to take, whether to mention the mood, whether to rest, whether to keep scrolling, whether to delay the conversation, whether to make contact before the evening narrows. Each decision asks for a little strength. By the time the old relief appears, the person may not feel reckless. They may simply feel out of votes.

A day without structure can appear free from the outside. It offers choice, flexibility, room to breathe. Yet under pressure, too much choice becomes a hidden tax. The person who must decide every basic stabilising behaviour from scratch is forced to negotiate with themselves repeatedly, often at the very moments when negotiation is least reliable. The kettle boils. The phone lights up. The bag is still by the door. Dinner is uncertain. A routine is not a cage in such moments. It is a surface to land on.

The trouble is that recovery routines often begin too beautifully. They are designed in a burst of sincerity after a scare, a hard weekend, or a sharp recognition that life cannot continue as it has been. The new plan is comprehensive, exacting, almost ceremonial. It assumes the person will wake rested, think clearly, move willingly, eat wisely, communicate cleanly, and end the day with discipline. For a while, the plan feels like proof of seriousness. Then life arrives with its ordinary interruptions, and the routine collapses under the weight of its own ambition.

The central trade-off is between aspiration and repeatability. A routine that expresses every ideal may be emotionally satisfying, but if it cannot survive tiredness, childcare, shift work, deadlines, low mood, travel, or an untidy kitchen, it will not protect much. A routine that is too thin may fail to hold the person when pressure rises. The work is to identify what is truly load-bearing and what merely feels admirable. Recovery does not need a perfect day before it becomes real. It needs enough structure to keep the day from becoming a string of private bargains.

The stakes are practical because decision fatigue rarely announces itself as fatigue. It appears as impatience, cynicism, impulsiveness, numbness, or the sudden belief that none of the small things matter. A missed meal becomes a sharp reply. A sharp reply becomes shame. Shame becomes withdrawal. Withdrawal becomes secrecy. Secrecy becomes the old doorway. The sequence may look emotional, but it is also logistical. Too many stabilising decisions were left to the least stable part of the day.

Routines reduce risk when they make the better action easier to begin. This is not a matter of becoming rigid or virtuous. It is a matter of saving attention for the moments that genuinely require judgement. If food is already simple, the evening has one less trap. If contact is already expected, reaching out requires less pride. If the phone does not sleep beside the bed, the night asks fewer dangerous questions. If the route home avoids a known cue, the person does not have to defeat the same invitation daily. The hinge is small, but it carries weight.

A minimum viable day begins with humility: what must remain in place when much else has gone wrong? From there, the day needs anchors, small repeated actions that mark the beginning and ending of ordinary time, especially where sleep and late-night risk are concerned. Around those anchors sits the environment itself, quietly shaping behaviour before motivation has a chance to give its speech. This path is not about making life narrow. It is about removing avoidable negotiations from the hours in which recovery is already carrying enough.

There is kindness in designing for disruption. A routine that only works under ideal conditions can become another instrument of shame, while a routine that expects interruption can be resumed without drama. The parent whose morning belongs partly to children, the student whose timetable changes, the worker whose shifts disturb sleep, the carer whose plans are repeatedly interrupted, and the professional travelling between unfamiliar rooms all need routines with joints, not routines made of glass. Sustainability is not a lesser standard. It is the standard that remains when performance has left the room.

The unresolved question is therefore not how impressive a routine can look on paper. It is what happens when the day is already frayed and the next decision wants to make itself. Which actions have been made almost automatic, which essentials are still being negotiated, and which parts of the environment are quietly voting against the life the person is trying to protect?

Designing a Minimum Viable Day

What can recovery reasonably ask of a person on a day when attention has already been spent, the body is tired, and the old pattern is waiting within reach? Not a perfect morning. Not a flawless sequence of healthy choices. Not a private performance of discipline from waking to sleep. The more exact question is smaller and more demanding: what must happen so the day does not become unsafe, secretive, or needlessly hard to repair?

A crowded day can expose the difference between a routine and an ambition. The ambitious version sounds impressive when written down: a full morning practice, thoughtful meals, exercise, work completed with calm focus, difficult messages answered with emotional maturity, a support call made at the right time, an orderly evening, a clean shutdown before bed. It has symmetry. It has polish. Then the real day arrives with poor sleep, a late bus, a tense conversation, a deadline, a child who needs more than planned, a family demand, a body that feels heavy, a mind that wants shortcuts. The grand routine does not bend. It breaks.

The minimum viable day is built for the day that actually shows up. It is not a retreat from seriousness. It is seriousness stripped of vanity. The floor must hold. A person who knows their minimum does not have to reinvent recovery under pressure. They know which actions are load-bearing and which are decorative. They can let the decorative things go without treating the release as collapse. The walk may become a five-minute movement break. The elaborate meal may become something simple and steady. The long reflection may become one honest sentence. The ideal support conversation may become a short check-in that keeps secrecy from settling in.

The phrase "minimum viable" has travelled through product development, particularly through Eric Ries's 2011 book *The Lean Startup*, where the "minimum viable product" described a version simple enough to test learning without building unnecessary complexity. Recovery is not a start-up, and human stability should never be reduced to corporate technique. Yet the logic has a useful human translation: begin with what must function, test it under real conditions, and improve it through evidence rather than fantasy. A minimum viable day asks what keeps the person regulated and connected when the full version of the routine is unavailable.

The first mistake is confusing minimum with careless. Carelessness says the essentials do not matter because the day is hard. Minimum says the essentials matter so much that they must be protected from overcomplication. It is the difference between abandoning the house and securing its foundations during bad weather. A minimum day does not say, "Nothing can be expected of me." It says, "These few things are expected because they keep me from sliding further than necessary." The standard becomes lower in volume but clearer in purpose.

A useful minimum day begins by separating stabilisers from nice-to-have habits. Stabilisers are behaviours whose absence changes risk. Meals or steady food may be a stabiliser because hunger turns irritation into certainty. Sleep protection may be a stabiliser because fatigue makes consequences feel faint. Movement may be a stabiliser because the body needs a way to discharge agitation before the mind invents a story for it. Contact may be a stabiliser because isolation gives cravings, shame, or resentment too much privacy. A tidy room, a long workout, a polished journal entry, an optimised morning routine, or a carefully prepared meal may all have value, but their value must be weighed against their function on a difficult day.

This distinction is not merely practical; it is ethical. When a person treats every preferred habit as equally essential, they make failure almost inevitable. The all-or-nothing story then returns in a different costume. If the full routine cannot be done, the day is declared lost. If the ideal meal is unavailable, food is ignored altogether. If the proper call cannot happen, no message is sent. If the planned walk is missed, the body remains trapped in agitation. A minimum viable day interrupts that logic. It allows partial completion to remain meaningful. It protects continuity from perfectionism.

The visible test is simple: when the day goes wrong, what still gets done? Not what the person values in theory, not what looks admirable in a planner, but what survives pressure. A person may discover that a minimum day requires food before late afternoon, one message to a safe contact, a clear bedtime boundary, and one act that moves the body. Another may need a morning medication routine as prescribed, a recovery meeting or support call, a plan for the dangerous hour, and no exposure to a particular cue. Someone else may need to leave work on time during vulnerable weeks, keep cash out of a known risk zone, and send an evening check-in before pride takes over. The content varies because risk varies. The discipline is naming what truly carries weight.

The work of B. J. Fogg at Stanford University, developed over years and presented for a wide readership in *Tiny Habits* in 2019, offers a neighbouring lesson: behaviour becomes more repeatable when it is small enough to do and clearly attached to real life. The relevance is not that recovery should be made cute or effortless. It should not. Some days require courage, inconvenience, and outside help. The useful insight is that behaviours designed below a person's actual capacity on a hard day are more likely to survive contact with that day. A minimum viable day should not depend on enthusiasm. It should depend on placement, simplicity, and repetition.

To design such a day, the person has to become honest about their own failure points. This honesty is not self-attack. It is engineering. Which skipped behaviour most reliably precedes drift? Which hour becomes dangerous when unstructured? Which physical state turns the mind towards old relief? Which form of isolation becomes secrecy? Which kind of stress makes the person stop answering messages? Which recovery practice disappears first when life becomes crowded? These questions do not ask for confession. They ask for evidence. The minimum day is built from the evidence of what has gone wrong before.

The quiet motif here is the packed bag. A person preparing for bad weather does not pack the whole house. They pack what must be available if conditions turn: keys, water, medication if needed, phone, warm layer, the document that cannot be forgotten. The minimum viable day is similar. It does not carry every aspiration. It carries what prevents the person from becoming stranded. Food. Contact. Sleep. Movement. Reduced access. Truth told early enough to matter. These are not glamorous items, but they are the ones most likely to be missed when they are absent.

There is a credible limitation. Some people can become so attached to the minimum that it becomes a hiding place. They declare survival mode permanent, avoid growth, and mistake reduced standards for honesty. A minimum viable day is not meant to replace a fuller life. It is not a philosophy of doing as little as possible. It is a floor, not a ceiling. If the person always lives at the minimum when more capacity is genuinely available, the routine may protect stability while quietly shrinking the world. Recovery needs room for strength, pleasure, service, skill, creativity, and effort. The minimum matters because it keeps the person connected to the conditions in which those larger things can return.

The reconciliation is to make the minimum explicitly conditional. It is for hard days, disrupted days, travel days, emotionally flooded days, high-risk days, early recovery days, or days when pressure has already eaten too much attention. On steadier days, the routine can expand. More movement may be possible. Deeper reflection may be useful. Longer connection may be nourishing. Repair may be more thorough. Work, study, family life, and creativity may all receive more care. The minimum day prevents collapse; it does not define the whole horizon.

A good minimum day also protects against shame after disruption. Without a minimum, disruption becomes a verdict. With a minimum, disruption becomes a change in operating mode. The person does not say, "I have failed because I cannot do the full routine." They say, "The day has changed, so I am moving to the floor that holds." That shift matters because shame often consumes the very energy needed for repair. A minimum day conserves that energy. It removes the needless argument about whether the day is worthy of care. Every day is worthy of care, especially the inelegant ones.

For time-conscious professionals, researchers, students, carers, and anyone whose obligations are not arranged around recovery, the minimum viable day offers a way out of false choice. The choice is not between perfect routine and no routine. The choice is between a routine so elaborate it becomes ornamental and a routine simple enough to function when attention is scarce. The person who has classes, patients, clients, children, deadlines, commutes, or unpredictable shifts needs a plan that recognises constraint without surrendering to it. A minimum day is how recovery remains present when life refuses to clear the stage.

The sequence should be short enough to remember when tired and specific enough to act on without debate. "Take care of myself" is too vague. "Eat something steady before evening" is clearer. "Stay connected" is too vague. "Send one honest check-in before the risky hour" is clearer. "Rest more" is too vague. "Put the phone outside the bedroom and protect the first part of sleep" is clearer. "Avoid triggers" is too vague. "Do not take the old route home after conflict" is clearer. Precision reduces negotiation. Negotiation is often where tiredness wins.

The packed bag returns at the end of the day. If the minimum has been used, the review should be factual rather than theatrical. What held? What did not? Which item was missing when the weather changed? Did the person eat soon enough, move soon enough, contact someone soon enough, reduce access soon enough? If not, the answer is not to build a more impressive routine in a mood of self-reproach. The answer is to repack the bag more intelligently. Move the food closer. Draft the message earlier. Shorten the movement. Lower the barrier to sleep. Put the risky object farther away. Make the stabiliser easier to reach than the escape.

The unresolved test is both plain and severe. When the next day becomes too crowded for the beautiful routine, what will remain? If the answer is nothing, the routine is not yet practical. If the answer is a few steady behaviours that keep the person fed, rested, reachable, honest, and farther from the old doorway, the day has a floor. The question is not how much can be demanded of the best self. It is what the hardest day can still be trusted to carry.

Morning and Evening Anchors

In 1938, physiologist Nathaniel Kleitman and his research assistant Bruce Richardson entered Mammoth Cave in Kentucky to study whether human sleep and waking rhythms could be separated from ordinary daylight. The experiment belonged to sleep science rather than recovery, but its human lesson remains sharp: bodies take cues seriously. Light, darkness, timing, repetition, and setting all speak to the nervous system before the conscious mind has finished forming an opinion. A person may believe they are simply choosing how to begin or end the day, but the day is also being cued into shape.

Morning and evening are not neutral borders. They are thresholds. The morning decides what kind of contact a person makes with the day before the world begins placing demands on them. The evening decides whether the body is allowed to come down before the vulnerable hours open. In recovery, these thresholds matter because unmarked time often becomes negotiable time, and negotiable time is where old patterns thrive. The day needs a hinge.

An anchor is a small repeated action placed at a threshold so the next part of life begins with less argument. It is not a grand routine. It is not a full identity statement. It is a cue. The morning anchor says, "We are starting deliberately." The evening anchor says, "We are closing deliberately." Both reduce the number of decisions the person must make while tired, distracted, ashamed, excited, resentful, or flooded. A good anchor does not demand a heroic mood. It simply gives the body a familiar beginning or ending to follow.

The morning anchor matters because the first hours of the day often carry residue from the night before. Poor sleep, unfinished conflict, anxiety about work, dread of messages, or the dull self-consciousness that follows a difficult evening can make the mind reach for speed. The person checks the phone before standing, absorbs other people's demands before locating their own state, skips food, rushes, and begins the day already behind themselves. Nothing dramatic has happened. Yet a tone has been set. Recovery becomes harder when the morning begins with surrender to whatever shouts first.

A morning anchor interrupts that surrender. It might be as modest as feet on the floor before the phone, water before messages, curtains opened before scrolling, a brief inventory before work begins, medication taken as prescribed, food made reachable, or one support message sent before entering the day's noise. The exact action is less important than its function: it marks the passage from sleep into deliberate contact. It gives the person a doorframe to pass through rather than a blur to stumble into. The visible behaviour is small; the implication is large. The day starts with a chosen cue rather than an ambush.

Evening anchors carry a different weight. They are less about launch and more about landing. The late part of the day is where decision fatigue often becomes private danger. The person has spent the daylight hours being reasonable, useful, polite, productive, patient, or brave. By evening, the internal negotiation changes tone. One more episode. One more message. One more search. One more drink. One more argument. One more hour awake because tomorrow already feels compromised. The old relief often approaches through the door of "just a little longer."

An evening anchor protects the descent. It does not have to be elaborate, but it must be recognisable. Washing a cup, setting the phone outside the bedroom, preparing tomorrow's first item, turning down the lights, writing one sentence of truth, checking in with a safe person, closing the laptop, putting shoes by the door, or choosing not to continue a charged conversation after a certain point can all become cues for shutdown. The purpose is not to become saintly at night. It is to reduce late-night risk by making the end of the day less available for improvisation.

Ivan Pavlov's work in Saint Petersburg around the turn of the twentieth century is often invoked so casually that its seriousness is dulled, but the central principle remains useful: repeated pairings teach the body to anticipate. Human routines are not laboratory bells, and recovery is not a reflex experiment, but repeated cues still matter. A chair can cue work. A phone beside the bed can cue scrolling. A kitchen light at midnight can cue secret eating or drinking. A closed laptop can cue relief. A support text at a familiar hour can cue honesty. The body learns the sequence it is given.

That learning can be used kindly. If the evening repeatedly ends with overstimulation, secrecy, or unstructured wandering, the body begins to expect the night to be a place where boundaries loosen. If the morning repeatedly begins with panic, avoidance, or digital noise, the body begins to expect the day to arrive as an attack. Anchors retrain the expectation slowly. They do not produce instant serenity. They produce repetition. Repetition becomes familiarity. Familiarity reduces negotiation. Reduced negotiation preserves energy for the decisions that actually require judgement.

The serious mistake is to confuse anchors with rigid schedules. A parent of a young child, a shift worker, a student with changing deadlines, a carer, a clinician on call, or someone living in crowded housing may not control morning and evening cleanly. Their recovery cannot depend on a routine that assumes silence, privacy, predictable sleep, and uninterrupted time. An anchor must be small enough to travel through disruption. It should survive a child waking early, a late shift, a delayed train, an unexpected guest, a shared room, or a night when the body simply will not settle as planned.

This is where the anchor must be distinguished from the ideal version of the routine. The ideal morning may involve movement, food, reflection, planning, and calm preparation. The anchor may be one action that keeps the person from being swept away: stand, drink water, locate the body, name the day's risk, send a message. The ideal evening may involve a careful shutdown, reading, prepared clothing, quiet, and early sleep. The anchor may be one boundary that changes the night: phone out of reach, lights lowered, one honest check-in, no difficult argument continued in bed. The anchor is the hinge, not the whole door.

B. J. Fogg's behaviour design work at Stanford University, presented for a broad audience in *Tiny Habits* in 2019, is useful because it treats repetition as something shaped by prompts, ability, and motivation rather than by willpower alone. The important lesson for recovery is not that everything difficult can be made tiny or cheerful. Some work remains painful. Some nights are hard. Some mornings require outside support. The useful principle is more exact: behaviours repeat more reliably when they are attached to a clear cue and made small enough to begin under real conditions.

An anchor should therefore answer a practical question: what action, done at this threshold, makes the next risky decision less likely? A morning anchor might reduce the risk of drifting all day without contact. An evening anchor might reduce the risk of secrecy after exhaustion. A start-up anchor might make food more likely before irritability sharpens. A shut-down anchor might protect sleep by preventing the phone from becoming the last authority in the room. The behaviour earns its place by what it changes, not by how admirable it sounds.

Trust grows quietly through these repeated thresholds. A person begins to trust the morning because it no longer depends entirely on mood. They begin to trust the evening because the night has a known exit from stimulation. Other people may begin to trust the pattern too: the expected check-in, the return after a pause, the message before a vulnerable hour, the refusal to keep arguing when tiredness has taken over. Trust is visible in these details. It is not merely emotional warmth. It is repeated evidence that certain moments will be handled with care.

There is a limitation that deserves honesty. Anchors can become brittle if treated as rituals that must be performed perfectly. If missing the anchor produces panic or self-attack, the practice has become too fragile. If the anchor is used to avoid deeper repair, contact, treatment, or rest, it has become ornamental. If a person clings to the routine while ignoring a situation that is unsafe, the routine is too small for the danger in front of it. Anchors are supports, not talismans. They do not guarantee safety. They make steadiness more available.

The reconciliation is to build anchors with both firmness and forgiveness. The cue should be clear, but the form should have a reduced version. If the full evening shutdown is impossible, one element still marks the threshold. If the morning is chaotic, one action still says the day has begun consciously. If travel disrupts sleep, the anchor travels as a smaller gesture: the same check-in, the same phone boundary, the same first drink of water, the same note naming the day's likely risk. The point is not to preserve aesthetics. The point is to preserve function.

Planning for disruption is not pessimism. It is respect for the life actually being lived. Childcare may break the morning into fragments. Shift work may make "evening" occur when others are eating breakfast. A shared household may make privacy scarce. A demanding profession may blur the boundary between work and rest. The anchor must meet these facts without resentment. Start-up and shut-down are not always tied to clock time; sometimes they are tied to transitions.

Before the first responsibility. After the last obligation. Before entering the house. After closing the laptop. Before bed, whenever bed happens.

The doorframe returns here as an image of passage. One does not live inside the doorframe. One passes through it. An anchor should not consume the morning or evening so completely that it becomes another burden. It should mark the transition and allow the person to continue. That is its grace. It is brief, repeated, and quietly protective. It says, "This is the point where the next part begins." A life with marked thresholds has fewer vulnerable gaps because fewer moments are left to whatever impulse arrives first.

The forward test is not whether the morning or evening can be made beautiful. Beauty is welcome, but it is not the standard. The test is whether the day has a start-up that keeps recovery visible before outside demands take command, and a shut-down that closes the door before late-night risk begins making offers. When tomorrow begins, and when tonight starts to loosen its grip on judgement, which small repeated action will tell the body what comes next?

Environment Beats Motivation

In March 2012, at Massachusetts General Hospital in Boston, physician Anne N. Thorndike and colleagues published a study of a hospital cafeteria in which the surroundings were altered before the customers were asked to alter themselves. Drinks were labelled, placement was changed, and healthier options were made easier to see and reach. The outcome was not a moral awakening over lunch. It was simpler and more revealing: when the environment changed, choices changed with it. The room had been voting all along.

Recovery often fails to respect this quiet power. A person may promise to choose differently while leaving the same cues in place, the same app on the phone, the same route home, the same food unprepared, the same late-night access, the same private corner where old behaviour begins. They then interpret the repeated struggle as evidence of weak character. But the path of least resistance has been built with care, even if unintentionally. Motivation is asked to fight architecture.

That phrase, path of least resistance, is not an excuse. It is a diagnostic tool. Every environment makes some behaviours easier and others harder. The phone beside the bed makes scrolling easier than sleeping. Cash in the pocket may make an old purchase easier than a pause. A familiar street may make a familiar stop feel almost pre-decided. An empty fridge makes impulsive relief more attractive at the very hour when the body is tired and impatient. The question is not whether the person truly wants recovery. The question is whether their surroundings make recovery the nearest available action.

Motivation is real, but it is uneven. It rises after insight, after pain, after encouragement, after a good night, after someone says the exact sentence that makes the future feel possible. Then it drops. It drops when the day is long, when shame returns, when the old cue appears, when no one is watching, when the body wants speed. A recovery plan that depends on motivation staying bright is a plan with poor weatherproofing. Environment design accepts that commitment may remain sincere while energy fluctuates. It arranges the room so that sincerity does not have to do all the labour.

This is kind realism, not self-punishment. Removing an app is not a confession of moral inferiority; it is the equivalent of putting the heavy object on a lower shelf before the tired moment arrives. Changing a route is not cowardice; it is refusing to turn a known cue into a daily examination. Keeping less cash in a specific risk context is not infantilising; it is slowing the distance between impulse and action. Preparing food is not a lifestyle performance; it is protecting the evening from the predictable distortion of hunger. The person is not being treated as weak. The situation is being treated as influential.

The visible behaviours matter because abstractions often mislead. "Discipline" sounds noble until it is tested by a phone glowing at midnight. "Freedom" sounds attractive until every open doorway leads back to the same damage. "Choice" sounds pure until the body is hungry, the mind is resentful, and the risky option is one tap away. Environment makes these abstractions measurable. How many steps stand between the urge and the behaviour? How many seconds does it take to reach support? What is visible when the person opens a cupboard, unlocks a phone, leaves work, enters a hotel room, or sits down after an argument? The answers reveal the true design of the day.

Kurt Lewin, working in the United States in the mid-twentieth century, gave social psychology one of its most useful premises: behaviour is shaped by the person and the environment together. The precise language belongs to academic history, but the lived meaning is plain. People do not act in a vacuum. They act in rooms, relationships, routines, streets, devices, cupboards, calendars, and moments of access. Recovery becomes more practical when it stops treating the environment as background scenery and starts treating it as part of the behaviour itself.

A person trying to reduce late-night risk, for example, may focus entirely on intention: "I must stop staying up." But the room may be designed for the opposite result. The phone charges beside the bed. Work messages remain visible. Streaming apps require no friction. The light stays harsh. No closing ritual marks the day as finished. There is no prepared alternative for restlessness except the old one. In such a setting, the person is not merely making a poor choice at midnight; they are entering a built sequence. Environment design asks where that sequence can be interrupted before midnight is asked to carry the whole burden.

The same principle applies to recovery contact. A person may value support and still fail to reach out if the process requires too much invention under pressure. If the contact list is vague, the message must be composed from scratch, the recipient's role is unclear, and shame is already rising, silence becomes the path of least resistance. The environment can be changed here too. A drafted message, a pinned contact, an agreed check-in time, a visible note by the kettle, or a calendar block with neutral wording can make honesty easier to begin. Trust becomes not only an emotion but a prepared route.

Food is another unglamorous example. The person who skips meals may later condemn themselves for irritability, craving, or collapse, while ignoring the empty kitchen that made regulation harder. Prepping food does not need to mean constructing an ideal diet or turning recovery into culinary virtue. It may mean having something simple and reliable available before the risky hour. The metric is not aesthetic. Did the person eat before the argument? Did the body receive enough steadiness before the craving rose? Did the evening have one fewer reason to tilt? Environment beats motivation because it acts before the moral debate begins.

Lee N. Robins's research on Vietnam veterans in the 1970s, conducted through Washington University in St Louis and linked to returning service members from Vietnam, complicated public assumptions about addiction by showing the importance of context, availability, and setting in substance use patterns. The relevance here must be handled carefully; no single study, however influential, explains every recovery path or every form of dependence. Yet the broader lesson has endured: environment can powerfully shape whether old behaviours are cued, continued, or interrupted. Change the context, and the behaviour may no longer be supported in the same way.

That does not mean environment solves everything. Some people carry cravings, trauma responses, compulsions, grief, or dependence across every setting. Some risks are internal, relational, economic, or physiological in ways that cannot be rearranged by moving furniture, blocking an app, or taking another street. A person may change the environment and still need clinical care, peer support, medication prescribed by a qualified professional, safer housing, legal protection, or a different relationship structure. It would be dishonest to turn environment design into a cure-all. A locked door does not heal the whole wound.

The reconciliation is to give environment its proper place. It is not the whole of recovery, but it is often the part most neglected because it looks too practical to be profound. The app removed from the phone may protect the moment before the craving becomes argument. The route changed after work may prevent a cue from becoming a ritual. The cash limit may add time between impulse and purchase. The meal prepared earlier may stop hunger from dressing itself as despair. These changes do not replace deeper work. They keep the person stable enough to keep doing it.

Friction is the central material. Add friction to the risky action; remove friction from the stabilising action. If support matters, make it reachable in one movement. If late-night phone use increases risk, make the phone less reachable when judgement is tired. If certain conversations become combustible after exhaustion, make the pause phrase visible before the conversation begins. If travel creates anonymity and drift, place check-ins and food before arrival rather than after the hotel door closes. Friction does not eliminate choice. It changes the slope.

The slope matters because many risky behaviours depend on speed. The faster the old action can begin, the less time there is for the two-minute inventory, the support message, the competing action, or the memory of consequences. A saved password, a stored payment method, a familiar shortcut, an unlocked cupboard, an unplanned evening: each shortens the runway. Recovery design lengthens it. The added minute may look trivial, but inside an urge, a minute can become the space in which another part of the self catches up.

Kind realism also refuses theatrical deprivation. Some people respond to fear by stripping their environment harshly, as if recovery must feel punitive to be serious. They remove too much, isolate too sharply, and create a life so narrow that resentment begins to grow. This is not sustainable. The aim is not to make the world bare. It is to make the next good action easier and the next harmful action slower. A recovery-friendly environment should still contain pleasure, comfort, beauty, humour, and rest. It should not feel like a cell designed by shame.

The path of least resistance returns in relationships too. If a household repeatedly drifts into late-night arguments, the environment is not only physical; it is temporal and conversational. The same room, the same hour, the same fatigue, the same unfinished grievances, and the same absence of a stopping rule may keep producing the same damage. A different environment may mean daylight conversations, chairs not arranged like a courtroom, a shared agreement to pause, or a support call after a hard exchange. The surroundings include the conditions under which speech happens.

Digital environments deserve particular scrutiny because they are built to be frictionless. A device can hold support, work, distraction, risk, memory, shopping, gambling, pornography, argument, comparison, and escape in the same hand. The issue is not the device as an object, but the absence of boundaries inside it. Recovery may require blunt interventions: deleting specific apps, moving them off the home screen, logging out, turning off notifications, using blocking tools, removing saved details, charging the phone elsewhere, or creating a no-phone threshold at night. These are not signs that the person cannot be trusted. They are signs that the environment has been made honest about its influence.

The most effective changes are often embarrassingly specific. "Be less impulsive" is vague. "Do not keep the triggering app on the phone" is specific. "Stop making bad choices after work" is vague. "Take the route that avoids the old stop on stressful days" is specific. "Look after myself better" is vague. "Have food available before the evening danger hour" is specific. Recovery improves when intentions are translated into placements, removals, routes, times, barriers, and prepared defaults. The environment understands nouns and verbs better than ideals.

There is also humility in letting the environment carry some of the burden. Many people want to prove they can stand beside the old doorway and not enter. Sometimes that proof is unnecessary, even vain. The goal is not to win a daily staring contest with risk. The goal is to live with less unnecessary exposure to it. A person who avoids a known cue is not less recovered than the person who walks past it and suffers theatrically. The question is not which choice looks stronger. The question is which choice better protects the life being built.

The forward test is practical and unsentimental. Walk through the day as it is actually arranged: the bed, the phone, the kitchen, the commute, the wallet, the calendar, the apps, the evening chair, the route home, the private hour after conflict. Which parts of the environment are making recovery the easier action, and which parts are quietly escorting the person back to the old door? Motivation may visit. It may even stay for a while. But when it leaves, as it often does, the room will still be voting.

Chapter 5
Stress Management Without Self-Improvement Pressure

What if the first useful sign of stress is not the breaking point, but the small behaviour that arrives hours earlier? The jaw tightens. The phone comes out for no clear reason. A message is read and left unanswered. A cupboard is opened, then closed. A harmless question receives a sharp reply. Nothing has collapsed. Nothing needs a dramatic label. Yet the body has already placed a marker on the floor.

Stress rarely begins where people say it begins. By the time someone announces that they are overwhelmed, the signal may have been sounding for some time: shoulders lifted at the desk, appetite gone blunt, irritation gathering in the throat, doom scrolling under the pretence of staying informed, withdrawal disguised as needing space. The trouble is not that people have no signals. The trouble is that they often mistrust the early ones because they seem too ordinary to deserve care.

There is a strange pressure to manage stress impressively. Rest must become a project. Self-care must look intentional, attractive, and morally improving. A walk must become a fitness habit; breathing must become a discipline; sleep must become a performance; food must become a philosophy. Under that pressure, people do not become steadier. They become self-conscious. The very practices meant to soften strain begin to ask for more effort than a strained person can give.

The central tension is between care and self-improvement theatre. Recovery needs stress management, but it does not need another stage on which the person proves discipline, depth, productivity, or enlightenment. It needs earlier detection and smaller responses. A stress signal is not a character flaw. It is information arriving while the situation may still be adjustable. The sooner the signal is trusted, the less heroic the intervention has to be.

The stakes are high because unmanaged stress does not remain neatly inside the category of stress. It travels. It turns into cravings, conflict, secrecy, avoidance, late-night risk, resentful generosity, poor judgement, and the private conviction that old relief is reasonable just this once. Stress changes how the body reads the room and how the mind reads other people. A neutral tone becomes criticism. A delay becomes rejection. A task becomes impossible. A temptation becomes comfort. The person may think the problem began at the moment they snapped, but the match was struck much earlier.

The longer stress goes unnamed, the more expensive it becomes. Small care is often cheap in time and pride: a pause before replying, a glass of water, a few minutes outside, a stretch at the kitchen counter, a message that says the day is getting sharp around the edges. Late repair costs more. It may require apology, cancelled plans, damage control, lost sleep, or a climb back from behaviour that could have been interrupted when the first signs appeared. Earlier care is not indulgence. It is thrift with one's future self.

The practical path begins by learning which stress signals are trustworthy, not because they are dramatic but because they reliably appear before drift. It then moves towards brief resets that can be used inside a real day rather than saved for an imaginary quiet one. From there, the question becomes whether the chosen form of relief leaves recovery stronger or weaker afterwards. Some relief clears the mind; some relief borrows peace and sends chaos back with interest.

This distinction matters because stress relief has a moral alibi. Almost anything can be defended under the sentence "I needed to relax." Yet recovery asks a sharper question: what did the relief do to the next hour? A behaviour that leaves the person more honest, more settled, more able to sleep, or more willing to connect belongs in a different category from a behaviour that leaves secrecy, agitation, shame, conflict, or a larger craving behind it. The after-effect tells the truth. The receipt is in the body.

The unresolved question is not whether stress can be removed from life. It cannot, and the attempt would make a narrow life. The question is whether stress can be noticed while it is still asking quietly. When the jaw tightens, the scrolling begins, the voice sharpens, or the body starts withdrawing from the day, will those signs be treated as accusations, or as prompts for care before the evening becomes harder to protect?

Stress Signals You Can Trust

In 1915, at Harvard Medical School in Boston, physiologist Walter Cannon published *Bodily Changes in Pain, Hunger, Fear and Rage*, giving scientific language to something human beings had long felt without being able to explain cleanly: the body begins preparing before the mind has finished deciding. Cannon's work on the fight-or-flight response did not belong to recovery culture, but its central lesson is useful here. Stress is not only an idea. It has posture, breath, appetite, muscle, attention, and impulse. It leaves fingerprints.

Those fingerprints often appear before the person admits that stress is present. The jaw tightens during a harmless email. The thumb opens the same app again and again. A small interruption produces a disproportionate snap. The body leans away from conversation. A task that would usually take little effort becomes strangely intolerable. The person says they are fine, and in one sense they may believe it. But the body has already placed a note under the door. Read the note early.

The problem is not that stress signals are absent. The problem is that many people have been trained to distrust them unless they become dramatic. Tension is dismissed as weakness.

Irritability is treated as proof of poor character. Withdrawal is renamed independence. Doom scrolling is explained as staying informed. Overwork is disguised as responsibility. The signal is therefore not answered when it is still small. It is ignored until it has to become louder, more expensive, and more likely to damage recovery.

A trustworthy stress signal is not always pleasant, noble, or convenient. It is reliable. It appears often enough before trouble that it deserves attention. For one person, the signal may be jaw tension and a sharpened voice. For another, it may be silence, cancelled plans, a sudden hatred of being asked questions, or a private need to control every detail. Someone else may notice that stress shows up as hunger ignored, music becoming irritating, messages left unopened, or the urge to buy, scroll, argue, drink, gamble, binge, disappear, or fix everyone else. The signal does not need to be impressive. It needs to be recognised.

This is where shame becomes a poor interpreter. If the first thought is "I should not be like this," the signal turns into an accusation. The person then has two problems: the original stress and the secondary shame of having a stress response at all. That second layer often makes recovery harder. A clenched jaw is no longer a prompt to pause; it becomes evidence that the person is failing. A sharp reply is no longer a sign that pressure is rising; it becomes a verdict on identity. The signal is useful only when it is treated as information arriving in time.

Hans Selye, working in Montreal in the mid-twentieth century, helped popularise the language of stress as a bodily process rather than merely a complaint or weakness. His work is not a complete map of human distress, and later research has refined many assumptions. Still, the broad shift matters: stress is not simply an attitude problem. It is a response involving the whole organism. That recognition lowers the temperature of self-judgement. It allows a person to ask, "What is my system doing?" rather than "What is wrong with me?" The first question opens a door. The second often locks one.

Early detection changes the size of the intervention required. When stress is caught as tight shoulders, the intervention may be a pause before replying, a brief walk, food, water, a boundary, a message, or a decision to postpone a difficult conversation. When stress is ignored until it becomes a late-night collapse, the repair may involve apology, lost sleep, secrecy, a craving plan, or damage control. The earlier signal is not trivial because the later consequence is larger. Recovery is protected by noticing the small hinge before the door strains.

The most trustworthy signals are behavioural because behaviour is harder to romanticise. A person may argue with their feelings, but it is more difficult to argue with repeated actions. If every period of high stress brings doom scrolling in bed, then the phone at night is not just a habit; it is an early warning. If snapping at a partner reliably follows skipped food and back-to-back obligations, then the sharp sentence is part of a sequence. If withdrawing from support comes before cravings, then silence is not neutral. It is a sign on the road. The body and behaviour are already drawing the map.

Doom scrolling deserves particular attention because it often feels passive. The person is not obviously acting out. They are sitting still. The screen glows. The hand moves. The mind is fed distress in fragments while the body remains tense and underused. What looks like rest can become agitation with a soft chair. The visible behaviour is simple: repeated checking without a clear purpose, inability to stop after receiving the necessary information, a mood that darkens with each scroll, sleep delayed while nothing nourishing is gained. The signal is not the phone alone. It is the combination of pressure, repetition, and worsening state.

Snapping offers a different kind of signal because it leaves evidence in the room. A voice hardens. A sentence comes out with unnecessary force. A question is heard as criticism. The person may be technically correct and still be emotionally unsafe in the way they deliver the truth. This matters for recovery because conflict can become a gateway to shame, secrecy, and old relief. The sharp reply is not merely a social mistake; it may be an early sign that regulation is thinning. When treated early, it can lead to repair. When defended, it can become a pattern.

Withdrawal can be more difficult to spot because it often carries dignity in its posture. The person says they need space. Sometimes they do. Space can be healthy, especially when it prevents reactive speech or gives the body time to settle. But withdrawal becomes a stress signal when it narrows contact, hides risk, or makes the person less reachable precisely when support would help. The difference is visible in follow-through. Healthy space has a return point. Risky withdrawal has fog. Healthy space says, "I need an hour and I will come back." Risky withdrawal stops answering and calls the silence recovery.

Jaw tension, tight chest, shallow breathing, stomach discomfort, restlessness, headaches, and fatigue can all function as early messages, but they should be read with humility. The body is not a simple codebook. A tight jaw does not always mean danger. A low mood does not always predict a setback. A restless evening may be ordinary human weather. This is the credible limitation: over-reading every sensation can create vigilance rather than steadiness. A person can become so alert to stress that they begin to fear normal fluctuation. That is not recovery; it is another form of captivity.

The reconciliation is to look for patterns, not isolated sensations. A single tense afternoon may mean little. Repeated tension before conflict deserves attention. One evening of scrolling may be ordinary fatigue. Repeated scrolling before late-night risk deserves attention. One cancelled plan may be rest. Repeated cancellation before isolation and craving deserves attention. The signal becomes trustworthy when it has a history. The person is not asked to panic over every flicker. They are asked to respect the signals that have repeatedly preceded drift.

This is why recording only a few observations can be more useful than conducting an exhaustive private audit. The person may note the cue, the body sign, the behaviour, and what followed. "Skipped lunch, jaw tight, snapped at home, wanted to disappear." "Long meeting, headache, scrolled for an hour, missed check-in." "Criticism at work, silent all evening, craving rose after ten." These are not confessions. They are field notes. Over time, they identify which signals can be trusted because they have led somewhere before.

The language used around the signal determines whether it becomes useful. "I am being ridiculous" pushes the person towards concealment. "My stress is showing in my jaw and my replies" points towards care. "I always ruin things" collapses the day into identity. "I am withdrawing and need a return point" creates a behavioural choice. The words do not need to be pretty. They need to keep the person close enough to reality to act before the situation grows teeth.

There is also a relational dimension. Other people often notice stress signals before the person is willing to name them. A partner hears the edge in the voice. A colleague notices unusual silence. A friend receives shorter replies. A child senses the room becoming brittle. This does not mean other people should be made responsible for managing someone's recovery. It means the person can learn from the evidence their stress leaves in shared space. If trusted others repeatedly describe the same signs, those signs deserve attention rather than instant defence.

For capable, high-functioning people, the hardest signal to trust may be competence itself. They continue performing while stress accumulates. Work is completed. Deadlines are met. Messages are answered. The public surface holds. Beneath it, food disappears, sleep shortens, patience thins, contact becomes performative, and the private hour grows risky. Competence can hide deterioration because it gives the person evidence that nothing is wrong. Yet recovery is not protected by output alone. It is protected by the condition in which output is being produced.

The aim is not to become fragile about stress. Life will continue to bring pressure, delay, conflict, disappointment, grief, boredom, and demand. The aim is to become more accurate. A stress signal is not a summons to abandon responsibility; it is a prompt to adjust before responsibility becomes harder to carry. Earlier detection means smaller care: step away before the voice becomes cruel, eat before irritation becomes certainty, answer one message before isolation becomes secrecy, pause the screen before the night is spent feeding dread.

The most reliable signals usually feel embarrassingly ordinary. The cupboard opened without hunger. The third check of the same news feed. The sentence typed and deleted with rising heat. The sudden conviction that everyone is demanding too much. The refusal to make eye contact. The wish to be unreachable. These are not moral failures. They are bells in the building. A bell does not put out a fire. It gives people a chance to move before the smoke fills the corridor.

The forward test is whether those bells will be trusted while they are still quiet. When stress first appears as jaw tension, scrolling, snapping, withdrawal, or the small private urge to make the day less honest, what meaning will be assigned to it? Character flaw, or timely information? Annoyance to suppress, or prompt for care? The answer will decide whether the intervention can remain small, or whether the body will have to shout before it is believed.

Micro-resets During the Day

In 1979, at the University of Massachusetts Medical Center in Worcester, Jon Kabat-Zinn began teaching a structured programme that asked people to bring disciplined attention to breath, body, and present-moment experience in the middle of pain and stress. Its later influence became far wider than the hospital setting, but the useful fact for recovery is modest: regulation does not always begin with a life overhaul. Sometimes it begins with a short, repeated return to the body before the day has gathered too much speed.

A busy person often imagines care as something that belongs to the margins: early morning, late evening, a quiet weekend, a room with no interruptions, a life temporarily cleared of other people's needs. That image can be soothing, but it is often impractical. The day does not wait until there is enough time to become manageable. It tightens at the desk, in the car, between classes, before a difficult call, after an irritating message, during the long stretch between food and rest. The reset must fit there. Two minutes can matter.

The word "micro" can sound faint, as though the action is too small for the seriousness of the pressure. That is the wrong measure. A micro-reset is not designed to solve the whole problem. It is designed to interrupt escalation while escalation is still cheap. A person who stands up before answering sharply, drinks water before the evening craving, breathes slowly before entering a tense room, or walks outside before the old story gathers force is not escaping responsibility. They are changing state before state becomes behaviour.

The body often needs repetition more than revelation. One long retreat from stress may be pleasant, but it cannot carry a week built from repeated strain. Micro-resets work differently. They enter the day as small corrections: shoulders lowered after an hour of tension, a breath lengthened before a meeting, hands unclenched after reading a message, a song used to mark the shift from work mode to home mode, a short walk taken before the known vulnerable hour. Each reset gives the nervous system a different cue. The cue says, "We are not waiting for collapse before we respond."

Paced breathing is one of the plainest examples because it uses something already present. No special equipment is required. No audience is needed. A person can lengthen the exhale, slow the rhythm, and allow attention to rest on the physical act of breathing. The value does not lie in achieving serenity. The visible measure is simpler: does the person pause before replying, lower the volume of speech, delay the risky action, or recover enough choice to make contact? Breathing becomes useful when it changes the next behaviour, not when it produces a perfect inner atmosphere.

Stretching and movement matter for similar reasons. Stress can trap the body in readiness: neck rigid, jaw set, back braced, hands busy, legs restless. A small movement breaks the posture that the mood has begun to inhabit. Standing, rolling the shoulders, stepping outside, walking to another room, loosening the hands, or moving the body for a brief interval can interrupt the physical script of stress. The body is not merely carrying the feeling; it is helping to maintain it. Change the posture, and the mind receives new information.

Hydration and food are sometimes treated as too basic to mention, which is precisely why they are often neglected. A person may conduct elaborate self-analysis while thirsty, hungry, and overstimulated, then wonder why every thought sounds sharper than it should. The micro-reset here is not a moral claim about perfect health. It is a practical recognition that the body's ordinary needs affect the quality of judgement. A glass of water, a simple meal, or a planned pause before the late-afternoon dip can reduce the number of unnecessary battles the mind has to fight. The ordinary is protective.

Music can reset the day because it changes tempo, attention, and emotional colour without requiring much language. A specific piece of music before walking home, after a demanding meeting, or during a transition from public competence to private vulnerability can mark a change in state. It should be chosen with care. Some music steadies; some intensifies agitation; some feeds resentment or longing until the old relief begins to look reasonable. The measure is the after-effect. Does the person become clearer, kinder, and more reachable, or more charged, more private, and more inclined towards the familiar spiral?

A brief walk is often powerful because it combines several useful changes at once: movement, different surroundings, altered light, a break from the immediate cue, and a pause in the conversation or screen loop. The walk need not become exercise in the heroic sense. Its purpose is to create enough distance for the next decision to improve. A person who walks round the block before sending a message may return with the same emotion but a different sentence. A person who steps outside before entering a risky hour may not feel transformed, but they may feel less trapped. That is enough.

Herbert Benson, a cardiologist at Harvard Medical School, published *The Relaxation Response* in 1975, helping to popularise the idea that simple, repeated practices could influence the body's stress response. The language and evidence around stress have developed since then, and no single technique should be treated as universally sufficient. Yet the practical lesson remains useful: small physiological shifts can alter the conditions under which decisions are made. Recovery often depends on those conditions. The person is not trying to become calm in the abstract; they are trying to become calm enough not to hand the next hour to impulse.

Timing is the hidden skill. A reset used after the collapse may still help, but a reset used before the known trigger can prevent the collapse from gaining authority. The noon reset before the difficult afternoon. The movement break before returning home. The water before the craving window. The breath before opening the message. The song before entering a family gathering. The brief walk after a meeting that has left the body hot with embarrassment. These are not decorative acts. They are placed interventions.

Known trigger moments deserve special respect because repetition teaches the body what to expect. If late afternoon reliably brings irritability, the reset belongs before late afternoon has fully formed. If the commute home becomes a corridor of craving, the reset belongs before the route begins. If conflict tends to flare when dinner is delayed, the reset belongs earlier than the first sharp sentence. If the evening becomes risky when the person moves from usefulness into emptiness, the reset belongs at the threshold. A well-placed reset is a hinge on the day.

The counter-example is real. Some stress cannot be reset away. A two-minute breath will not fix chronic overwork, unsafe relationships, poverty, grief, clinical anxiety, traumatic stress, discrimination, unstable housing, or medical conditions. It would be insulting to suggest otherwise. Micro-resets become harmful when they are used to make an unbearable structure more bearable without questioning the structure itself. They can be supports, but they should not become a polite way to endure what needs protection, change, treatment, or help beyond the individual.

The reconciliation is to give micro-resets their proper scale. They are not a replacement for boundaries, therapy, medical care, financial planning, safer conditions, repair, rest, or community. They are the smaller actions that keep the person from becoming too flooded to use those larger supports. They preserve access to choice. They reduce the heat in the room. They keep a difficult state from becoming an automatic sequence. Their power lies not in grandeur, but in placement and repetition.

For the time-conscious person, the appeal is not efficiency for its own sake. Efficiency can become another pressure, another demand to optimise suffering neatly. The point is mercy. A reset that fits inside a real day is more compassionate than a perfect practice that can only be performed in ideal conditions. The professional between meetings, the student before an exam, the parent in a noisy kitchen, the worker on a split shift, the carer with no clean edge to the day: each needs practices that do not require life to stop before support can begin.

The tone of the reset matters. If it is used as punishment, it will not last. "Calm down" spoken inwardly with contempt is not care. "Pause now, before this gets harder" is different. The same action can carry different meanings depending on the voice attached to it. A stretch can be an act of irritation at the body, or a brief return to it. A walk can be escape, or a deliberate break before repair. Water can be a rushed gesture, or a signal that the body is not being abandoned while the mind is busy.

The most reliable micro-resets are paired with existing transitions. After closing the laptop, stand and breathe before reaching for the phone. Before entering the house, pause and name the mood. After reading a difficult message, put both feet on the floor before replying. Before the evening begins, eat something simple. After an argument starts to heat, change rooms and set a return point. The reset attaches to a hinge already present in the day. It does not require a new life. It uses the life that is already happening.

The motif of the hinge is useful because the reset does not carry the whole door. It helps the door move differently. A day without hinges becomes force: pushing, slamming, sticking, breaking. A day with hinges allows transition. Work to home.

Public self to private self. Irritation to speech. Craving to delay. Shame to contact. Fatigue to sleep. The reset belongs at these points of motion, where a small change can alter the direction of what follows.

A person will not always want to reset. That is why the reset must be small enough to begin without enthusiasm. Motivation is welcome, but it is unreliable. Repetition is sturdier. The person who has practised the noon pause, the pre-commute breath, the after-message walk, or the evening water-and-phone boundary does not need to invent care when the day is already sharp. The body recognises the cue. The action begins before the argument inside has become elaborate.

The forward test is not whether a micro-reset can make a hard life feel easy. It cannot. The test is whether a small action, placed before the known danger point, can keep the next hour from becoming more costly than it needs to be. When the first signal arrives and the day is still adjustable, will the person wait for a collapse worthy of care, or take the brief, unglamorous hinge that may stop the collapse from needing to happen?

Choosing Recovery-Friendly Stress Relief

What if the relief that works fastest at 8 p.m. is also the relief that makes 11 p.m. more dangerous? The question is not theoretical. A person comes home tense, hungry for quiet, and worn thin by restraint. Their body asks for release. The mind offers the familiar menu: scroll until numb, eat without tasting, pour the drink, start the argument, buy something, disappear into a screen, send the message that will complicate the morning. For a few minutes, the pressure drops. Then the receipt arrives.

The receipt is the most honest part of stress relief. Not the promise before it, not the pleasure during it, not the story the mind tells to justify it, but the after-effect. Is the body clearer or more agitated? Is sleep nearer or further away? Is the person more reachable or more secretive? Is there less repair to do, or more? Relief is not automatically recovery-friendly because it feels good at the start. Some forms of relief soothe the system. Others simply postpone discomfort and add interest.

The old mistake is to divide stress relief into virtue and vice too quickly. That approach often produces shame, and shame is a poor designer of behaviour. The more useful distinction is functional: what does this form of relief tend to create afterwards? A brief walk may leave the person calmer and more able to speak without injury. Music may soften the day enough to make dinner and sleep possible. A support call may reduce isolation. A hot shower may bring the body down from readiness. Yet the same categories can turn. Music can feed resentment. A walk can become avoidance. A conversation can become reassurance-seeking without action. A screen can become a tunnel. The behaviour must be judged by its pattern, not by its label.

A recovery-friendly form of relief does not need to be impressive. It needs to leave the next hour cleaner. That cleanliness is visible in behaviour: the person answers honestly rather than hiding, eats rather than grazing in distress, rests rather than stimulating the nervous system further, pauses rather than escalating conflict, contacts support rather than staging a private collapse. The stress may not vanish. The day may remain difficult. But the chosen relief does not multiply the difficulty. It lowers the temperature without setting fire to another room.

Richard Lazarus and Susan Folkman's work on stress and coping, especially their 1984 book *Stress, Appraisal, and Coping*, remains useful because it treated coping not as a single moral category but as a set of responses shaped by how a person appraises a situation. Some coping aims to change the problem; some aims to manage the emotional strain around it. Recovery requires both, but it also requires discernment. A coping method that reduces feeling while increasing risk is not the same as one that reduces feeling while preserving judgement. The after-effect separates them.

The body often knows the difference before pride admits it. After recovery-friendly relief, breathing may slow, speech may soften, and the person may become more willing to do the next honest thing. After risk-friendly relief, the mind often becomes foggier, more entitled, more defensive, or more secretive. The person may need to explain why it was "not that bad". They may avoid a message, hide a detail, extend the behaviour beyond what they intended, or resent anyone who interrupts it. These are not subtle philosophical signals. They are footprints.

A useful way to evaluate stress relief is to compare the first five minutes with the following hour. The first five minutes may say, "This is working." The following hour may say, "This has made me less able to care for myself." Fast relief is not automatically false, but it deserves inspection because speed can flatter the old pattern. The familiar behaviour often knows how to create immediate contrast: tension falls, boredom breaks, loneliness gets covered, anger finds a target, shame gets hidden. Recovery-friendly relief may be less dramatic. It may not provide a rush. It may simply make the person more capable of not worsening the night.

This is where a menu becomes useful. A menu is not a rigid prescription; it is a set of options chosen before the nervous system starts bargaining. Different moods need different forms of relief. Anger may need movement, space, cold water on the hands, or a pause before words. Sadness may need warmth, contact, music that does not deepen the wound, or a simple task that restores a sense of agency. Anxiety may need grounding, reduced stimulation, a written next action, or a reliable person who will not amplify urgency. Boredom may need novelty without risk: a change of setting, a practical errand, a creative task, a brief walk, a different room. Loneliness may need contact that is real enough to interrupt secrecy, not contact that produces more longing.

The menu should be built from evidence, not fantasy. Many people list the activities they think ought to help, rather than the ones that actually do. They imagine reading, running, cooking, meditating, phoning a friend, stretching, cleaning, praying, writing, walking, resting, or listening to music, then discover under pressure that some of these require too much energy or produce the wrong after-effect. The honest question is not "What sounds healthy?" It is "What reliably leaves me clearer, safer, and more willing to stay connected?" A person may find that a brief shower works better than a long journal entry, or that gentle tidying steadies them while intensive planning makes them harsher. The evidence should be allowed to win.

There is a quiet discipline in removing ambiguous options from high-risk windows. A person may be able to use a certain form of entertainment well on a calm Saturday afternoon but not late at night after conflict. They may be able to enjoy online browsing in a public space but not alone in bed. They may be able to socialise safely when rested but not when resentful and hungry. The same behaviour can have different consequences depending on timing, mood, company, and access. Recovery-friendly relief therefore asks not only "What?" but "When, where, and after what kind of day?"

Mihaly Csikszentmihalyi's research on flow, developed over decades and widely known through his 1990 book *Flow*, offers a useful distinction. Some activities absorb attention in a way that leaves a person more ordered afterwards: making, practising, repairing, learning, gardening, playing music, sport, craft, or focused work that has clear boundaries. This is not a claim that everyone should pursue flow as a remedy, nor that productive absorption is always healthy. It can also become avoidance. But the principle matters: relief that engages attention, skill, and embodied presence often differs from relief that merely numbs. One leaves a trace of agency. The other may leave appetite without satisfaction.

The receipt appears again here. After numbing relief, the person may feel oddly unfinished. More is needed, though more does not satisfy. After recovery-friendly relief, the person may still be tired, but the next right action is easier to see. They may be able to eat, apologise, sleep, answer one message, leave the room, or stop the behaviour before it turns into a spiral. That is the practical measure. Relief is not judged by purity. It is judged by what it makes possible next.

A credible limitation must be kept in view. Some stress is not a matter of choosing a better form of relief. Chronic overload, grief, unsafe relationships, trauma, discrimination, financial strain, untreated illness, or working conditions that grind people down cannot be solved by a menu of calming activities. To suggest otherwise would be cruelly tidy. Recovery-friendly relief can reduce damage and preserve capacity, but it should not be used to disguise the need for wider change, appropriate professional support, safer conditions, or genuine rest. A person should not be asked to breathe their way into tolerating the intolerable.

The reconciliation is to treat stress relief as both immediate and diagnostic. Immediate relief asks, "What can reduce risk in the next hour?" Diagnostic relief asks, "What does my repeated need for this relief reveal?" If the person needs a micro-reset after every conversation with a particular person, the issue may not be poor stress management. If every workday ends with collapse, the structure of the day deserves scrutiny. If every night requires numbing, the life may be asking for more than a better evening routine. Recovery-friendly relief should steady the person without silencing the larger evidence.

The menu also needs low-energy options. Under stress, people often list activities that require the very capacity stress has removed. A long walk may be excellent, but on certain days the workable version is standing outside for a few minutes. Cooking may help, but on a hard day the workable version is eating something already prepared. Calling someone may be right, but the workable version may be a text that says, "I am tense and need to stay accountable." Reading may be restorative, but the workable version may be one page rather than a chapter. Relief that cannot be begun under strain is mostly decorative.

There is also a difference between privacy and secrecy. Some stress relief should be private: a bath, prayer, music, stretching, reading, a quiet walk, time alone after social demand. Privacy restores. Secrecy hides. The dividing line is often visible in the after-effect. Privacy makes a person more able to return. Secrecy makes return feel intrusive. Privacy has edges. Secrecy blurs them. Privacy can be named without panic. Secrecy requires editing. Recovery-friendly relief may occur alone, but it does not need to be protected by dishonesty.

For professionals, researchers, students, carers, and people carrying visible responsibility, stress relief can become entangled with identity. They may mistrust anything that looks unproductive. They may push themselves towards "improving" relief: educational podcasts, fitness goals, skill development, purposeful reading, domestic efficiency. There is nothing wrong with useful activities. But not all relief has to earn its place through productivity. Sometimes recovery-friendly relief is deliberately unproductive because the body has spent the day being used as an instrument. Sitting quietly, looking out of a window, listening to music, walking without measuring it, or making something badly for pleasure may be more restorative than another optimised task.

The strongest menu contains variety without chaos. It includes options for the body, for contact, for environment, for attention, and for rest. It is not a list to complete. It is a set of prepared alternatives to the old reflex. When anger arrives, the menu reduces the chance that anger chooses the relief. When loneliness arrives, the menu reduces the chance that loneliness chooses the person. When fatigue arrives, the menu reduces the chance that fatigue negotiates with access. A menu gives the steadier self a voice before the strained self starts improvising.

The language of "deserving" relief should be handled carefully. People under stress often say, "I deserve this," just before choosing something that will cost them. There is truth inside the sentence: human beings do deserve rest, pleasure, softness, interruption, and care. But the old behaviour may exploit that truth. A sharper question is, "What kind of relief would treat me as someone I am responsible for protecting?" That question does not deny pleasure. It asks pleasure to remain on recovery's side.

Stress relief and recovery belong together when relief restores choice rather than steals it. The person does not need to become suspicious of every comfort. Comfort is part of a liveable recovery. Warmth, humour, beauty, movement, food, friendship, quiet, art, nature, faith, play, and sleep are not indulgences to be rationed only after perfect behaviour. They are part of how people remain human under pressure. The test is whether the comfort leaves the person more present to their life or more absent from it.

The unresolved test is written on the receipt. After the next form of relief, what will be easier: honesty or hiding, sleep or stimulation, repair or avoidance, steadiness or another round of bargaining? The answer may not be available in the first pleasant minutes. It will appear in the hour that follows, in the body's tone, in the phone's pull, in the willingness to connect, in the amount of damage left to clean up. Relief will always make its offer. Recovery asks what it costs.

Chapter 6
Setbacks: Repair, Not Shame

What if the most dangerous moment after a setback is not the setback itself, but the story told in the hour that follows? A person breaks a boundary, returns to an old behaviour, hides something, says the cruel sentence, cancels the support they needed, or steps through a doorway they had promised to avoid. Then the mind rushes in with its courtroom. One voice minimises. Another condemns. Neither tells the whole truth.

Minimising says the event was nothing, that everyone overreacts, that naming it properly would create unnecessary drama. Catastrophising says the event proves everything, that the work was false, that repair is pointless, that one breach has swallowed the entire future. Both stories protect the person from accuracy. One protects them by shrinking the event until it cannot teach. The other enlarges it until it cannot be touched. Shame and denial look like opposites, but both can keep recovery from moving.

The first task after a setback is therefore not self-punishment, and it is not instant analysis. It is contact with reality. What happened? Where? When? With whom? What was felt before, during, and after? What behaviour needs to be named without theatrical language? The broken plate on the kitchen floor is still a plate, not a prophecy. It needs to be seen clearly enough that no one cuts themselves on it while pretending it is either harmless dust or proof that the whole house is ruined.

The central tension is between responsibility and collapse. Recovery needs the person to take the event seriously, but seriousness is not the same as self-attack. A shamed person may perform remorse, promise too much, hide the next warning sign, or try to earn their way back into safety through exhaustion. A responsible person steadies the immediate situation, reduces further risk, tells the truth to the right people, and waits until the body is calmer before turning the event into instruction. Repair has a sequence. Shame has a spiral.

The stakes are immediate because one event can become a week when the first response is poorly designed. A slip followed by secrecy grows roots. A harsh exchange followed by pride becomes distance. A missed routine followed by all-or-nothing thinking becomes abandonment of the whole structure. A risky evening followed by sleep loss, hunger, isolation, and more exposure to the same cues becomes less like a single incident and more like a system temporarily losing power. The first day matters because it can either shorten the damage or give it room to spread.

The stakes are also relational. Setbacks rarely remain private, even when they are hidden. They change tone, availability, truthfulness, patience, and trust. Other people may feel the disturbance before they know its name. Repair begins when the person stops asking shame to be the evidence of accountability and offers something more useful: accurate language, stabilising action, reduced risk, and a change that can be observed. Trust does not require a dramatic confession every time. It requires fewer distortions and more dependable returns.

The path begins with naming the event in language clean enough to support change, neither polished into innocence nor inflated into identity. From there, attention turns to the first day after the slip, when food, sleep, safety, contact, and distance from triggers may matter more than the deep autopsy the mind is eager to conduct. Only after steadiness returns does reflection become useful: the lead-up, the decision points, the missed exits, and the single system change most likely to reduce repetition. The work is not to write ten new rules in shame. It is to alter the conditions that made the old rule collapse.

There is a discipline in refusing drama after damage. Drama can feel like moral seriousness because it is loud, but loudness is not repair. The person who says, "I am terrible," may still avoid naming the actual behaviour. The person who says, "It was nothing," may still leave others carrying the consequences. The steadier sentence is harder because it permits neither escape: "This is what I did, this is what it affected, this is what I am doing now to reduce further harm." That sentence has edges. It can be tested.

The unresolved question is what will happen when the next setback tries to become a verdict. Will the event be minimised until nothing changes, or magnified until change feels impossible? Or will it be lifted, carefully and without ceremony, like broken glass from the floor: named, contained, and studied only after everyone has stopped bleeding?

Naming What Happened Accurately

On 1 February 2003, the Space Shuttle Columbia broke apart during re-entry over Texas and Louisiana, and NASA's later accident investigation did not stop at the comforting phrase "something went wrong." The Columbia Accident Investigation Board examined foam strike, organisational culture, missed signals, assumptions, communication patterns, and decision-making under pressure. The moral force of the inquiry came from its refusal to settle for either a scapegoat or a shrug. Accuracy mattered because future safety depended on it.

A setback in recovery is smaller in scale, but the same discipline applies. The mind wants speed after damage. It wants a verdict, an excuse, a punishment, a disappearance, a speech. It does not naturally want a clear account with edges: what happened, where it happened, when it happened, who was involved, what was felt, what was chosen, and what now requires repair. Yet the clear account is where recovery begins again. The facts need a clean table.

That table is easily disturbed by two opposite impulses. Minimising sweeps the event into vague language: "It was not that bad," "I was just stressed," "It sort of happened," "I only slipped a bit," "They are making too much of it." Catastrophising throws the event into identity: "I have ruined everything," "I am hopeless," "This proves I never change," "There is no point now." Both are evasions, even when one sounds gentle and the other sounds brutally honest. Minimising avoids consequence. Catastrophising avoids detail. Neither gives the person a usable map.

Accurate naming begins with observable behaviour. Not "I lost control," but "I stayed online after I agreed to stop." Not "I was awful," but "I shouted during the conversation and then refused to answer for the rest of the evening." Not "I relapsed because everything was too much," but "I went to the place I had agreed to avoid after work, when I was angry and had not eaten." The wording may feel plain almost to the point of discomfort. That is its strength. Plain language removes the fog without adding theatre.

The distinction between behaviour and identity is not a sentimental courtesy. It is a practical necessity. Behaviour can be examined, repaired, interrupted, and planned around. Identity, once condemned, becomes a prison cell with no workbench inside it. A person who says, "I lied about where I was," has a difficult but workable fact. They can identify the fear, the moment of choice, the person affected, and the repair required. A person who says, "I am a liar," may feel morally serious, but the sentence is too large to guide the next hour. It invites shame rather than action.

Daniel Kahneman and Amos Tversky's work on judgement under uncertainty, developed from the 1970s onwards, is useful here because it showed how human judgement can be distorted by mental shortcuts, especially under pressure. Recovery after a setback is full of such shortcuts. The mind overweights the most vivid moment, forgets the lead-up, edits out protective actions that still held, or exaggerates the meaning of one failure until the whole life is coloured by it. The point is not that feelings are false. The point is that feelings are not a complete record. Accuracy asks the person to compare the feeling with the sequence.

The sequence matters because setbacks usually have ancestry. A person may describe the event as sudden, but the day may tell another story: poor sleep, skipped food, resentment after a meeting, no contact after work, a risky route taken, an argument continued too late, a phone kept close, a support message delayed. None of these details excuses the behaviour. They explain the conditions in which the behaviour became more likely. Explanation is not acquittal. It is the beginning of prevention.

The clean table requires more than the external facts. It also requires an account of the inner weather without allowing that weather to become a defence. "I felt ashamed," "I felt cornered," "I felt lonely," "I felt entitled," "I felt numb," "I felt angry and wanted to make them understand," "I felt embarrassed and wanted to hide." These statements matter because emotions often shape the route towards harm. Yet they must be held in the right place. "I felt angry" is not the same as "therefore I had to shout." "I felt ashamed" is not the same as "therefore I had to lie." Feeling names the pressure. Behaviour names the choice made under pressure.

There is an important difference between detail and drama. Detail says, "After the call, I sat in the car for twenty minutes, opened the app I had deleted before, reinstalled it, and ignored the check-in." Drama says, "I completely destroyed everything." Detail may be painful, but it remains close to reality. Drama may feel intense, but it often reduces responsibility because it makes the event too enormous to handle. When everything is ruined, one specific repair can seem pointless. When the facts are named, repair becomes possible because the damage has boundaries.

The legal world offers a useful parallel, though recovery is not a courtroom. A witness statement that says "there was a disturbance" is weaker than one that describes who did what, where they stood, what was said, and what followed. The aim is not emotional punishment; the aim is reliability. In recovery, a similarly reliable account prevents the person from becoming both unreliable witness and harsh judge. The account should be specific enough that another responsible person could understand the risk, the impact, and the next practical step.

There is a credible limitation. Some people are not ready to name everything immediately after a setback, especially when the body is flooded, sleep-deprived, frightened, or in an unsafe setting. Forcing a full account too soon can produce panic, denial, or a rehearsed confession that satisfies no one. Some situations also require outside support, professional care, or protection before reflection can be useful. Accuracy should not become another demand placed on a person who first needs safety, food, rest, distance from the trigger, or help from someone qualified to provide it.

The reconciliation lies in timing and scale. Immediately after the event, the first account may be brief: "Something happened. I am not steady. I need to reduce risk and tell the truth to the right person." Later, when the body has settled, the fuller account can be built. Accuracy does not require instant completeness. It requires refusal to distort. A first sketch can become a clearer map once the person is no longer shaking, defending, or drowning in shame.

The words chosen after a setback teach the nervous system what kind of world recovery is. If the words are savage, the person learns that truth leads to punishment and may hide sooner next time. If the words are vague, the person learns that truth has no consequences and may repeat the same pattern with little adjustment. If the words are accurate and humane, the person learns that reality can be faced without collapse. That is a serious kind of trust. It is built each time the person names behaviour without turning it into a life sentence.

A useful account often includes the cost, but cost must also be named precisely. "It cost me trust with my partner because I concealed where I had gone." "It cost me sleep because I stayed online until the early hours." "It cost me money I had planned to use elsewhere." "It cost me confidence because I delayed support and then felt more ashamed." The cost should not be inflated for emotional effect. Inflated cost can become another form of self-absorption. The aim is not to suffer impressively. The aim is to understand consequence well enough to act differently.

Separating behaviour from identity also protects other people from being drawn into the wrong repair. When someone says, "I am terrible," the injured or affected person may feel pressured to comfort them rather than discuss the actual harm. The focus shifts from impact to reassurance. More accurate language keeps the burden where it belongs: "I said I would be home, and I was not. I understand that made you anxious and damaged trust. I am taking these steps tonight." The sentence does not beg to be contradicted. It stands where repair can begin.

The table returns here as a place of sorting. Facts on one side. Feelings on another. Impact in full view. Next action within reach. Identity statements are not placed at the centre because they are too blunt to do careful work. "I am broken," "I am selfish," "I am hopeless," "I am cured," "I am fine" all leave too much out. The table needs smaller, truer items: the hour, the place, the cue, the person affected, the bodily state, the thought that gave permission, the support not used, the action now required.

This kind of accuracy can feel cold at first, especially to someone used to proving remorse through emotional intensity. Yet it is not cold. It is respectful. It respects the harm enough to name it. It respects the person enough not to reduce them to it. It respects the future enough to ask what can be changed. Self-attack may burn brightly, but it often leaves ash where structure should be. Accuracy builds with material that can hold.

There is also freedom in giving up the exaggerated story. A setback may be serious without being total. A mistake may require repair without becoming an identity. A slip may reveal weakness in a system without proving that recovery was false. A hard fact may hurt and still be survivable. The person does not need to make the event smaller than it was, and does not need to make themselves smaller than they are. They need to tell the truth at the size truth actually is.

The forward test is exacting. After the next setback, the mind will probably reach for its familiar script: minimise, dramatise, defend, condemn, vanish, perform. The work is to bring the facts back to the clean table before those scripts take over. What happened? Where? When? With whom? What was felt? What was chosen? What did it cost? What needs repair now? The answer will not erase the setback. It will decide whether the setback becomes evidence for shame, or material for change.

The 24-hour Stabilisation Plan

What if the first 24 hours after a slip matter less because they explain the slip, and more because they decide whether it spreads? The person wakes, or sobers, or comes back into themselves after the argument, the binge, the lie, the risky visit, the old purchase, the night of scrolling, the missed commitment, the private collapse. The facts are still tender. Shame is awake before breakfast. The mind wants a trial.

That trial can wait. Not forever. Not as an avoidance of truth. But long enough for the body to stop shaking, for food to enter the system, for sleep to become possible, for the next dangerous cue to be moved farther away, for one honest person to know enough to help interrupt the spiral. The first day after a setback is not the best time to write a grand theory of failure. The first day is for containment. Put down the matches.

The mistake many people make after a slip is mistaking intensity for repair. They want to analyse everything while exhausted, confess everything while flooded, promise everything while ashamed, or punish themselves hard enough to feel purified. Yet the body in the first hours after a setback is often a poor witness and a worse judge. It may be hungry, dehydrated, sleep-deprived, frightened, defensive, overstimulated, or still close to the cue that started the sequence. Deep analysis conducted in that state can become another form of acting out: dramatic, sincere, and badly timed.

Stabilisation is not denial. It is triage. The word may sound clinical, but the principle is ordinary: deal first with the condition that could worsen fastest. If the person is unsafe, safety comes before reflection. If the body has been neglected, basic care comes before moral investigation. If the old behaviour is still within reach, access must be reduced before the mind starts negotiating again. If secrecy is growing, one trustworthy contact must be made before shame builds a private room around the event. The purpose is not to make the setback disappear. It is to stop one event becoming a week.

Judith Herman's 1992 book *Trauma and Recovery*, written from the context of psychiatric and feminist clinical work in the United States, helped popularise a phased understanding of recovery from traumatic experience: safety and stabilisation precede deeper remembrance and integration. Setbacks in everyday recovery are not the same as trauma treatment, and the distinction matters. Still, the order is instructive. The human system often needs enough safety before it can usefully examine pain, responsibility, memory, and change. If the ground is still moving, the first task is not interpretation. It is footing.

The first stabilising question is therefore plain: is anyone, including the person themselves, at immediate risk? The answer determines the scale of response. Sometimes ordinary support, distance from a cue, and reduced access will be enough. Sometimes the situation requires urgent professional help, emergency services, medical attention, or removal from a dangerous setting. A recovery plan should never romanticise self-management when outside help is needed. Safety is not a mood. It is visible in concrete conditions: no ongoing exposure to the risky object, place, person, platform, substance, route, conflict, or decision that could extend the damage.

Once safety is addressed, the body deserves attention before the story does. This can feel almost insulting to someone who wants to discuss meaning, blame, or identity. Yet setbacks often leave the body in a state that makes every interpretation harsher. Food may have been missed. Water may have been neglected. Sleep may be damaged. The nervous system may still be braced. A person trying to understand their life while physically depleted may end up mistaking depletion for truth. Hydration and food do not absolve behaviour; they make the next responsible behaviour more likely.

Sleep belongs in the same category of unglamorous repair. After a slip, many people either avoid sleep because shame keeps them restless, or use exhaustion as evidence that they must solve everything immediately. But a tired mind tends to widen despair and narrow options. It is more likely to catastrophise, more likely to seek quick relief, and less able to remember the larger pattern accurately. Protecting sleep during the first day is not an indulgence. It is a risk reduction measure. The person is not trying to sleep their way out of responsibility. They are trying to become fit enough to meet it.

Connection must come early enough to prevent secrecy from becoming a second problem. The message need not be dramatic. It does not need to contain every detail. It does need to be honest enough to change the situation. "I had a slip and I am not steady. I am safe at the moment, reducing access, and need a check-in later." "I argued badly and want to keep it from becoming a worse night. I am taking space and will return to repair when calmer." "I missed the plan and am tempted to disappear. Please ask me whether I have eaten and gone offline." These sentences do not perform shame. They create contact.

The bridge motif matters here because the first day after a setback is often a crossing between two versions of the event. On one side is the incident itself, still hot, still carrying its immediate consequences. On the other side is the review, the repair, the system change, the clearer account. The bridge is made of safety, food, water, sleep, contact, and reduced access. Without that bridge, the person may try to leap directly from harm to insight and fall into self-attack, denial, or another round of the same behaviour.

Reduced exposure to triggers is not cowardice. It is containment. If the setback involved a place, do not keep passing it while shame is fresh. If it involved a device, do not keep the device in the same position with the same permissions. If it involved a person, do not continue the conversation while flooded. If it involved money, route, app, substance, secrecy, boredom, conflict, or late-night access, place distance there before the next urge arrives. A person after a slip is not in a neutral state. The familiar cue may still carry heat. The environment should be asked to help.

There is a subtle form of pride that resists this. It says, "I should be able to handle it." Perhaps, on a steadier day, the person can. The first 24 hours after a slip are not the ideal time to test that claim. A person does not prove strength by standing beside the open door that has just caused damage.

They prove seriousness by closing it while they recover enough judgement to understand why they opened it. The issue is not moral toughness. It is timing.

The plan must also include what to cancel or postpone. This is where many people hesitate, because cancelling can feel like failure or exposure. Yet some commitments are simply unsafe in the immediate aftermath of a setback. A late-night social event, a difficult conversation, a high-pressure meeting that can be moved, a journey through a known risk zone, an unnecessary errand, an emotionally charged visit, or an unstructured evening alone may need to change. Cancelling is not always avoidance. Sometimes it is the first honest act after a dishonest one.

Of course, responsibilities cannot always be dropped. Children still need care. Work may still demand attendance. Bills do not pause. Exams do not reorganise themselves around emotional weather. The 24-hour plan must therefore distinguish between what must be done and what can be simplified. Necessary duties may need support, shorter edges, or fewer added demands. Optional strain should be removed where possible. The question is not "How can I escape the day?" It is "How can I make the day less likely to produce further harm?"

The counter-example is important. Some people may use stabilisation to avoid accountability indefinitely. They say they are "not ready" to discuss the harm, then remain permanently unavailable for repair. They focus on their own distress so completely that the impact on others is pushed aside. They use the language of care to protect themselves from consequence. That is not stabilisation. That is evasion in softer clothing. A 24-hour plan is a bridge, not a hiding place. It delays deep analysis until it can be useful; it does not cancel responsibility.

The reconciliation is to place a clear return point inside the first day. "I will stabilise tonight and speak to the person affected tomorrow morning." "I will contact support now and review the sequence after sleep." "I will reduce access for the next 24 hours and write the factual account when I am rested." This return point protects both the person and those affected by the setback. It says that immediate care is being used to support accountability, not to escape it. Time becomes structured rather than vague.

A strong stabilisation plan also limits the appetite for new rules. Shame loves to write constitutions after a setback. Never again. Everything changes. Ten new commitments. No exceptions. Total transformation by Monday. These vows may feel bracing, but they are often too heavy to carry once the shame burns off. The first day should not be spent designing an entire new life from the emotional wreckage of one event. It should be spent restoring enough steadiness to identify one or two changes that are actually likely to hold.

The same caution applies to confession. Telling the truth matters, especially when others have been affected, but indiscriminate disclosure can create more harm than repair. The person needs to consider who truly needs to know, who can help with immediate stabilisation, and who might be unfairly burdened by details they cannot use. A support person may need enough information to help reduce risk. An affected person may need an accurate acknowledgement of impact. A professional may need fuller context. Not every person needs every detail in the first hours. Honesty and dumping are not the same.

The plan should therefore be written in language that is both firm and humane. "For the next 24 hours, I protect safety, reduce access, restore the body, contact support, and postpone deep analysis until I can think clearly." This is not a slogan. It is an operating order. It prevents the mind from making the same four mistakes: minimising, catastrophising, isolating, and improvising. Each mistake worsens the odds. Each stabilising action improves them.

A person with a history of setbacks will often know their post-slip danger signs. Some become secretive. Some become punitive. Some try to repair too quickly and flood other people with emotion. Some seek another round of the same relief because the shame of the first round feels unbearable. Some decide the week is ruined and abandon every routine that might have limited the damage. These patterns should be named before the next slip, not after. The stabilisation plan is most useful when it anticipates the second wave.

The second wave is the reaction to the setback: shame, panic, defensiveness, craving, self-pity, anger, despair, or an urge to make the event either disappear or mean everything. Often this second wave causes more damage than the first. A single lapse becomes a weekend because the person cannot tolerate the story they are telling about it. A harsh sentence becomes a relationship crisis because pride refuses to pause and return. A missed commitment becomes withdrawal because embarrassment feels fatal. Stabilisation is designed for this second wave. It keeps the aftermath from becoming the real disaster.

The bridge returns at the close of the first day. The person does not have to feel proud of crossing it. Pride is irrelevant. They need to be on the other side with enough honesty and steadiness to review what happened. Did they make themselves safer? Did they eat and drink? Did they sleep or at least protect rest? Did they contact someone appropriate? Did they reduce exposure to the cue? Did they cancel or simplify what would likely deepen the spiral? These are not glamorous questions. They are the questions that keep one event from recruiting the next.

The unresolved test is what will happen in the hours after the next slip, when shame asks for a trial and the old pattern asks for a sequel. Will the person attempt deep analysis while still flooded, or build the bridge first? Safety, body, sleep, contact, distance from triggers, and a clear return point for repair:

these are the planks. The question is whether they will be placed quickly enough for the person to cross before one event becomes a week.

Turning Setbacks into Data

On 7 December 2000, in Washington, D.C., the Institute of Medicine published *To Err Is Human*, a report that changed how many health systems spoke about mistakes. Its central force was not that error had suddenly been discovered, but that error was treated as something to be studied through systems, conditions, signals, and safeguards, rather than only through blame. The report did not make harm less serious. It made seriousness more useful.

Recovery needs the same discipline after a setback. Once the first day has been stabilised, once the body is safer, the immediate trigger is farther away, and one honest contact has interrupted secrecy, reflection can begin to do its proper work. Not punishment. Not theatre. Not a grand inquiry into whether the person is good or bad. A setback, examined at the right time, becomes material. It can show where the system thinned, where the warning signs were missed, where the old door remained open, and where one change would carry more weight than ten dramatic vows.

Data is not cold. It is humble. It says, "Something happened, and I am willing to learn from the actual sequence rather than from the shame-cloud around it." The person sits with the facts already named: what happened, where, when, with whom, and what was felt. Now the question changes. Not "How could I?" as a cry of self-condemnation, but "How did this become more likely?" That question does not excuse the behaviour. It refuses to waste it.

The first useful line of inquiry is the lead-up. A setback usually has a weather pattern before it has an event. There may have been poor sleep, skipped food, an unspoken resentment, a run of overwork, an argument left unresolved, too much time alone, a support call missed, an app reinstalled, a risky route taken, a familiar story rehearsed. These details can feel ordinary enough to dismiss, yet ordinary details often build the bridge to old behaviour. The visible sequence matters: Monday sleep shortened, Tuesday contact avoided, Wednesday evening left unstructured, Thursday craving treated as private, Friday slip.

Lead-up factors should be described without turning them into excuses. "I was tired" is not a defence. It is a condition. "I felt criticised" is not a licence. It is a trigger. "I was alone in the hotel room after a difficult day" is not fate. It is a high-risk setting. Mature reflection holds two truths at once: the person is responsible for what they did, and the conditions around the behaviour influenced how easy it became to do. If either truth is removed, learning weakens. Pure blame teaches fear. Pure explanation removes agency. Recovery needs the harder middle.

Decision points are the next layer. These are the small exits that existed before the setback became a setback. A decision point might be the moment the person noticed they had not eaten but continued anyway. It might be the moment they took the old route home, kept the phone in bed, answered while angry, cancelled the meeting, ignored the support text, walked into the shop, stayed in the argument, or decided not to mention the craving because it felt embarrassing. Decision points are rarely cinematic. They are quiet hinges. That is why they matter.

Aviation offers a useful parallel. After the Tenerife airport disaster on 27 March 1977, in the Canary Islands, aviation training and investigation placed increasing emphasis on communication, hierarchy, cockpit resource management, and the chain of small conditions that can precede catastrophe. The lesson for recovery is not that personal setbacks are equivalent to public disasters. They are not. The useful principle is narrower: when serious outcomes are reviewed well, the inquiry does not stop at the final act. It examines the chain. It asks where confusion, pressure, assumption, silence, fatigue, or authority shaped the next move.

The chain is where change becomes possible. If the person only studies the final behaviour, the answer will often be vague: "I must not do that again." True, but weak. If the chain is studied, the answer becomes more precise: "I need to move difficult conversations to daytime," "I need support lined up after family visits," "I need to eat before the commute," "I need to remove access before travel," "I need to send the check-in when shame first appears, not after I have already hidden." Precision turns regret into design.

This is where the temptation to write ten new rules must be resisted. Shame loves abundance. It creates an entire constitution overnight: no more late nights, no more phones, no more mistakes, no more anger, daily exercise, perfect honesty, total discipline, immediate transformation. The list feels powerful because it is severe. Yet severity is not the same as durability. A person flooded by remorse can design a life no ordinary human will maintain. Then, when the impossible system breaks, shame gains fresh evidence. One system change is often braver than ten declarations.

A system change alters the conditions under which future choices happen. It is not a mood. It is not merely a promise. It shows up in the calendar, the room, the route, the contact plan, the timing of conversations, the placement of the phone, the availability of food, the removal of access, the expectation of a check-in, the decision to avoid a particular setting at a particular hour. "I will try harder" is a wish. "I will not have that conversation after ten at night, and I will text support afterwards" is a system change. The difference is visible.

The review should also ask what held. This may feel counterintuitive after a setback, but it matters. If something prevented the setback from becoming worse, that information belongs in the data. Perhaps the person eventually told the truth. Perhaps they stopped after one event rather than continuing for days. Perhaps they contacted support sooner than last time. Perhaps they removed access after the slip. Perhaps they slept instead of arguing through the night. Noticing what held is not self-congratulation. It identifies the supports worth strengthening. A damaged bridge may still have beams that carried weight.

There is a credible limitation in turning setbacks into data. Some pain should not be rushed into lessons. A person who has harmed someone, broken trust, or created serious consequences may be tempted to convert the event into learning too quickly, as if insight could settle the moral account. "I learned a lot" can become another way of stepping around impact. Reflection must not replace repair. Nor should the language of data be used to sound detached from responsibility. A harmed person does not need a lecture on patterns when what is required is acknowledgement, changed behaviour, and patience with the consequences.

The reconciliation is order. Stabilise first. Name accurately. Repair where repair is due. Then review the system with enough humility to change it. Data is not the opposite of remorse; it is remorse made useful. It does not ask the affected person to be grateful for the lesson. It asks the person in recovery to stop wasting pain on self-attack and to convert it into observable prevention. The work must show up later, when the same conditions return and the old exit is no longer left unguarded.

A brief review can be more powerful than a long emotional autopsy. The mind after shame may want to search every corridor of childhood, personality, relationship history, stress, and meaning. Some of that deeper inquiry may have its place, especially with appropriate support. But immediate recovery learning often needs narrower questions: what led up to the setback, where were the decision points, what did I believe the old behaviour would give me, what did it actually cost, what one condition will I change before the next similar day? These questions keep reflection tied to behaviour.

Cost deserves a clear place in the review. Not inflated cost, not melodrama, but actual cost. Time lost. Trust weakened. Sleep damaged. Money spent. Health affected. Work disrupted. Emotional distance created. Support avoided. Self-respect shaken. The cost should be named because memory can become selective later. A craving remembers relief. A pattern remembers permission. The written cost gives the future self a more honest record to consult when the old door starts to look harmless again.

The review should also examine expectation. What did the person think would happen if they acted on the urge, concealed the truth, continued the argument, skipped the call, or entered the risky setting? Did they expect relief, control, privacy, revenge, comfort, numbness, excitement, escape, or proof that no one could reach them? Expectation is often the sales pitch of the old behaviour. It promises one thing and delivers another. A useful review compares promise with receipt. The behaviour promised relief; it delivered secrecy. It promised control; it delivered repair work. It promised comfort; it delivered a longer climb back.

There is also the question of timing. Many setbacks are less about a single weak moment than about placing a demanding situation in the wrong part of the day. A difficult conversation held late at night. A stressful errand attempted hungry. A travel day left without contact. A family visit followed by solitude and an open phone. A high-pressure week treated as if it were a normal week. Timing is not a minor detail. It can decide whether a tool is available or useless. Moving a difficult conversation to daylight, with food beforehand and support afterwards, may be the one change that prevents a repeat.

The motif of the bridge returns, but now its purpose is inspection. After crossing the first 24 hours, the person looks back at the bridge and asks where the supports were missing. Was there no rail at the high-risk hour? Was contact too far away? Was the environment still voting for the old behaviour? Was the person trying to carry a full load with no sleep, no food, and no honest witness? The inspection is not performed to admire the damage. It is performed so the next crossing is less fragile.

Data must remain small enough to use. A spreadsheet of suffering may look rigorous while producing no change. A single clear sentence may alter the next month. "I am most at risk after conflict when I am alone and tired; the system change is no serious conversation after nine, and a check-in afterwards." That sentence has a trigger, a condition, a boundary, and a support. It can be remembered under pressure. It can be tested. It can be revised if it does not hold. Good recovery data is not impressive; it is actionable.

This approach also changes how the person relates to repetition. If the same setback recurs, shame says, "You learned nothing." Data asks a harder question: "Was the system actually changed, and was the change close enough to the risk?" Perhaps the rule was too vague. Perhaps the support came too late. Perhaps the environment still allowed easy access. Perhaps the person changed the wrong variable because it was more comfortable than changing the real one. Repetition is painful, but it can become more precise if the person refuses to hide inside global despair.

For intelligent, time-conscious people, this may feel almost too plain. They may prefer a more elaborate theory, a deeper narrative, an elegant explanation of personality, attachment, motivation, or stress. Those frameworks can be useful, but recovery after a setback often turns on blunt practicalities. Did you eat? Did you sleep? Did you tell the truth early? Did you stay near access? Did you go alone into a high-risk hour? Did you confuse shame with accountability? Did you write a plan you would actually follow when tired? The plain questions are not beneath serious people. They are often what serious people avoid.

The forward test is whether the next setback, if one comes, will be permitted to teach something specific. Not everything. Not a grand doctrine. One useful change. One moved conversation. One earlier text. One blocked route. One meal placed before the danger hour. One reduced access point. One support person given clearer instructions. The event cannot be undone. The question is whether it will remain only a wound, or whether, once stabilised and repaired, it will become evidence that changes the design of the next hard day.

Chapter 7
Shame Reduction and Self-Talk

What if the voice that claims to keep you accountable is the same voice that keeps the cycle alive? A person makes a mistake, breaks a promise, hides a risky thought, speaks with cruelty, returns to an old behaviour, or lets a hard day become a secret one. Then the inner verdict arrives quickly: not "that action needs repair", but "this is who you are". The sentence lands heavily. It feels severe enough to be true.

Shame is persuasive because it borrows the clothing of conscience. It sounds morally serious. It appears to demand better behaviour. Yet its usual effects are strangely unhelpful: secrecy, isolation, defensiveness, collapse, and the dangerous little phrase that has ruined many recoveries, "I might as well." Once the self has been sentenced, the next harmful action can feel almost logical. Why protect a life already declared guilty? Why tell the truth if the truth will only confirm the worst story?

Guilt and shame are often tangled together, but recovery needs the distinction. Guilt points towards behaviour: what was done, what it cost, who was affected, what repair is required. Shame attacks identity: what kind of person this proves you are, why change is impossible, why being seen would be unbearable. Guilt can become a doorway into responsibility. Shame often becomes a locked room. The difference is visible in the next action. One moves towards repair. The other moves towards hiding.

The central tension is that recovery requires honest self-assessment without self-destruction. Too little responsibility leaves harm unnamed. Too much self-attack makes learning impossible. The person must be able to say, "I did something that needs repair," without adding, "therefore I am beyond care." That line is not sentimental. It is exact. A person who can remain present after a mistake is more likely to tell the truth, reduce risk, and make amends that do not demand emotional rescue from the very people affected.

The stakes are high because inner language becomes outer behaviour. A harsh internal script does not stay private. It changes posture, eye contact, tone, timing, honesty, and willingness to be reachable. The person who is calling themselves disgusting may delay the apology because being seen feels unbearable. The person who is calling themselves hopeless may abandon the evening routine because the day has already been condemned. The person who is replaying an old shame script may interpret concern as accusation and support as intrusion. A sentence inside the mind can become a room no one else is allowed to enter.

There is also a relational cost. Shame can make apology dramatic, excessive, and strangely self-centred. The person apologises in a flood, repeats their remorse until the other person feels pressured to comfort them, or turns repair into a performance of suffering. That may look like accountability from a distance, but it often shifts attention away from the impact and back towards the person who caused it. Clean repair is quieter. It names the impact, states what will change, and leaves room for the other person's response without demanding immediate absolution.

The path here moves through the mechanism of shame before it tries to change the language around it. The inner script has to be heard clearly: the old phrases, the body sensations that accompany them, the moments when they intensify, and the behaviours they tend to produce. From there, responsibility needs a different voice, one that can acknowledge harm without turning the self into a case for permanent condemnation. Repair then has to leave the private mind and enter relationship, where apology becomes grounded action rather than self-erasure.

The motif is a receipt. Shame hands over a receipt with only one word printed on it: failure. Recovery asks for an itemised account. What happened? What did it cost? What needs repair? What risk needs reducing today? The itemised account may be uncomfortable, but it is usable. It prevents the person from paying endlessly for a vague sentence while leaving the actual damage unattended.

The unresolved question is whether the next mistake will be allowed to become an identity, or whether it will remain a fact that can be faced. When the old script rises in the body, tightening the chest, lowering the eyes, pushing the person towards secrecy or over-apology, what will speak next: the voice that condemns, the voice that excuses, or the steadier voice that can repair without disappearing?

How Shame Fuels Cycles

In 1971, in *Shame and Guilt in Neurosis*, British psychoanalyst Helen Block Lewis drew a distinction that still cuts cleanly through recovery work: guilt concerns what one has done; shame concerns what one is. The distinction may sound delicate on the page, but in lived experience it is the difference between a door and a trapdoor. Guilt can lead a person towards repair. Shame often drops them into hiding.

A person does not usually experience shame as a concept. They feel heat in the face, a heavy chest, a wish to be unseen, a sudden hatred of being asked a simple question. The eyes lower. The shoulders curl inward. The phone goes unanswered. A message that might have been sent early is delayed until the facts are harder to tell. The inner voice does not say, "A behaviour needs attention." It says, "You are the problem." The room gets smaller.

That shrinking is why shame can become so dangerous in recovery. It rarely stops at remorse. It reorganises the next decision. A person who feels guilt may say, "I acted against my values; I need to name the impact and change the conditions." A person drowning in shame may say nothing, avoid everyone, seek relief from the feeling, and then feel even worse when the relief creates more damage. The original setback becomes only the first turn of the wheel. Shame supplies the next one.

The wheel has a recognisable pattern. A behaviour causes distress or consequence. Shame turns the behaviour into identity. Identity feels unbearable. The person seeks escape through secrecy, withdrawal, numbing, defensiveness, over-apology, or another familiar relief. That relief creates more consequence. More consequence confirms the shame story. The cycle is not mysterious once seen, but it is powerful because each step feels like a reaction rather than a choice. The person does not think, "I will now fuel the pattern." They think, "I cannot stand being seen like this."

This is where guilt is useful and shame is not. Guilt can be morally intelligent. It points towards the broken promise, the sharp sentence, the concealed truth, the missed responsibility, the boundary crossed, the support avoided. It can motivate apology, restitution, renewed structure, and reduced risk. Shame, by contrast, blurs the evidence. It turns "I lied" into "I am rotten", "I shouted" into "I am unsafe to love", "I slipped" into "I have ruined everything". The behaviour disappears inside the sentence about the self. Once that happens, learning becomes harder because the thing to be changed has become too large to touch.

Psychologist June Price Tangney and her colleagues, writing extensively from the 1990s onwards on shame, guilt, and moral behaviour, helped clarify this distinction in empirical psychology. Their work has repeatedly treated guilt as more closely tied to reparative action, while shame is more often associated with avoidance, defensiveness, and distress. The practical meaning is not that guilt is always clean or shame is always simple; human emotion is rarely that tidy. The useful point is sharper: when the self is globally condemned, the person's capacity to learn from a specific act often narrows.

Shame also distorts time. It makes the present mistake feel ancient and permanent, as though every earlier failure has returned to testify and every future effort has already been discredited. A missed check-in becomes proof that the person never changes. A craving becomes evidence of secret corruption. A conflict becomes confirmation that relationships are unsafe because the person themselves is unsafe. Shame stacks the evidence badly. It gathers every old receipt, throws them onto the table, and says the account can never be settled.

The receipt motif matters because shame often refuses itemisation. It hands over a total and calls it truth. Recovery requires the itemised account: what happened, what it cost, who was affected, what condition made it more likely, what repair is due, what support is needed now. Itemising does not minimise the cost. It makes payment possible. A vague life sentence cannot guide repair. A specific account can. "I ignored two messages after the argument and stayed alone with a craving" is painful but useful. "I am impossible" is painful and useless.

The body often reveals the shame script before the mind has words for it. Some people feel shame as heat: face burning, ears hot, skin prickling. Others feel it as collapse: heavy limbs, lowered gaze, a wish to sleep or disappear from contact. Others feel it as attack: sudden irritation, contempt, a need to blame someone else before they are blamed. Some feel it as frantic repair: apologising repeatedly, explaining too much, demanding reassurance, trying to settle everyone else's feelings at once. These bodily signatures are not character flaws. They are early warnings that the cycle is trying to recruit the person again.

Shame scripts tend to be short, absolute, and familiar. "I always do this." "No one would stay if they knew." "I am too much." "I am not serious about recovery." "I ruin everything." "There is no point now." Their power lies partly in speed. They arrive before the fuller record can assemble itself. A script does not need to be original to be convincing; in fact, its familiarity is part of the spell. It feels true because it has been rehearsed. The task is not to argue with every word at the level of philosophy. The task is to notice the script as a script before it becomes instruction.

The phrase "might as well" is one of shame's most efficient tools. It sounds casual, almost lazy, but it is a hinge into further damage. "I have already missed the meeting, so I might as well avoid everyone." "I have already eaten badly, so I might as well keep going." "I have already lied once, so I might as well hide the rest." "I have already broken the routine, so I might as well abandon the day." The phrase converts an initial breach into permission for expansion. It turns a crack into a corridor.

All-or-nothing thinking and shame make a natural alliance. All-or-nothing thinking supplies the verdict; shame supplies the identity wound; old relief supplies the anaesthetic. The person then confuses intensity with inevitability. Because the feeling is so painful, the next escape seems reasonable. Because the escape creates more pain, the shame story seems confirmed. The wheel turns, and the person may describe the pattern as weakness when it is also a sequence. Seeing the sequence does not erase responsibility. It locates the next possible interruption.

Secrecy is the chamber where shame grows most persuasive. Alone, a person can rehearse the worst sentence without interruption. Alone, they can edit out the facts that would complicate the verdict. Alone, they can imagine the reaction of others as harsher than it may be, or avoid the reactions that are legitimately difficult but necessary. This is why even a brief contact can weaken shame's authority. A message sent early, plain and undramatic, can bring the event back to scale. "I am ashamed and want to hide. I need to stay accountable tonight." That sentence is not glamorous. It opens a window.

Isolation is not always physical. A person can sit in a room full of people and still be isolated if the truth has gone underground. They can answer work emails, attend a lecture, care for a child, lead a meeting, smile at a neighbour, and still be carrying a private verdict that no one is allowed to challenge. This is one reason shame is so compatible with high functioning. Performance continues while contact thins. Recovery risk may rise precisely because the outside world still appears orderly.

There is a credible limitation in talking about shame reduction. Some people use the language of shame to avoid confronting guilt. They say they feel ashamed when the more urgent matter is that someone else was hurt, misled, frightened, ignored, or left carrying consequences. In such cases, reducing shame must not become a way of reducing accountability. The answer is not to replace shame with comfort, but to replace shame with responsibility. The question is not "How can I stop feeling bad as quickly as possible?" It is "How can I stay present enough to repair what is mine to repair?"

The reconciliation is to let guilt do its work while refusing shame the authority to define the self. Guilt says, "Name the behaviour." Shame says, "Become the behaviour." Guilt says, "Repair the impact." Shame says, "Hide, collapse, or perform." Guilt says, "Change the condition that made this more likely." Shame says, "You are the condition." Recovery needs the person to hear guilt clearly and shame sceptically. Not because the person is innocent of harm, but because harm is less likely to be repaired by someone who has disappeared into self-condemnation.

Understanding the mechanism reduces its power because shame depends on being mistaken for truth. Once the person sees the sequence, the sequence becomes less automatic. Heat in the face can be read as "my shame script is starting", not "I must hide". A heavy chest can be read as "I need contact before this becomes secrecy", not "I cannot face anyone". A surge of defensiveness can be read as "I am trying to outrun guilt", not "they are attacking me". The body signal becomes a prompt rather than a sentence.

The most practical question after shame appears is not "How do I feel better?" but "What does shame usually make me do next?" For some, it makes them avoid. For others, confess excessively. For others, attack. For others, numb. For others, make new rules they will later resent. The answer identifies the risk. A person who knows shame makes them withdraw can arrange contact early. A person who knows shame makes them over-apologise can pause before repair. A person who knows shame makes them seek quick relief can reduce access before the craving gathers force. Insight becomes useful when it changes the next move.

Shame also blocks learning by making evidence feel dangerous. To review a setback honestly, the person must look at details: timing, choices, triggers, impact, cost, and missed exits. Shame makes those details feel like weapons. The person either refuses to look, or looks with such cruelty that nothing can be understood. Learning requires a steadier posture. The event must be close enough to examine and far enough away not to engulf the whole self. This is why stabilisation comes before reflection. A flooded person does not learn well; they survive, defend, or submit.

There is a strange humility in accepting that self-attack is not the same as moral seriousness. Many people cling to harsh self-talk because they fear that without it they will become careless. Yet harshness often produces the very carelessness it claims to prevent. It exhausts the person, drives secrecy, and makes the next repair feel unbearable. Responsibility requires staying in the room. Shame tries to remove the self from the room entirely, either by hiding or by turning the self into the only subject worth discussing.

The receipt returns one last time. When shame hands over the single-word bill, the person can ask for the itemised version. What was the behaviour? What was the impact? What feeling preceded it? What did shame urge afterwards? What is the next honest action? This is not softness. It is accuracy with a spine. The total may still hurt. Some costs do. But an itemised receipt can be paid, disputed where it is distorted, and used to prevent the same charge appearing again.

The forward test is whether shame will be recognised at the point where it begins to steer. Not after the week has vanished. Not after secrecy has hardened. Not after "might as well" has opened every old door. At the first heat in the face, the first urge to hide, the first global sentence about the self, the question is waiting: is this guilt asking for repair, or shame asking for a cycle? The answer may decide whether the next action moves towards honesty or back into the wheel.

Writing a Repair-Focused Inner Script

In 1962, at the University of Pennsylvania in Philadelphia, psychiatrist Aaron T. Beck began developing what would later become cognitive therapy after noticing that people in distress often carried swift, automatic thoughts beneath their visible emotions. The importance of the discovery was not that inner language controlled everything, nor that a sentence could magically heal pain. It was more exacting than that: the words a person accepts as true can shape what they notice, what they avoid, and what they do next.

Recovery has always known this in a rougher, more intimate way. After harm, risk, secrecy, or a setback, the mind starts speaking before the person has decided what kind of leader they intend to be. One voice says, "You are disgusting." Another says, "It does not matter." Another says, "You have ruined everything, so why bother now?" These voices may feel different, but they can produce the same result: less honesty, less repair, less steadiness. The script becomes the hand on the wheel.

A repair-focused inner script does not pretend that nothing happened. It is not a scented veil thrown over consequence. It does not ask the person to recite comforting nonsense while trust is damaged, risk is rising, or an apology is overdue. Its purpose is more serious. It gives the person language sturdy enough to keep them responsible without pushing them into collapse. The sentence has to hold both weight and movement: "I did a risky thing; I will repair and reduce risk today." There is no sparkle in it. That is part of its dignity.

The old harsh script often disguises itself as accountability. "I am hopeless" can sound morally alert because it hurts. "I always ruin things" can seem honest because it refuses comfort. "I do not deserve support" can feel like humility because it lowers the self. Yet these sentences are rarely accountable in practice. They do not name the behaviour, the impact, the person affected, the next repair, or the risk that must be reduced. They create heat without direction. They burn the room and call it truth.

A functional inner script begins by separating the act from the identity while keeping the act fully visible. "I lied about where I was" is different from "I am a liar." "I shouted and frightened someone" is different from "I am a monster." "I ignored my plan and increased risk" is different from "I never change." The behaviour sentence is harder because it can be acted upon. It points towards acknowledgement, repair, changed access, contact, apology, sleep, food, distance from the trigger, or a review of the lead-up. The identity sentence may feel larger, but it is less useful. It offers drama instead of traction.

Albert Ellis, working in New York in the 1950s, developed rational emotive behaviour therapy around the idea that beliefs and self-statements shape emotional and behavioural consequences. His style was famously direct, sometimes too blunt for some temperaments, but the relevant inheritance is practical: people can learn to dispute self-defeating inner claims and replace them with language that supports better action. The value here is not mere optimism. It is behavioural consequence. Does the sentence make truth-telling more likely? Does it make repair more possible? Does it help the person reduce the next risk? If not, its harshness has not made it wise.

The repair-focused script has three quiet tasks. It names the behaviour without euphemism. It names the next responsibility without theatrical punishment. It names the immediate risk without pretending the person is either safe forever or doomed already. A sentence such as "I crossed a boundary last night; I need to apologise clearly and avoid that setting today" performs all three tasks. It neither collapses nor excuses. It stands up, looks at the broken piece, and reaches for the broom.

The broom is the motif because repair-focused language should be practical enough to clean with. It is not a banner. It is not a hymn to self-worth. It is a tool held after something has been spilt, cracked, or scattered. "I made a harmful choice; I will tell the truth before noon." "I am ashamed and want to hide; I will contact one safe person now." "I am angry and tempted to punish with silence; I will pause and set a return time." "I slipped yesterday; today I will stabilise, reduce access, and review when rested." The sentences are plain because the moment does not need decoration. It needs direction.

This is why fake positivity fails. A person who has caused harm does not need to be told, "Everything is fine." Everything may not be fine. Trust may have been weakened. Someone may have been hurt. A plan may need to change. A risky cue may need to be removed. The self may feel shaken because the event matters. To deny that is not kindness; it is avoidance with a softer voice. Repair-focused language is warmer than shame, but stricter than denial. It says, "This is serious enough to handle, and I am not allowed to disappear."

The same principle applies after near-misses, not only obvious setbacks. A person may not have acted out, but they may have hidden a craving, walked towards a risky place, rehearsed a lie, kept access open, or delayed contact until the situation grew hot. A shame script might say, "I cannot believe I am still like this." A repair-focused script says, "The risk rose, and I noticed late; I will move support earlier next time." This language protects learning. It prevents the person from needing full damage before they feel authorised to adjust the system.

There is a credible limitation. Inner scripts cannot be expected to solve severe distress, unsafe environments, addiction, trauma, coercion, deprivation, or clinical conditions by themselves. A sentence is not treatment. It is not shelter, medication, legal protection, a recovery meeting, a crisis service, or a trustworthy relationship. Some people need forms of help far beyond self-talk, and it would be dishonest to imply that better wording can carry what a wider structure must carry. Language is powerful, but it is not omnipotent.

The reconciliation is to place the script where it belongs: between the feeling and the next behaviour. It is a hinge, not the whole door. It can help a person reach for support rather than hide, apologise without self-erasure, cancel the high-risk plan, eat before the evening collapses, put the phone away, leave the argument, or tell the truth while it is still small. It should not be asked to do the work of an entire recovery system. It should help the person use the system already in place.

A repair-focused script also needs to match the level of harm. If the sentence is too mild, it becomes evasion. If it is too savage, it becomes shame. "I made a mistake" may be accurate for a missed check-in, but too thin for deception that affected someone else. "I destroyed everything" may be emotionally tempting after a painful setback, but too global to guide repair. The right sentence names the actual weight. "I concealed something that mattered, and trust has been affected. I will name it clearly and accept that repair may take time." This is not self-attack. It is adult language.

For thoughtful people, there is another trap: turning inner work into endless commentary. The mind writes a paragraph when one sentence would do. It explains history, intention, stress, pain, motives, and context until the repair gets pushed further away. Understanding matters, but timing matters more. In the hot moment, the inner script should be brief enough to remember and strong enough to interrupt the old sequence. Later, reflection can widen. At the point of action, the sentence must be clean.

The script should also be written in verbs. Verbs prevent moral fog. "Repair." "Tell." "Pause." "Leave." "Contact." "Eat." "Sleep." "Cancel." "Return." "Apologise." "Reduce." "Review." A sentence that contains no verb may create atmosphere without movement. "I feel terrible about what happened" may be sincere, but it does not yet know where to go. "I feel terrible, and I will contact the person affected after I have stabilised enough to speak cleanly" has a path. The broom has found the floor.

Functional self-leadership sounds different from both indulgence and abuse. It does not say, "You poor thing, nothing is your fault." It does not say, "You are beyond repair." It says, "Look directly. Stay present. Do the next clean thing." That tone may feel unfamiliar to people who grew up with criticism, chaos, emotional withdrawal, or praise that depended on performance. Some may equate kindness with softness because the only authority they knew was harsh. Others may equate responsibility with panic because mistakes were treated as disasters. A repair-focused script creates a different authority inside the person: firm, brief, fair, and oriented towards action.

The body will often resist the new script before the mind trusts it. Shame may still tighten the chest. The face may still burn. The old urge to disappear may still arrive. The new words may feel artificial at first because they have not yet been rehearsed under pressure. That does not make them false. It means the nervous system is learning a different route. Repetition matters. A sentence used only once is a phrase. A sentence used repeatedly at the hinge between shame and action becomes part of recovery architecture.

The most reliable scripts are prepared before the worst moment. A person should not expect themselves to invent fair language while flooded. The old script has had years of rehearsal; the new one deserves rehearsal too. It can be written on paper, placed in a phone note, spoken after a check-in, or attached to known risk states. After anger: "I can be angry without causing more harm." After secrecy: "The longer I hide this, the larger it becomes." After a slip: "Stabilise now; review later." After hurting someone: "Name the impact, state the change, do not demand reassurance." These sentences are not magic. They are prepared rails.

The repair-focused script must also leave room for consequences. Some people unconsciously use kinder self-talk to rush past the discomfort of being held accountable. "I am not a bad person" may be true, but it is incomplete if someone else is waiting for acknowledgement. The better sentence is fuller: "I am not only this behaviour, and this behaviour still requires repair." That structure prevents both collapse and escape. It allows the person to remain human without becoming vague.

There is a particular strength in the phrase, "Today." Shame loves forever. It says always, never, ruined, hopeless, permanent. Recovery often needs a shorter unit of time. "Today I will reduce risk." "Today I will tell the truth." "Today I will eat and sleep before reviewing." "Today I will not turn one slip into a week." The word does not deny the longer arc. It returns authority to the next set of actions. A life changes through many todays that refuse to become verdicts.

The broom returns in the final measure of the script: what is cleaner after the sentence has been used? Not perfect. Cleaner. Is the person more likely to be honest? More likely to contact support? More likely to repair impact without theatrics? More likely to reduce access? More likely to sleep rather than spiral? More likely to review the sequence when steadier? If the answer is yes, the sentence is doing useful work. If the sentence leaves the person more hidden, more defended, more dramatic, or more likely to act out, it may be familiar, but it is not fit for recovery.

The forward test is whether the next inner sentence will help or harm the next outer action. After the risky choice, the sharp word, the concealed truth, the craving, the near-miss, or the setback, the mind will speak. It always does. The question is whether it will hand the wheel to shame, to excuse, or to the steadier voice that can say, without ornament, "I did something that needs repair; I will reduce risk and take the next honest step."

Making Amends Without Self-Erasure

In December 1995, in Cape Town, South Africa's Truth and Reconciliation Commission began its public work under the chairmanship of Archbishop Desmond Tutu. Its scale belonged to national history, not private recovery, and no intimate apology should be confused with the gravity of political violence. Yet one principle travels carefully: repair requires more than feeling bad in public. Testimony had to name harms, locate responsibility, and place truth where denial had once stood. Emotion mattered, but emotion alone was not repair.

The same distinction applies in smaller rooms. A person who has caused hurt may enter the conversation already flooded with shame, eager to apologise before the other person has finished speaking, desperate to be forgiven quickly so the body can stop burning. They may say "I am sorry" repeatedly, explain too much, promise too much, cry so hard that the injured person becomes the comforter, or collapse into self-attack. The apology fills the room. The impact disappears.

This is how over-apologising becomes another form of drama. It looks humble, but it can quietly move attention away from the person affected and back towards the person apologising. The exchange becomes less about repair and more about emotional relief. The injured person is asked, sometimes without words, to reduce the apologiser's shame, confirm that they are not terrible, and shorten the discomfort of consequence. That is not clean accountability. That is self-erasure demanding an audience.

A clean apology has a different shape. It names the impact, states the change, and sets a follow-up. The language is plain because repair needs fewer decorations than shame wants to add. "When I disappeared after the argument, it left you anxious and alone with the conflict. I am changing the way I pause: I will give a return time and keep it. I will check in tomorrow after work to talk about what support would help rebuild trust." This sentence does not grovel. It does not excuse. It does not ask to be rescued. It gives the other person something observable.

The first element is impact because harm must not be buried beneath intention. Many apologies fail at this point. They begin with the apologiser's stress, history, fear, tiredness, or remorse, all of which may be real, but none of which should take the first chair. Impact asks what the other person experienced because of the behaviour: uncertainty, embarrassment, fear, inconvenience, disappointment, extra labour, loss of trust, emotional whiplash, or the burden of guessing what was true. Naming impact does not mean pretending to know exactly how another person feels. It means making a responsible attempt to locate the effect of one's actions outside one's own inner weather.

The second element is change because apology without altered behaviour becomes noise. "I am sorry" may matter, but repeated apologies attached to the same unchanged pattern lose moral force. Change has to become visible in decisions: replying when agreed, pausing with a return time, moving a difficult conversation to daylight, reducing access to a known trigger, arranging support after high-risk situations, telling the truth earlier, or setting a boundary before resentment turns into punishment. Trust is rebuilt by evidence. The evidence may be small at first, but it must exist.

The third element is follow-up because repair is rarely completed in a single exchange. A person harmed by secrecy, volatility, avoidance, or broken promises may need time before they know what they need. The apologiser may also need time to prove that the stated change is not merely a shame-driven performance. A follow-up creates a sober bridge between words and practice. "I will check back on Friday." "I will show you the change for the next week and then ask how it is landing." "I will not press you to respond tonight." Follow-up gives repair a calendar, not a spotlight.

Aaron Lazare, a psychiatrist and former chancellor of the University of Massachusetts Medical School, examined apology in his 2004 book *On Apology*, emphasising recognition of offence, responsibility, remorse, and reparative action. The relevance here is practical rather than ceremonial. Apology is not merely expression; it is a social act that can either restore dignity or deepen injury. A vague apology asks the affected person to do the interpretive work. A clean apology carries its own weight. It says, in effect, "I understand enough of what I did to begin repairing it, and I will not make you manage my shame before your own hurt has been acknowledged."

Self-erasure often enters through the back door of remorse. The person says, "I am awful," "I do not deserve you," "You should hate me," or "I ruin everything." Such statements may feel like accountability because they are severe, but they often create a burden for the listener. The other person must either contradict the sentence, absorb its intensity, or sit in the discomfort of someone condemning themselves in the middle of a conversation about harm. Self-condemnation can become a way of avoiding the harder sentence: "I did this, it affected you in this way, and I am taking this action."

The difference is not softness. It is precision. "I am a terrible partner" is emotionally large and practically vague. "I raised my voice and then refused to return to the conversation; that made the conflict less safe and left you carrying it alone" is harder to say because it is exact. It cannot hide behind personality. It cannot demand reassurance as easily. It points towards change. Self-erasure says, "Make me vanish because I cannot bear what I did." Repair says, "Let me stay present long enough to become responsible for what I did."

The broom returns here as the quiet motif of repair. After something breaks, waving the broom in panic does not clean the floor. Neither does weeping over the shards while others step around them. The broom has to touch the ground. It has to move the pieces carefully. Apology is the same. Feeling sorry may bring the person to the room, but it does not sweep. Naming impact, stating change, and returning to follow up: that is the motion across the floor.

There is also a time to pause before apologising. This may sound counterintuitive, especially to someone terrified of seeming evasive, but immediate apology is not always the cleanest apology. When the body is flooded, the voice may shake with panic, the words may become excessive, and the person may seek relief rather than repair. A pause can allow the person to stabilise, speak to support, separate behaviour from identity, and decide what actually needs to be said. The pause must not become disappearance. It needs a boundary: "I want to apologise properly, and I am too activated to do that cleanly right now. I will come back at seven."

Support before repair can be wise when shame is likely to distort the conversation. A trusted support person, therapist, sponsor, mentor, or recovery peer can help the person sort facts from self-attack, identify the real impact, and avoid using apology as a demand for absolution. This is not about outsourcing responsibility. It is preparation for taking responsibility without turning the affected person into a regulator of the apologiser's nervous system. Grounded accountability is steadier because it has been settled enough to listen.

The restorative justice movement offers another useful, though not identical, example. New Zealand's Children, Young Persons, and Their Families Act 1989 helped establish family group conferences in youth justice, placing structured attention on accountability, victims, families, and agreed plans for repair. Private recovery conversations are not legal processes, and they should not borrow that gravity carelessly. Yet the principle is relevant: repair works best when it moves beyond apology as feeling and towards acknowledgement, responsibility, practical commitments, and follow-through. A harmed person should not be handed only emotion when what is needed is changed conduct.

A credible limitation must be named. Not every relationship is safe enough for direct amends. In situations involving coercion, abuse, harassment, manipulation, legal risk, active danger, or patterns where contact itself causes harm, apology may require professional guidance, distance, indirect repair, or no contact at all. The desire to apologise does not override another person's safety or boundaries. Nor does someone's need to repair grant them a right to access the person they harmed. Accountability includes respecting the limits of the person affected.

The reconciliation is to define amends more broadly than emotional access. Sometimes repair means returning money, correcting a record, respecting distance, changing shared arrangements, telling the truth to the appropriate person, ceasing contact, seeking treatment, or altering conditions so the harm is less likely to recur. A direct apology can be powerful when it is safe, wanted, and grounded. When it is not, repair must find a form that does not make the affected person pay again for the apologiser's need to feel resolved.

A clean apology also avoids the trap of over-explanation. Context can matter, especially when a pattern needs to be understood and changed, but context should not crowd out responsibility. "I was exhausted and ashamed" may be relevant. It becomes evasive if it functions as a plea to lower the cost of the behaviour. The order matters. Impact first. Responsibility next. Context, if useful, later and briefly. Change always visible. The person affected should not have to dig through paragraphs of explanation to find the apology.

The language of apology should be concrete enough to be tested. "I will do better" is often too vague. "I will not continue serious conversations after midnight; I will ask for a pause and return the next day" can be observed. "I will be more honest" is a worthy intention, but "I will tell you when I am craving rather than pretending I am fine" is more useful. "I will respect your boundaries" becomes real when the person stops sending repeated messages after being asked for space. Repair lives in verbs.

There is a particular danger in apologising to end discomfort. The person wants the room to soften, the face across from them to relax, the relationship to feel restored, the shame to quieten. Those wishes are human. They are not the other person's obligation. An apology offered cleanly must leave room for the possibility that forgiveness is slow, partial, uncertain, or not available. It must not demand the very trust it damaged. The person making amends can control the honesty of the apology and the consistency of the change. They cannot control the timeline of another person's healing.

This is where self-erasure can appear noble but actually become impatient. "I will do anything" may sound devoted, but it can place a frightening and unrealistic burden on the other person. "I do not matter" may sound remorseful, but it may invite unhealthy dynamics and further instability. Grounded repair is more respectful. "I care about the harm I caused. I will make this specific change. I understand you may need time, and I will not pressure you to reassure me." That sentence preserves responsibility without making the self disappear.

The broom works slowly. It does not restore the floor by declaring itself sorry for the glass. It moves, gathers, checks corners, returns to the place where a shard may still be hidden. Amends are like that. The first apology may clear the visible pieces. Follow-up finds what remains: the altered routine, the boundary that needs strengthening, the question the other person was not ready to ask, the evidence that change is still holding after the emotion of the moment has faded.

For thoughtful people, the temptation may be to produce the perfect apology. That impulse should be treated with suspicion. Perfection can become another way to centre the self: the flawless wording, the morally elegant tone, the exact degree of remorse. The affected person does not need a prize-winning sentence. They need the truth, proportion, changed behaviour, and room to respond honestly. A clean apology may be awkward. It may not resolve the tension quickly. It may feel insufficient because repair is larger than words. That does not make it weak. It makes it real.

The forward test is whether the next apology will reduce harm or simply redistribute shame. When repair is needed, will the person rush in seeking relief, vanish behind self-condemnation, or arrive grounded enough to name the impact, state the change, and set a follow-up? The difference will be visible afterwards: in whether the affected person has been heard, whether the behaviour has a new boundary, and whether the broom has touched the floor.

Chapter 8
Relationship Boundaries That Hold

You say yes before the request has finished arriving. The voice on the other end is tired, disappointed, familiar. Your own body gives its answer first: shoulders tightening, stomach sinking, a small inward flinch that knows the cost before the mind begins explaining it away. You had planned to rest, eat, make the call, keep the evening clean. Now the room shifts. Someone else's urgency has entered and quietly rearranged the furniture.

A boundary problem rarely announces itself as a crisis at first. It often looks like kindness, loyalty, patience, flexibility, being easy to live with, being the reasonable one, being the person who can absorb just a little more. Then the pattern begins to show its underside. The yes becomes resentment. The explanation becomes pleading. The silence becomes disappearance. The relationship remains outwardly intact, but recovery starts paying the bill in private.

The most difficult boundaries are not always the dramatic ones. They are the ordinary thresholds where affection, fear, guilt, duty, and old habit meet. A person may know exactly what would protect their steadiness and still abandon it when someone sighs, presses, accuses, withdraws, flatters, or keeps asking after the answer has already been given. The problem is not lack of intelligence. It is pressure at the hinge of connection. Many people would rather betray themselves quietly than risk disappointing someone openly.

The central tension is that recovery needs relationship, but not every relational pattern supports recovery. Connection can steady a person, bring truth into the open, and interrupt secrecy. It can also become the place where old roles return: rescuer, appeaser, avoider, fixer, performer, defendant, ghost. A boundary is not a wall against love. It is the line that allows love, duty, friendship, family, and care to remain honest without turning into self-abandonment.

The stakes are high because boundary leaks often become recovery leaks. A person who over-gives may later seek relief from the resentment they never named. A person who over-explains may become exhausted and easier to pull into conflict. A person who avoids hard conversations may carry unspoken anger into cravings, shutdown, or secrecy. A person who stays too long in chaos may begin to confuse intensity with importance. The visible behaviours matter: answering messages at unsafe hours, continuing circular arguments, cancelling stabilising routines, hiding stress from support, or saying yes and then numbing the resentment afterwards.

Boundaries also reveal the difference between discomfort and danger. Some guilt is simply the feeling of leaving an old role. Some pushback is an ordinary reaction from people adjusting to a new limit. But some dynamics are more serious: repeated pressure after a clear no, punishment for needing space, ridicule of recovery routines, threats, monitoring, manipulation, or demands for access that leave the person less safe and less honest. Clarity matters because recovery cannot afford to treat every request as harmless or every discomfort as a warning to retreat. The gate must be able to open and close.

The work begins with recognising where the gate has been left half-open: the places where over-giving, over-explaining, conflict avoidance, or vanishing have become habitual. From there, language has to become shorter and steadier, because boundary-setting under stress is rarely helped by speeches. Then comes the harder test: remaining grounded when another person dislikes the limit, questions it, or tries to make guilt do the work that persuasion could not.

A boundary that holds is often plain enough to feel almost disappointing. "I am not discussing this while we are shouting.

I will talk after dinner." "I cannot help tonight." "I need space, and I will reply tomorrow." "No, that does not work for me." Such sentences are not cold. They are clean. Their strength lies partly in what they refuse to carry: the courtroom defence, the anxious biography, the frantic effort to make the other person comfortable with the limit before the limit is allowed to exist.

The unresolved question is where recovery is currently being negotiated away in the name of keeping peace. Which relationships ask for more access than is healthy? Which conversations keep circling until the body is flooded? Which guilt reliably makes the boundary collapse? The next boundary will not be tested by whether it sounds good in private, but by whether it still stands when someone pushes against the gate.

Identifying Boundary Problems

What if the relationship pattern that looks like kindness at 6 p.m. becomes recovery risk by midnight? The request is ordinary. Someone needs a favour, a reply, a second chance, an explanation, a longer conversation, a softer version of your no. You feel the familiar pressure in the body before the mind has finished deciding. The stomach drops. The shoulders brace. The answer forms itself: yes, perhaps, all right, I can manage. Seven words can change a night.

A boundary problem does not always begin with obvious mistreatment. It may begin with a person who wants to be good, loyal, calm, generous, easy, forgiving, mature, or needed. These are not bad desires. They become dangerous when they repeatedly require self-abandonment. The person says yes and later feels resentment. They stay in a circular argument and later need relief from the emotional noise. They over-explain until exhausted. They disappear because saying the truth feels impossible. The boundary leak is not merely relational. It becomes physiological, behavioural, and eventually part of the recovery landscape.

The word "boundary" can sound cold, as if care must be measured with a ruler and tenderness kept behind a locked door. That misunderstanding has done real damage. A healthy boundary is not a withdrawal of humanity. It is a line that tells the truth about capacity, safety, responsibility, and choice. It allows generosity without resentment, intimacy without engulfment, and repair without surrender. A boundary is the gate, not the wall. It exists so that contact can happen honestly rather than through pressure, performance, or fear.

The gate becomes visible when it fails. A person agrees to help when they have not eaten, have not slept well, and have already missed the stabilising call they promised themselves. They answer a provocative message at night because silence feels rude, then spend an hour defending a position that needed only one sentence. They lend money they cannot spare, disclose more than feels safe, absorb another person's crisis, or keep listening after their body has started sending clear signals of overload. The visible behaviour may look caring. The after-effect tells a different story: irritability, secrecy, craving, numbness, blame, exhaustion, or the private conviction that old relief is deserved.

People-pleasing is often the most socially rewarded boundary problem. It can be mistaken for warmth because it produces immediate comfort for other people. The person anticipates needs, smooths tension, says yes quickly, remembers everyone's sensitivities, and becomes skilled at sensing disappointment before it is spoken. The cost is that their own needs become negotiable before they have even been named. In recovery, that cost is not abstract. It may show up as missed meals, cancelled meetings, delayed rest, increased cravings, resentment after family contact, or a pattern of helping others while quietly drifting from the routines that keep them steady.

Conflict avoidance has a different texture. It presents as peacekeeping, but often stores conflict for later. The person does not say what bothered them. They smile, withdraw, change the subject, minimise, or tell themselves it is not worth discussing. Then the unsaid thing travels underground. It becomes sarcasm, coldness, fantasy, compulsive distraction, or a sudden disproportionate reaction to a small prompt. Avoided conflict does not disappear because no one named it. It waits in the body. Recovery suffers because the person is left managing the emotional residue of conversations they refused to have honestly.

Staying in chaos is perhaps the most exhausting pattern because it can feel like loyalty. The relationship is always urgent, always dramatic, always on the brink of rupture or rescue. There are late-night arguments, repeated crises, accusations, apologies, promises, reversals, and a sense that stepping away would be cruel. The person becomes trained to respond to intensity rather than truth. Their routines shrink around someone else's volatility. Meals, sleep, recovery contact, and quiet judgement are repeatedly sacrificed to the latest emotional emergency. Over time, chaos begins to feel like connection, and steadiness begins to feel strangely empty.

Over-explaining is another leak in the gate. A clear boundary might require one sentence, but fear adds paragraphs. The person explains their motives, their history, their guilt, their affection, their schedule, their exhaustion, their reasons for needing space, and their hope that the other person will understand. Explanation is not inherently wrong; relationships need context. But over-explaining often reveals that the person does not believe their limit is allowed to stand unless it is approved by the person pressing against it. The more they explain, the more there is to argue with. The boundary becomes a debate rather than a decision.

Disappearing is the opposite performance and often grows from the same fear. The person cannot tolerate the guilt of a limit, so they avoid the conversation altogether. They stop replying, become vague, miss plans, delay honesty, or hope the other person will somehow understand a boundary that was never spoken. Disappearing may feel safer than saying no, but it creates confusion and often damages trust. It also leaves the person alone with shame, which can become its own recovery risk. A boundary that is never named cannot be respected; it can only be guessed at, resented, or violated unintentionally.

Family systems thinker Murray Bowen, working in the United States in the mid-twentieth century, gave enduring attention to how people manage closeness, anxiety, and individuality within relationships. His language was clinical and rooted in family therapy, yet the practical insight is widely recognisable: people can become entangled in emotional patterns where another person's tension feels like their assignment. Recovery requires enough differentiation to notice where care ends and self-erasure begins. The person is still connected, but no longer fused to every demand, mood, or crisis around them.

The body often identifies boundary problems before the intellect admits them. A request arrives, and the body tightens. A name appears on the phone, and breathing changes. An invitation is extended, and resentment appears before the answer. A conversation starts looping, and the person feels a desperate urge either to win, appease, or vanish. These sensations are not final proof that the other person is wrong. They are signals that capacity, safety, or honesty may be under pressure. The body's signal deserves investigation, not automatic obedience and not automatic dismissal.

Red-flag dynamics need firmer language. A relationship becomes risky when a clear no is repeatedly challenged, when privacy is treated as betrayal, when recovery routines are mocked or undermined, when contact is demanded at unsafe hours, when guilt is used to extract compliance, when anger punishes ordinary limits, or when the person feels they must hide stabilising behaviours in order to keep peace. These patterns are not merely uncomfortable. They may increase relapse risk, emotional flooding, secrecy, and self-abandonment. Clarity is protective because vague discomfort can be argued away; named patterns are harder to dismiss.

There is a credible limitation. Not every uncomfortable relationship is unhealthy, and not every request that stretches a person is a boundary violation. Real intimacy sometimes asks for patience, compromise, inconvenience, and repair. A friend's need may arrive at a poor time. A partner may ask a difficult question. A family member may be disappointed by a limit without being manipulative. Recovery should not become a language for avoiding all discomfort or treating every emotional demand as a threat. Boundaries are not excuses for selfishness dressed in therapeutic clothing.

The reconciliation is to look at pattern, pressure, and after-effect. Pattern asks whether this situation repeats. Pressure asks whether the person feels free to say no, pause, or ask for time. After-effect asks what happens inside recovery afterwards. Does the person feel clearer, connected, and able to return to routines, even if the exchange was difficult? Or do they feel resentful, flooded, secretive, depleted, ashamed, craving relief, or pulled away from essential supports? The gate is assessed not by one moment alone, but by what repeatedly happens when it opens too far or stays closed too long.

Mapping boundary problems requires a sober inventory of where the self keeps disappearing. Some people over-give with family, over-explain with partners, avoid conflict with colleagues, and disappear from friends when ashamed. Others hold boundaries well at work but collapse in romance, or speak clearly with peers but become a child again around a parent's disappointment. The map should name the person, setting, request, body signal, usual response, and after-effect. "When my sibling calls late and sounds distressed, my chest tightens, I stay on the phone past my limit, then I miss sleep and feel resentful the next day." That sentence contains a map. It is more useful than "I need better boundaries."

Resentment is often the smoke from a boundary fire. It should not be worshipped, but it should be read. Sometimes resentment reveals entitlement or unwillingness to be inconvenienced. Often, however, it reveals repeated consent given without honesty. The person said yes while meaning no, stayed while wanting to leave, listened while becoming depleted, gave while keeping an invisible invoice. Resentment then becomes proof that a boundary was needed earlier. If ignored, it may seek relief through withdrawal, contempt, passive aggression, or old coping patterns.

Relapse risk rises when boundaries fail because the person's internal state becomes less honest. People-pleasing teaches the body that other people's comfort outranks recovery. Conflict avoidance teaches the mind that truth is dangerous. Staying in chaos teaches the nervous system to live at a high pitch and then search for a way down. Over-explaining teaches the person that limits require permission. Disappearing teaches secrecy. Each pattern weakens the ordinary structures that keep recovery practical: sleep, food, contact, truthful language, reduced exposure to triggers, and the ability to pause before acting.

The gate returns here as a question of maintenance. A gate that never opens becomes isolation. A gate that never closes becomes exposure. A gate that opens only when someone pushes hard enough teaches people to push harder. A gate with a clear handle, a clear hinge, and a clear stopping point allows relationship without constant negotiation. Boundaries that hold are not necessarily dramatic. They are often boring, repeated, and calm. Their calmness is part of their strength.

The forward test is to notice where the next boundary problem begins: not at the explosion, but at the first small betrayal of capacity. The quick yes. The extra explanation. The ignored body signal. The late-night argument allowed to continue. The crisis that becomes more important than sleep, food, contact, or truth. When that moment appears, the question is not whether the other person deserves care. They may. The question is whether care is being offered through honesty or through self-abandonment, and what recovery will be asked to pay afterwards.

Boundary Scripts for Common Situations

What if the most important sentence in a difficult relationship is not the most eloquent one, but the one you can still say when your pulse is up and the room has become too loud? A familiar request arrives. A conversation starts looping. Someone pushes past the first no. The body reacts before the mind organises itself: throat tight, face warm, thoughts crowded, old roles waking. In that moment, improvisation is expensive.

A boundary without language often remains only a private wish. The person may know they need space, but stay in the room. They may know the answer is no, but keep explaining until the no becomes negotiable. They may know the argument has become circular, but continue because leaving feels like losing. Stress narrows speech. It makes people either overtalk or vanish. A prepared sentence gives the boundary a handle.

The point of a script is not to make human relationships mechanical. It is to protect clarity when the nervous system is under pressure. A good script is short enough to remember, plain enough to repeat, and specific enough to be tested in behaviour. It does not carry a courtroom defence. It does not require the other person to agree before the limit becomes real. It says what will happen next: "I cannot do that tonight." "I need an hour, and I will come back at seven." "I am not discussing this while we are shouting. I will talk after dinner."

The practical power of such sentences can be understood through the work of psychologist Marsha M. Linehan, whose 1993 treatment manual for borderline personality disorder helped formalise dialectical behaviour therapy skills, including interpersonal effectiveness. The relevance here is not diagnostic. It is behavioural. Under emotional strain, people need language that can hold both self-respect and relationship respect. A boundary script does that by reducing the burden on a flooded mind. It turns an inner intention into an outer action.

Saying no is often the place where the old pattern reveals itself. The request may be minor, but the body responds as though affection, approval, or safety depends on compliance. A person who has learned to please may feel that a bare no is rude, so they add reasons, apologies, alternative offers, emotional cushioning, and a hopeful little invitation for the other person to understand. Sometimes explanation is appropriate. Often, however, the extra language opens doors that the boundary was meant to close. "I cannot help tonight" is clearer than "I am so sorry, I wish I could, but I have had a difficult day, and I know you need me, and maybe I could later if things change." The second sentence sounds kinder. It may be less honest.

A clean no should be proportionate to the relationship and the request. In ordinary situations, warmth can sit beside firmness: "I cannot do that, but I hope it goes well." "That does not work for me." "I am not available tonight." "I cannot lend money." "I am not the right person for this conversation." The voice may tremble. The sentence can still stand. The important visible behaviour is that the person does not keep negotiating after giving the answer. A no repeated calmly is not aggression. It is maintenance.

Asking for space requires a different kind of precision because space can easily be confused with abandonment. Recovery often needs pauses, especially when conflict, shame, cravings, or emotional flooding begin to narrow choice. Yet a vague retreat can create anxiety and mistrust. "I need space" may be true, but it is incomplete. Better language gives the pause a shape: "I am getting too heated to speak well. I am taking twenty minutes and will come back." "I need quiet before I answer. I will reply tomorrow morning." "I care about this, and I cannot handle it properly while I am flooded." The return point matters. It turns disappearance into regulation.

The pause script is especially important for people who either stay too long or leave too completely. Staying too long may lead to sharp words, old coping, or a night spent recovering from an argument that should have been paused much earlier. Leaving too completely may look like punishment, avoidance, or secrecy. A grounded pause is neither. It names the state, states the limit, and commits to a return. That commitment rebuilds trust because others are not left guessing whether the person is regulating or escaping.

Ending circular arguments is a particularly demanding skill because circularity can feel like urgency. The same point returns in different clothing. Evidence is reintroduced. Tone becomes the new subject. The past is summoned. Apologies are challenged. Motives are cross-examined. The person may keep speaking because silence feels like surrender, or because the other person's distress feels like an order. A script cuts across the loop: "We are repeating ourselves. I am stopping this conversation now." "I will not continue while we are shouting." "I have answered that. I am not going to keep defending it tonight." "I will discuss the next practical step, not replay the whole argument."

Short scripts protect recovery because they reduce exposure to the conditions that make old behaviour more likely. A circular argument at night can lead to shame, craving, secrecy, or retaliatory silence. A no that becomes an hour-long defence can leave the person depleted and resentful. A request for space without a return time can create further conflict, which then becomes its own trigger. The script is not merely about communication style. It is about risk management in relationship form.

There is a lesson here from nonviolent communication, developed and popularised by Marshall B. Rosenberg through work that became widely associated with his 2003 book *Nonviolent Communication: A Language of Life*. Its emphasis on observation, feeling, need, and request has helped many people speak with less blame and more clarity. Yet boundary scripts in recovery must remain even leaner under pressure. A person may not have the capacity to produce a fully reflective statement when flooded. The practical inheritance is the preference for clean, non-accusatory language: describe what is happening, name the limit, make the next step clear.

Still, a script is not a spell. It cannot guarantee that the other person will respond well. Some people will accept the boundary with disappointment but respect. Some will feel hurt and need time. Some will argue. Some will mock, escalate, guilt, or push harder. The script's success cannot be measured only by whether the other person becomes calm. That would return power to the very dynamic the boundary is meant to interrupt. The more useful measure is whether the person stayed clear, proportionate, and aligned with recovery.

This is where repetition becomes a skill. Many people state a boundary once, then collapse when it is challenged. They assume that if the other person asks again, they owe a new explanation. Often they do not. Repetition can be calm and almost boring: "I understand you are disappointed. I am still not available." "I hear that you want to keep talking. I am still pausing now." "I know you disagree. I am not changing my answer." The sentence returns to the gate and closes it again. There is no need to decorate the second closing.

Over-explanation is tempting because it promises relief from guilt. If the other person fully understands, perhaps they will not be upset. If every reason is laid out, perhaps the boundary will feel less selfish. If the person can prove they are kind, perhaps the no will not cost connection. But explanation does not always create respect. Sometimes it creates material for cross-examination. The more detail offered, the more opportunities the other person has to dispute, minimise, or bargain. A short explanation may be enough. Sometimes no explanation is required beyond the limit itself.

The script must also be adapted to risk. In a generally safe relationship, a boundary can include warmth and collaborative repair. In a volatile or controlling dynamic, brevity and safety become more important than emotional nuance. If a person repeatedly ignores no, punishes space, monitors contact, mocks recovery, or escalates when limits are set, scripts alone may not be sufficient. The situation may require outside support, professional guidance, legal advice, or a safety plan. A boundary sentence is useful only when the context is safe enough for a sentence to function.

This limitation matters because popular boundary language can be dangerously simplistic. It may imply that every problem can be solved if the person speaks clearly enough. That is not true. Some people are not confused by a boundary; they oppose it. Some dynamics are not messy; they are coercive. Some arguments are not misunderstandings; they are attempts to exhaust resistance. Recovery requires the humility to know when communication is the wrong tool for the level of risk. A script can hold a gate. It cannot turn an unsafe person into a safe one.

For ordinary but difficult relationships, however, scripts can transform the pressure of the moment. A person who has rehearsed "I cannot take this on today" is less likely to discover their limit only after resentment has set in. A person who has rehearsed "I need a pause and will come back at seven" is less likely to disappear into silence. A person who has rehearsed "I will talk when we are not shouting" is less likely to sacrifice the whole evening to escalation. Rehearsal is not artificial. It is respect for the fact that stress steals language.

The handle motif returns here. A boundary without a prepared sentence is like a door with no handle: the person can see the exit but cannot easily use it under pressure. A script gives the hand somewhere to go. It does not force the other person outside. It does not shut down all intimacy. It allows the person to open, close, pause, or return with more control over their own participation. The handle is plain because it must work quickly.

The most effective scripts often share a structure so simple it can feel almost too blunt. They name the limit, state the next action, and stop. "I am not available." "I am leaving now." "I will answer tomorrow." "I am not continuing this conversation." "I can talk for ten minutes, not longer." "I can listen, but I cannot solve this." "I will not lend money." "I need support for my recovery, so I am keeping that appointment." Each sentence creates a boundary that can be observed. Each reduces the room available for vague pressure.

Tone matters, but tone cannot be asked to do the work of the boundary. A person can speak gently and still be firm. They can sound nervous and still be clear. They can feel guilty and still hold the line. Many people wait until they can state a boundary without discomfort; meanwhile the pattern continues. The body may feel uneasy because it is leaving an old role. Unease is not evidence that the boundary is wrong. It may be evidence that the boundary is new.

There is also a place for repair after a clumsy boundary. No one speaks perfectly under pressure. A person may sound sharper than intended, leave too abruptly, or use a script in a way that feels stiff. That does not mean the boundary was false. It means the delivery may need repair. "I was right to pause, but I was abrupt. I am back now and can speak calmly." Such language protects both recovery and relationship. It refuses the old pattern in which one imperfect boundary becomes proof that no boundary should have been set.

Scripts become stronger when they are paired with action. "I am ending this conversation now" must be followed by ending it. "I will reply tomorrow" must be followed by not replying all night and then returning when promised. "I cannot help today" must be followed by not offering hidden labour through guilt. Without action, scripts become performance. With action, they become evidence. Trust grows not from the elegance of the sentence, but from the consistency between sentence and behaviour.

The forward test is whether the next pressure moment will require invention or use. When the request arrives, when the guilt rises, when the argument circles, when the body wants either to appease or disappear, will there be a handle within reach? A short sentence. A calm repetition. A stated return. A no that does not ask permission to exist. The boundary will not be proven by how little discomfort it creates. It will be proven by whether it still holds when discomfort arrives.

Handling Pushback and Guilt

What if the guilt that arrives after a boundary is not proof that the boundary is wrong, but proof that an old role has been interrupted? The request has been declined. The conversation has been paused. The late-night call has not been answered. The explanation has been kept short. For a few seconds there is relief, almost physical, like putting down a bag carried too long. Then the reply comes back: disappointment, silence, accusation, confusion, a softer appeal, a sharper demand. The body tightens. The gate begins to shake.

That moment matters because many boundaries do not fail at the first sentence. They fail in the echo. A person can say no clearly and still collapse when the other person looks hurt. They can ask for space and still return too soon because silence feels cruel. They can end a circular argument and then re-enter it because the unanswered message sits on the phone like a test of love. The boundary itself may have been sound. What was unprepared was the after-pressure.

Pushback is not automatically evidence of wrongdoing. Other people are allowed to feel disappointed, inconvenienced, confused, or unhappy when a limit changes the usual arrangement. A person who has benefited from easy access may need time to adjust. Someone who expected help may feel let down. Someone who is anxious may ask for reassurance. These reactions are not necessarily manipulative. They are human. The problem begins when the reaction is used to make the boundary illegitimate: when disappointment becomes punishment, confusion becomes interrogation, hurt becomes control, or urgency becomes a reason that the limit must disappear.

Guilt is the lever most likely to move the old pattern because guilt often feels morally intelligent. It says, "A good person would answer." "A loyal person would stay." "A loving person would explain until everyone understands." "A responsible person would absorb this." But guilt is not always conscience. Sometimes it is the withdrawal symptom of people-pleasing. Sometimes it is the body remembering that safety once depended on keeping someone else calm. Sometimes it is fear wearing ethical clothing. The task is not to silence guilt immediately, but to examine what it is asking for and what recovery will pay if it is obeyed.

There is a crucial difference between a reasonable request and control. A reasonable request leaves room for an answer. It can include disappointment without retaliation. It may ask for clarification, propose another time, or name a real impact. Control presses past the answer. It repeats the demand until exhaustion looks like consent. It treats privacy as betrayal, recovery routines as selfishness, or a pause as abandonment. It punishes the boundary with coldness, threats, ridicule, public embarrassment, emotional withdrawal, or escalating urgency. The visible behaviour reveals the difference.

Reasonable pressure still recognises the gate. Control tries to remove it.

This distinction has deep roots in how people learn relationships. Family systems thinker Murray Bowen, working in the United States in the mid-twentieth century, described how anxiety in relationships can pull people back into familiar roles, especially when one person tries to become more differentiated. The language belongs to clinical theory, but the ordinary truth is recognisable. When one person stops automatically appeasing, rescuing, explaining, or disappearing, the system may protest. The protest does not always mean harm is being done. It may mean the pattern has noticed that it is being changed.

The body often interprets that protest as danger. The heart speeds up. The stomach drops. The throat tightens. The mind starts composing long explanations. The hand moves towards the phone. The person may feel an almost urgent need to repair the discomfort by withdrawing the limit. This is the old script trying to restore the old peace. Yet the old peace may not have been peace at all. It may have been the absence of visible conflict purchased through private resentment, fatigue, secrecy, or relapse risk.

Tolerating guilt does not mean becoming hard. It means allowing discomfort to exist without letting it take over decision-making. The person can care that someone is disappointed and still maintain the limit. They can acknowledge impact without surrendering capacity. They can offer an alternative without reopening the original demand. They can say, "I understand this is frustrating, and I am still not available tonight." The sentence is simple because the work is difficult. It holds two truths in one hand: your feeling matters, and my limit remains.

This is where choosing the response in advance becomes essential. Under pressure, the mind tends to overcorrect. The person either becomes too soft and collapses, or too harsh and later feels ashamed. Prepared responses create a middle path. "I am not changing my answer." "I can talk tomorrow, not now." "I hear that you are upset. I am still taking space." "I will not continue if I am being insulted." "I can offer this much, not more." These sentences are not designed to win admiration. They are designed to keep the gate from being negotiated away by panic.

The gate motif matters because a gate can be pressured from both sides. Other people may push from outside; guilt may push from inside. A boundary that holds has to answer both. If the outside pressure is mild and respectful, the gate may remain closed without drama or open later by choice. If the pressure becomes coercive, the gate may need a firmer lock, more distance, or outside support. If the internal pressure becomes shame, the person may need to steady themselves before replying. The gate is not a symbol of rejection. It is a structure that protects honest contact from becoming invasion.

There is a credible limitation. Some people use boundary language to avoid ordinary responsibility, intimacy, apology, or compromise. They call any discomfort "pressure" and any request "control". They refuse to be inconvenienced and describe the refusal as self-respect. That is not recovery. Healthy boundaries do not remove the person from all obligations. They clarify which obligations are truly theirs, which belong to others, and which must be shared honestly. A boundary that never allows generosity, repair, sacrifice, or mutual adjustment may be less a gate than a sealed room.

The reconciliation is to test the boundary by pattern, proportion, and purpose. Pattern asks whether the request is part of a recurring dynamic that leaves recovery weakened. Proportion asks whether the limit matches the situation, or whether the person is using an excessive defence where a smaller truth would do. Purpose asks what the boundary protects: sleep, safety, sobriety, honesty, emotional regulation, recovery contact, or the ability to speak without harm. A boundary grounded in purpose is easier to hold because it is not merely a preference. It is attached to a stabilising function.

Pushback often becomes more manageable when it is separated into categories. Some pushback is disappointment, which can be allowed. Some is negotiation, which may be answered once. Some is confusion, which may deserve brief clarification. Some is pressure, which needs repetition. Some is punishment, which may require distance. Some is danger, which requires support beyond the conversation. The person does not need to treat every reaction as an emergency. They need to recognise what kind of reaction is in front of them.

The most seductive pushback is often not anger but sadness. Anger may make the boundary easier to defend because the pressure is visible. Sadness activates guilt. The disappointed voice, the long pause, the message that says "I thought I could count on you", the quiet withdrawal after a no: these can pull the person back into over-giving more effectively than a shouted demand. Compassion is appropriate. Collapse is not. A person can care about another's sadness without volunteering their own stability as the solution.

Recovery requires this distinction because resentment is not harmless. The yes given under guilt often returns later as anger, secrecy, craving, or avoidance. The person may tell themselves they were being kind, but the body knows the truth: the boundary was crossed, even if the crossing was self-administered. Over time, repeated guilt-based consent teaches the nervous system that relationships are places where recovery is repeatedly traded for approval. The cost is not only emotional. It becomes behavioural.

There is also the guilt of being changed. As recovery becomes steadier, some old patterns no longer fit. The person may become less available for late-night drama, less willing to argue endlessly, less open to vague demands, less tolerant of chaos, less willing to hide their routines. Others may experience this as loss. They may prefer the old version: more flexible, more porous, more easily recruited. The guilt that follows can be sharp because it feels like disloyalty. Yet growth always disappoints the parts of a relationship that depended on self-abandonment.

Steady boundaries do not require perfect harmony. This is a hard truth for people who have survived by keeping the emotional weather mild. Harmony achieved through silence, compliance, and private collapse is not harmony; it is emotional debt. A relationship may become more visibly tense when boundaries are introduced, but also more truthful. The aim is not to make everyone comfortable at all times. The aim is to make contact honest enough that recovery does not have to happen in secret underneath it.

Choosing a response in advance also protects tone. A person who waits until resentment peaks may speak with unnecessary force. A person who prepares language can remain briefer and cleaner. "I cannot take this on" is better than an explosion after an hour of trapped listening. "I am leaving this conversation now" is better than staying until the cruel sentence arrives. "I will not be available after ten" is better than answering at midnight and resenting every word. A boundary spoken early often sounds less dramatic because it has not yet been charged by endurance.

Some pushback should be met with a broken-record response: calm repetition without adding new material. The phrase may feel awkward at first, especially to those trained to explain until understood. But repetition is often what keeps a boundary from becoming a debate. "I know this is not the answer you wanted. I am still not available." "I have explained what I can. I am not discussing it further tonight." "I will talk tomorrow. I am not replying again now." The point is not to sound superior. The point is to stop feeding the loop.

There is a moment when guilt begins to fade not because the other person approves, but because the person has survived disapproval without abandoning themselves. That experience is instructive. The body learns that disappointment is not necessarily danger. The relationship learns that pressure no longer guarantees access. The recovery system learns that it can remain visible even when someone else is unhappy. This is how a boundary becomes less theoretical. It is held once, then again, then through a harder reaction, then with repair if the delivery was imperfect.

Repair may still be needed after a boundary, but repair is not the same as reversal. A person can say, "I was abrupt earlier, and I am sorry for my tone. The limit still stands." They can acknowledge impact without reopening the decision. They can return after a pause without apologising for needing the pause. They can clarify without defending their entire character. This distinction prevents guilt from smuggling collapse back into the conversation under the name of kindness.

The forward test is whether the next wave of pushback will be allowed to redefine the boundary. When disappointment appears, will it be treated as information or as an order? When guilt rises, will it be read as conscience or as the old role protesting? When the other person pushes again, will the answer become longer, softer, and less true, or shorter, steadier, and more grounded? The gate will not prove itself in silence. It will prove itself when it is pressed.

Chapter 9
Support Systems That Are Consistent

What if the problem is not that support is absent, but that it has never been assigned a job? The phone contains names. Some belong to people who care deeply. Some belong to people who answer quickly but do not know what to say. Some are good in a crisis and poor with ordinary sadness. Some can listen but cannot challenge. Some love you, yet become frightened, vague, preachy, or unavailable at precisely the hour when recovery needs steadiness. A contact list is not a support system.

Stress exposes this difference quickly. A person feels the old drift begin and reaches for help, but the choice itself becomes another burden. Who will understand without panicking? Who can be asked for accountability without turning it into a lecture? Who can help with a practical task rather than a long emotional conversation? Who should not be contacted late at night because the exchange will become more complicated than the original problem? Without a map, support becomes improvisation, and improvisation under pressure tends to favour delay.

There is a quiet loneliness in having people but not knowing how to use their care. The person may hint at distress and feel disappointed when no one reads it correctly. They may ask too intensely, too late, or too vaguely, then resent the imperfect response. They may expect one person to be listener, witness, adviser, emergency contact, practical helper, truth-teller, and emotional shelter all at once. When that person fails, the mind draws a sweeping conclusion: no one is there. The conclusion feels convincing. It may also be badly designed evidence.

The central tension is that recovery needs other people, but not in a sentimental or shapeless way. Support must be human enough to hold fear, shame, boredom, anger, and uncertainty, yet practical enough to function under strain. It cannot depend on one perfect person always answering in the right tone. It needs distribution: different people, different roles, different levels of access, different expectations. Consistency is not created by intensity. It is created by structure that remains available when feelings are unreliable.

The stakes are immediate because unsupported stress often turns private. A craving kept private gathers authority. A shame script kept private becomes a verdict. A boundary problem kept private becomes resentment. A setback kept private becomes a second event. Recovery weakens when the person has to translate distress, choose a helper, overcome pride, draft the perfect message, and manage the other person's reaction all while already under pressure. A support system reduces the number of tasks inside the vulnerable moment.

The stakes also reach into trust. Other people are more able to help when they know what kind of help is being requested. "I am struggling" may be honest, but it leaves the listener guessing. "Can you listen for ten minutes without advice?" is clearer. "Please ask me at eight whether I went to the meeting" gives the other person a useful role. "I need practical help getting through the next hour" sets a different expectation from "I need reassurance that I am not awful." Specificity protects both sides. It lowers resentment because no one is being asked to perform mind-reading under emotional weather.

The path begins with a realistic map: who can listen, who can help practically, who can hold accountability, and who belongs in a genuine crisis plan. From there, the work turns to the language of requests, where honesty needs time frames, options, and respect for the other person's limits. Then comes the harder truth that support will sometimes disappoint, not because recovery is doomed, but because human systems have weak points that must be repaired, diversified, and adjusted.

The motif is a switchboard. Not glamorous. Not intimate in itself. Useful because it routes the signal. A good switchboard does not pretend every call belongs to the same line. Loneliness does not always need the same person as accountability. A practical emergency does not need the same response as a hard mood. A crisis contact is not the same as someone who can talk during a commute. When the signal is routed well, help becomes less dramatic and more dependable.

The unresolved question is whether support is currently real enough to use before the hour becomes dangerous. Who knows what role they play? Who is being asked to do too much? Where are the gaps, the fantasy, the unspoken expectations, the names that look reassuring but do not function when tested? The next difficult day will not ask whether care exists in theory. It will ask whether the right person can be reached for the right kind of help at the right time.

Mapping Your Support Realistically

What if the weakest point in a support system is not the number of people in it, but the assumption that care will automatically know what to do? The phone is full of names. There is the friend who answers quickly but becomes anxious. The colleague who is practical but emotionally blunt. The sibling who loves you but turns every difficulty into advice. The recovery peer who understands cravings but is not available during work hours. The person who says, "Call anytime," yet rarely answers at night. The list looks reassuring until pressure arrives.

A difficult hour exposes the difference between having contacts and having support. The person is restless, ashamed, tired, or tempted, and now they must choose whom to tell, how much to say, what to ask for, how to handle a missed reply, and whether the helper can tolerate the truth. That is too much design work for a moment already under strain. Support should not have to be invented at the point of need. The map belongs in the pocket before the weather turns.

Support is often treated sentimentally, as though love and goodwill are enough to make a person useful in any role. They are not. Good people can be poor listeners. Loving people can panic. Wise people can be unavailable. Generous people can overstep. Someone may be excellent for humour, ordinary companionship, and relief from loneliness, yet entirely wrong for a craving disclosure. Another may be awkward with feelings but reliable for practical help: a lift, a meal, a check-in, a reminder, a place to sit quietly until the dangerous hour passes. The question is not who cares. The question is what their care can actually do.

A realistic support map begins by respecting function. Listening is one function. Practical help is another. Accountability is another. Crisis contact is another again. These should not be blurred simply because the same person sometimes performs more than one role. The listener helps the person feel less alone without rushing to solve. The practical helper assists with concrete barriers: transport, childcare, food, leaving a risky setting, attending an appointment, getting through an awkward transition. The accountability person can ask direct questions without shaming. The crisis contact belongs in the category of serious risk, where the situation requires immediate, appropriate help rather than ordinary reassurance.

This distinction protects relationships as much as recovery. When one person is expected to do everything, resentment grows on both sides. The supporter feels overwhelmed, inadequate, or trapped in a role they never clearly accepted. The person in recovery feels abandoned when the supporter cannot provide every kind of help at every hour. A map reduces this unfairness. It says, in effect, "You are not my entire system. You are one valued part of it." That sentence is kinder than it may first appear. It releases people from being perfect.

The switchboard is the useful image here. A switchboard does not create the message; it routes it. Loneliness does not need the same line as crisis. A craving does not need the same line as a practical errand. A bad mood does not need the same response as immediate danger. When the signal is routed poorly, the person may receive care that is real but mismatched: advice when they needed witness, comfort when they needed accountability, silence when they needed an agreed check-in, intensity when they needed calm. The right line matters.

Listening support is often misunderstood because it can look passive. In fact, good listening can prevent escalation by reducing secrecy and shame before they harden. The visible behaviour is simple: the person tells the truth earlier than they would have alone. The listener does not moralise, interrogate, or rush to rescue. They reflect enough to show they have understood, and they remain steady enough that the person does not have to manage their panic. This kind of support is especially useful when the need is to stay connected while the feeling moves through the body. It may not solve the problem. It keeps the person from disappearing into it.

Practical support is less dramatic but often decisive. A person may not need a deep conversation; they may need someone to sit with them while they delete an app, collect them from a risky place, bring food, help cancel a plan, walk with them before the dangerous hour, or remain present while they make a necessary call. Practical help turns recovery from an inner ideal into a changed situation. The door is no longer open. The route has changed. The person has eaten. The appointment is attended. The evening is no longer unstructured. These are not symbolic victories. They alter the conditions under which the next decision is made.

Accountability support requires a particular temperament. It is not scolding. It is not surveillance. It is the ability to ask clean questions and tolerate honest answers. "Have you contacted your support group?" "Are you near the place you agreed to avoid?" "Have you told the whole truth, or the easier version?" "What is the next action, not the next explanation?" Accountability works when it is specific, agreed, and bounded. Without agreement, it can feel intrusive. Without specificity, it becomes vague encouragement. Without warmth, it becomes policing. The best accountability has a firm hand and no appetite for humiliation.

Crisis contact belongs in a separate category because ordinary support is not always enough. Some situations require emergency services, professional crisis lines, clinical care, safeguarding, medical attention, or immediate removal from danger. It is unwise and unfair to make a friend the sole plan for moments beyond their capacity. A realistic map names what counts as urgent, who is appropriate to contact, what information they may need, and what professional or emergency resources exist in the person's location. This is not pessimism. It is respect for scale. Serious risk deserves a serious route.

The work of Alcoholics Anonymous, which began in Akron, Ohio, in 1935, offers one historical example of support becoming structured rather than merely affectionate. Whatever one thinks of its spiritual language or fellowship model, its enduring practical insight is clear: people often need repeated contact, shared language, role clarity, and access to others who understand the pattern from the inside. Support becomes stronger when it is not left to chance. The same principle can be adapted without copying any single tradition. Recovery needs reliable points of contact, not vague hope that someone will be free.

SMART Recovery, incorporated in the United States in 1994, gives another example of structured support, this time through a secular, skills-based model that emphasises tools, meetings, and self-management. Its relevance here is not that one model suits every person, but that support can be organised around function rather than sentiment. A person can seek skills in one place, peer understanding in another, professional guidance elsewhere, and practical help from people in daily life. A mature support map is rarely one circle. It is several circles, each with a different purpose.

There is a credible limitation to mapping support: people are not instruments. They are not entries in a private service directory, waiting to perform assigned tasks whenever needed. They have limits, moods, responsibilities, histories, and boundaries of their own. A support map becomes unhealthy when it turns others into equipment or when it assumes that naming a role creates an entitlement to access. Consent matters. Availability matters. So does reciprocity, even if reciprocity looks different in different seasons of life. Support that ignores the supporter's humanity will eventually weaken the very system it tries to build.

The reconciliation is to map support through conversation, not fantasy. It is one thing to decide privately that a friend is your accountability person; it is another to ask whether they are willing to receive a brief message during high-risk evenings and what they can realistically offer. It is one thing to assume a family member can help with practical tasks; it is another to clarify what kind of help is possible without resentment. A realistic map is negotiated. It is also revised. People's capacity changes. Relationships change. Recovery needs change. The map should be treated as a living document, not a monument.

Gaps matter because unnamed gaps become emergencies. A person may have several listeners but no one who can provide practical help. They may have a therapist but no one available between appointments. They may have friends who care but no one who understands recovery language. They may have a partner who is deeply involved but no diversified support beyond the relationship. They may have daytime support and no evening plan, or crisis contacts and no ordinary maintenance contact. The gap is not a failure. It is a place where the map is telling the truth.

Weak points deserve the same honesty. A supporter may be kind but unreliable. Another may be available but too entangled in family patterns. Another may keep confidences poorly. Another may make every conversation about themselves. Another may be excellent in calm times but reactive when risk is named. These observations can feel disloyal, especially when the person cares. But a support map is not a judgement of anyone's worth. It is a record of fit. The person who is not suited for accountability may still be beloved. The person who cannot handle crisis may still be good for laughter, companionship, and ordinary life.

Trust becomes visible when roles are matched well. The person in recovery stops expecting the wrong thing from the wrong person. They no longer ask the anxious friend to remain calm during a high-risk disclosure. They no longer ask the emotionally distant relative for tender listening. They no longer ask the over-involved partner to be the entire safety system. Instead, they route the signal. The switchboard does its work. Fewer conversations end in disappointment because fewer conversations are built on unspoken expectations.

A support map should also include timing. Some people are available in the morning but not at night. Some are reachable by text but not by phone. Some can meet weekly but not respond spontaneously. Some are only appropriate for non-urgent updates. Some should not be contacted during certain hours because the relationship will become strained or the person is caring for others. Timing is not a minor detail. A support option that is unavailable during the high-risk hour is not useless, but it cannot be the only support assigned to that hour.

The map should distinguish between emotional privacy and dangerous secrecy. Not every feeling needs to be shared with everyone. Privacy is healthy; it preserves dignity and choice. Secrecy becomes risky when it hides urges, setbacks, shame, boundary problems, or conditions likely to lead to old behaviour. A realistic map helps the person decide what information must leave the private room and where it should go. "I am tired and sad" may belong with a friend. "I am near a known trigger and bargaining with myself" may belong with an accountability contact. "I may be unsafe" belongs with urgent support.

For intelligent, capable people, the hardest part may be admitting that competence is not the same as having a support system. They may manage demanding work, study, research, parenting, caring, or leadership roles while quietly improvising support in the most vulnerable parts of life. Public competence can hide private fragility. A map does not insult competence. It protects it from becoming isolation with a polished surface. The person who knows how to direct a project, supervise others, or conduct complex analysis can also learn to direct support with equal seriousness.

Last-minute scrambling is costly because it adds decisions when decision-making is already compromised. Under stress, the person must not only admit need but design the response. That is why support mapping belongs to calm hours. The names, roles, permissions, contact methods, and backup options should be identified before the craving, conflict, or shame spiral begins. A map made in a calm state becomes an act of care towards the future self who will not have the same clarity.

The forward test is not whether many people care. Care matters, but care without routing may still fail at the decisive hour. The test is whether the next signal can travel to the right place quickly: listening when the person needs to be heard, practical help when conditions must change, accountability when the truth is at risk, crisis contact when the situation exceeds ordinary support. When the difficult hour arrives, will the person open a contact list and scramble, or reach for a map that already knows which line should carry the call?

Asking for Specific Support

What if the sentence "I need help" is honest, but still too vague to be useful in the hour when help is needed? A person stands in the kitchen after a difficult day, phone in hand, shoulders tight, old relief within reach. They do not want to be dramatic. They do not want to be ignored. They do not want to explain everything. So they send a message that says, "I am struggling." Then they wait, hoping the other person will somehow know whether to call, listen, challenge, distract, reassure, ask direct questions, or simply stay nearby. The request has left the room, but the need has not been translated.

This is where many support attempts fail. Not because people are uncaring, and not because the person in recovery is unreasonable, but because stress makes language either too small or too large. Some people hint. They mention being tired, make a dry joke, send a vague "rough day" message, or withdraw and hope someone notices the absence. Others demand. They contact someone in panic, expect immediate availability, flood the conversation with urgency, or become hurt when the response is imperfect. Both patterns are understandable under pressure. Neither is dependable.

The middle path is specific support: a clear request that names what is happening, what kind of help is wanted, the time frame involved, and whether there are options. Specificity is not cold. It is considerate. It reduces mind-reading, protects the supporter's limits, and increases the chance that help will actually fit the need. A precise request does not make the person needy. It makes the need workable.

A vague request often carries a hidden wish: "Please understand me without making me say it plainly." That wish may come from shame, exhaustion, pride, old disappointment, or the fear of being too much. Yet unspoken expectations easily become resentment. The person hints, the supporter misses the signal, and the old story begins: no one is there, no one understands, support does not work. But the experiment was flawed. A foggy signal was sent into ordinary human busyness and expected to return as perfect care. A clearer signal would have given the relationship a fairer test.

Demanding has its own hidden wish: "Please prove I am safe by responding exactly now." In genuine crisis, urgent help may be necessary, and appropriate emergency or professional support should be used when ordinary support is not enough. But many non-emergency support demands come from panic rather than proportion. The person may ask for immediate emotional rescue when what they need is a defined next step: a ten-minute call, an accountability check, a practical lift, a reminder to eat, or someone to stay on the phone while they leave a risky setting. Urgency is real. It still needs shape.

The request should begin close to evidence. "I am ashamed and want to hide." "I am craving and near access." "I am angry and tempted to send a message I will regret." "I am overwhelmed and starting to shut down." "I have not eaten and I can feel myself getting sharp." These sentences do not dramatise; they locate. They tell the supporter what kind of weather has arrived. The map becomes visible. From there, the person can ask for a concrete form of help rather than placing the entire emotional burden in someone else's hands.

A useful support request includes a time frame because open-ended need can frighten or exhaust people. "Can you talk for ten minutes?" is easier to answer than "Can you be there for me?" "Can you check in at nine?" is more workable than "Please make sure I do not mess up." "Can I send you a message after I leave this place?" gives the supporter a role and an endpoint. Time frames do not make the need less serious. They make it easier for another person to enter without feeling swallowed.

Options matter because support is a relationship, not a command centre. A request that allows another person to choose is more respectful and often more successful. "Are you free for a ten-minute call, or would a quick text check-in be easier?" "Could you ask me directly whether I have gone home, or should I contact someone else tonight?" "If you cannot answer, I will message my recovery contact next." This language does two important things at once: it tells the truth about need, and it does not make one person responsible for the entire outcome.

The work of Marshall B. Rosenberg, widely known through his 2003 book *Nonviolent Communication: A Language of Life*, offers a useful principle here: requests become clearer when they are separated from blame and made specific enough to be acted upon. Recovery does not require perfect conversational technique, and the urgency of a craving or shame spiral may make polished language impossible. Still, the practical inheritance is valuable. A request is stronger when it describes the situation, names the need, and asks for a doable action. "You never care when I am struggling" traps the conversation in defence. "I am having a risky evening; can you ask me in half an hour whether I have gone offline?" gives the other person a door.

Specificity also protects dignity. When a person asks for exactly what they need, they do not have to perform distress to prove the request is valid. They do not need to exaggerate, collapse, or make the situation sound worse than it is in order to be taken seriously. "I am not in immediate danger, but I am not steady, and I need accountability tonight" is a strong sentence. It respects the truth. It prevents overreaction while still preventing secrecy. It also helps the supporter respond at the right level.

The switchboard motif returns here because a specific request routes the signal correctly. Listening, practical help, accountability, and crisis support are different lines. If the person needs listening, they might say, "Can you hear me out for ten minutes without advice?" If they need practical help, they might say, "Can you sit with me while I block this app?" If they need accountability, they might say, "Please ask me whether I have cancelled the risky plan." If the situation is urgent or unsafe, the line must move beyond ordinary friendship to appropriate immediate help. Routing well is not dramatic. It is efficient in the humane sense: less confusion, less resentment, less delay.

There is a subtle courage in asking for accountability rather than comfort. Comfort says, "Tell me I am not awful." Accountability says, "Help me do the next honest thing." Comfort may be necessary, especially when shame is loud, but comfort alone can leave the pattern untouched. A recovery-friendly request often combines warmth with direction: "I am ashamed and could use kindness, but I also need you to ask whether I have told the truth." This protects the person from drowning in shame while still keeping responsibility in the room.

The supporter's consent remains essential. A specific request is not a disguised entitlement. Other people may be unavailable, tired, in their own difficulty, or not suited to the role being asked of them. A respectful request leaves room for no. "Are you able to help with this tonight?" is different from "I need you, so you must respond." The first honours the relationship. The second may create pressure, especially if repeated often or delivered with panic. Recovery support becomes more consistent when it is based on clear agreements rather than emotional coercion.

This is where a credible limitation must be named. Some people do not have enough safe, reliable support in their personal lives. Others have relationships shaped by control, criticism, stigma, or instability. A person may make a clear request and still receive silence, poor advice, minimising, gossip, spiritual platitudes, blame, or alarm. Specificity improves the odds of useful help, but it does not turn every relationship into a safe one. In some circumstances, support must be sought through trained professionals, peer groups, crisis services, community organisations, or carefully chosen formal structures rather than through family or friends.

The reconciliation is to treat each request as both help-seeking and information-gathering. If someone responds well to a clear, bounded request, they may belong on the support map for that function. If they repeatedly respond poorly, the map should change. This is not a verdict on their worth. It is evidence about fit. A person who cannot handle craving accountability may still be a good companion for ordinary life. A person who gives awkward advice may still be willing to provide practical help. A person who cannot answer at night may still be reliable during the morning. The request tests the line.

Specific requests also reduce resentment in the supporter. People are often more willing to help when they know the task, the time, and the boundary. A friend may not be able to hold a two-hour emotional conversation after work, but they may gladly send a check-in at nine. A sibling may not be able to discuss recovery in depth, but they may be able to collect groceries. A partner may not be able to absorb another circular apology, but they may be able to agree on a return time after a pause. When the ask is bounded, care becomes less frightening.

The person asking is also protected from resentment. Clear requests make it harder to build a case against others for failing at a job they were never given. If the request was "Can you ask me at eight whether I went to the meeting?" and the person forgot, the problem can be addressed plainly. If the expectation was never spoken, disappointment becomes murkier. The mind may turn the missed support into evidence that no one cares, when the more accurate account is that no one was clearly asked. Precision protects reality from the drama of inference.

There is an art to keeping the request short. Under stress, intelligent people often explain too much. They include context, apology, history, caveats, worry about burdening the other person, and pre-emptive reassurance that the request is not a big deal. By the time the message ends, the actual ask is buried. A cleaner message might read: "I am having a craving and I am near access. Are you able to stay on text with me for ten minutes while I leave?" Or: "I am ashamed and tempted to hide. Can you ask me at nine whether I have sent the honest update?" The shorter message is not less thoughtful. It is easier to answer.

Tone matters. A support request should not punish the person being asked for not already knowing. "I guess I am alone again" may express pain, but it makes support harder. "I am having a hard hour and could use a check-in if you are free" opens a clearer door. "You need to stop me" places too much power on the other person. "Please help me follow the plan by asking one direct question" keeps agency where it belongs. The request should invite support without handing over responsibility for the entire recovery.

The best requests often include the action the person is already taking. "I am walking away from the shop; can you stay on the phone until I reach the bus stop?" "I am putting the phone outside the bedroom; can I text you when it is done?" "I am going to eat before replying; can you check in after dinner?" This prevents support from becoming passive reassurance. The person is not waiting to be rescued. They are using contact to strengthen movement already begun.

When support is needed repeatedly, it may help to create agreed templates in calmer moments. A supporter can learn that "yellow light" means the person is drifting and needs a low-key check-in, while "red light" means the situation is urgent and requires a different response. The exact language can vary, but the principle is useful: pre-agreed signals reduce the burden of explanation when stress is high. They also prevent ordinary supporters from being surprised by requests they did not know they were being asked to handle.

There is also value in naming what is not needed. "I do not need advice right now." "Please do not reassure me that it is fine; I need help staying accountable." "I am not asking you to solve this." "I need practical help, not analysis." These statements may sound unusually direct to people accustomed to hinting, but they can spare both sides frustration. The supporter does not waste energy offering the wrong kind of care, and the person in recovery does not become resentful because the care missed the mark.

The forward test is whether need can become language before pressure becomes behaviour. When the next difficult hour arrives, will the person hint and hope, demand and resent, or send a request with a shape: what is happening, what is needed, when help is needed, and what option exists if that person cannot respond? The support may not always arrive perfectly. It may not arrive from the first line called. But a clear signal gives the system a chance to work before the old pattern answers on its behalf.

When Support Disappoints

What if the person you finally ask for help says the wrong thing, answers too late, or does not answer at all? The message has been sent with effort. The need has been made visible. The phone is face up on the table, screen dark between glances, while the body waits for proof that reaching out was worth the discomfort. Then comes the awkward advice, the nervous joke, the silence, the reply that misses the point entirely. The old story wakes quickly: see, this is why you should handle things alone.

Support disappoints because support is human. People forget, misread, panic, overreach, minimise, preach, become busy, become frightened, or bring their own history into the moment. Someone may care deeply and still be clumsy with need. Someone may intend to help and still offer a sentence that lands badly. Someone may be reliable most days and unavailable on the day the craving, shame, or conflict happens to rise. The failure may be small, but its timing can make it feel enormous. Disappointment has leverage.

That leverage matters in recovery because failed support can become a trigger. A missed call may turn into isolation. Awkward advice may become resentment. A poorly handled disclosure may become secrecy. Conflict within a support network may make the person feel foolish for needing anyone at all. The mind moves fast from one event to a global verdict: nobody understands, people always leave, help is useless, I am too much, I should not have asked. These sentences feel protective, but they often escort the person back towards the very patterns support was meant to interrupt.

The first task is to distinguish disappointment from abandonment. A supporter who replies late may have failed a time-sensitive need without rejecting the person. A friend who gives awkward advice may be anxious, inexperienced, or trying too hard rather than uncaring. A recovery peer who is unavailable may still be part of the system, just not the whole system. This distinction does not ask anyone to excuse repeated unreliability or harmful responses. It asks for proportion. A single failed connection should not be allowed to define the entire map.

The switchboard motif returns because failed support often reveals a routing problem. The wrong line was used. The person asked a comfort-giver for accountability, an anxious relative for calm containment, a busy friend for urgent response, or a romantic partner to become the whole safety system. When the response failed, the pain was real, but the design also deserves review. Support disappointment is not only an emotional event. It is data about fit, timing, role, and backup. The signal may need another route.

Missed calls require a plan because silence can become a dangerous amplifier. If one person does not answer, the next action should already be known. The person should not have to decide, while activated, whether to wait, interpret, resent, hide, or escalate. A backup line prevents the mind from turning delay into destiny. The practical sequence might be internal rather than written in list form: send the agreed message, wait the agreed span, contact the next appropriate person, move away from access, use a public or safer setting, and seek urgent support if the level of risk demands it. The point is not to make people instantly available. The point is to prevent one unavailable person from becoming the whole plan.

Awkward advice is a different disappointment. It may arrive as "just stay positive", "do not think about it", "you are stronger than this", "pray harder", "go for a run", "that does not sound so bad", or "you need to stop making excuses". Sometimes the advice contains a small grain of usefulness wrapped in poor timing. Sometimes it is simply unhelpful. The recovery task is to avoid turning the irritation into another injury. The person can register the mismatch without swallowing it as truth. "That advice did not help" is more accurate than "no one can help me." One sentence keeps the door ajar. The other bolts it shut.

Repair may be appropriate when a support attempt goes badly, especially in relationships worth preserving. Repair should be specific and modest. "When I asked for accountability and received reassurance instead, I felt more alone. Next time, could you ask me the direct question we agreed on?" Or: "I know you were trying to help. Advice makes me defensive when I am flooded; listening for a few minutes works better." Such sentences can feel vulnerable because they ask twice: once for help, and again for better help. Yet this is how support systems mature. People are rarely excellent supporters by instinct. They learn from clear feedback.

There is a necessary boundary here. Not every disappointing supporter deserves further instruction. Some people repeatedly mock recovery, spread private information, turn disclosures into gossip, shame the person, make the crisis about themselves, minimise serious risk, or respond with control rather than care. In those cases, the lesson is not to explain more elegantly. The lesson is to move the role elsewhere. Repair is for relationships capable of repair. Repeated harm is information. A support map should not keep routing sensitive signals through a line that keeps damaging them.

John Bowlby's work on attachment, developed in Britain across the mid-twentieth century, offers a useful frame without reducing adult support to childhood theory. Human beings seek proximity under threat. When the hoped-for response fails, the nervous system may react strongly, especially if old experiences of rejection, inconsistency, or humiliation are near the surface. This does not make the reaction irrational in the dismissive sense. It makes it historically charged. A missed text may hurt because of the present moment and because it touches an older pattern. Recovery needs enough self-understanding to separate the two.

That separation prevents support disappointment from becoming a relapse script. The present fact may be: one person did not answer. The old script may be: nobody comes. The present fact may be: the advice was clumsy. The old script may be: being known is unsafe. The present fact may be: there was conflict with a supporter. The old script may be: support always turns into control. When the script is named, the person can respond to the present more accurately. The hurt is still real. It is not allowed to write the whole policy.

Adjusting expectations is not cynicism. It is respect for reality. Some people can offer scheduled check-ins but not spontaneous calls. Some can listen but not hold accountability. Some can offer practical help but not emotional nuance. Some can understand addiction but not family conflict. Some can support recovery as long as the conversation stays within their capacity. Expecting people to perform outside their true range creates repeated disappointment. Naming their range allows care to be used where it actually works.

This adjustment can bring grief. It may be painful to realise that a parent cannot provide the kind of tenderness hoped for, that a partner cannot be the only support, that a close friend panics around cravings, or that a trusted person is better at ordinary companionship than accountability. The grief should not be mocked or rushed. It is a loss to see someone clearly when fantasy had been carrying hope. But clarity also releases energy. The person stops returning to an empty shelf expecting a different item to appear. They build the support system from what exists, not from what should have existed.

Diversifying support is the structural answer to human limitation. Stability should not rest on one perfect person because no such person exists. A diversified system includes different kinds of contact: peer understanding, professional guidance where appropriate, practical help, ordinary friendship, accountability, crisis routes, and spaces where the person can be more than their recovery. This does not mean broadcasting private struggles indiscriminately. It means not asking one relationship to bear every function. A bridge with several supports is less likely to collapse when one beam weakens.

There is a credible limitation to diversification. More people do not automatically mean better support. A large circle can become noisy, inconsistent, or unsafe if roles are unclear and privacy is not protected. The person may start collecting opinions instead of taking the next responsible action. They may shop for reassurance, avoid accountability, or become overwhelmed by conflicting advice. Diversification must therefore be organised, not scattered. The question is not how many people know. The question is whether the right people know enough to perform the right roles.

Conflict within support networks needs particular care because it can feel like betrayal. A sponsor, therapist, friend, partner, group member, or relative may say something difficult. They may challenge minimisation, miss a nuance, set their own boundary, or disagree with the person's preferred interpretation. Some conflict is harmful and should be taken seriously. Some conflict is the discomfort of being known by people who are not there merely to soothe. The person in recovery must learn to distinguish between support that wounds and support that refuses to collude. The difference is visible in tone, pattern, respect, confidentiality, and whether the challenge points towards safety and responsibility.

When support disappoints, the immediate response should protect the day from all-or-nothing thinking. The person may need a short inner script: "This support did not land; I still need support." Or: "One missed reply is not the whole system." Or: "I am hurt, and I will use the next line." Such language is not fake calm. It is a guardrail against escalation. The disappointment can be addressed later. The craving, conflict, shame spiral, or risky hour may need attention now.

The support map should be updated after disappointment, but not in the heat of it. When steadier, the person can review what happened. Was the request clear? Was the person suited to that role? Was there a time frame? Was there a backup? Did the supporter violate trust, or merely lack the skill being asked of them? Does the relationship need a repair conversation, a narrower role, or removal from sensitive support? These questions turn hurt into design. They prevent the map from becoming either fantasy or rubble.

There is also a responsibility to supporters. People who help need boundaries, appreciation, and freedom to be unavailable. Recovery support should not quietly become emotional employment without consent. A supporter who misses a call may already feel guilty. A supporter who gives poor advice may be trying from limited knowledge. A supporter who sets a boundary may be protecting the relationship from resentment. Respecting these realities makes the system more sustainable. Dependence that cannot tolerate another person's limits eventually becomes another form of pressure.

The most resilient support systems make room for imperfection without making room for repeated harm. That distinction is essential. Imperfection is the late reply, the clumsy phrase, the tired tone, the misunderstood request that can be corrected. Harm is ridicule, coercion, betrayal of confidence, persistent shaming, manipulation, or repeated unreliability in a role that requires reliability. Imperfection may be repaired. Harm may require distance. A mature support map has enough honesty to tell the difference.

The switchboard appears one last time at the point of disappointment. A line fails, crackles, or carries the wrong voice. The answer is not to smash the whole board. Nor is it to keep using a broken line because loyalty demands it. The answer is to reroute, repair where possible, label the line accurately, and add another route before the next storm. Stability comes from systems because systems expect parts to fail sometimes. A system is not offended by contingency. It is built for it.

The forward test is what will happen after the next failed reply, awkward comment, or strained support conversation. Will disappointment become proof that help is pointless, or will it become information about the map? Will the person retreat into secrecy, or reach for the next line? Will they demand perfection from one person, or build a structure humane enough to include human limits? Support will disappoint at times. The question is whether recovery has to fall with it.

Chapter 10
Managing Conflict and Emotional Flooding

What if the most dangerous part of an argument is the moment when the body becomes certain before the mind has finished thinking? The voice rises. The room narrows. A sentence that would usually be edited arrives already sharpened. The phone feels like a weapon or an escape hatch. The other person's face becomes evidence for a whole story: they do not care, they are attacking, they never listen, this must be settled now. The argument is no longer only about the subject on the table. It has become weather inside the nervous system.

Flooding does not always look dramatic from the outside. Sometimes it looks like rapid speech, interrupting, pacing, repeating the same point with increasing force. Sometimes it looks like silence so dense it becomes punishment. Sometimes it looks like a sudden need to leave, slam a door, send a long message, prove a case, search for old evidence, or make the other person understand before anyone is allowed to rest. The body has moved into emergency, but the person may call it clarity. That is the danger.

Conflict becomes especially risky in recovery because it can create a tunnel between emotional pain and familiar relief. A hard exchange can produce shame, anger, loneliness, entitlement, fear, or the private conviction that old coping is justified. The person may not intend to act out, withdraw, lie, drink, scroll, binge, disappear, or escalate. They may simply be trying to get out of the unbearable state created by the argument. When flooding is mistaken for truth, relief begins to look like logic.

The central tension is that relationships need honest conflict, but recovery cannot afford unmanaged escalation. Avoiding every difficult conversation breeds resentment and secrecy. Staying in every conversation past the point of regulation breeds damage. The skill is not to become untouched by emotion or perfectly calm under pressure. The skill is to notice when the conversation has stopped being a place where thinking can happen. At that point, the task changes. It is no longer to win the point. It is to protect the relationship, the recovery, and the next hour from the flooded state.

The stakes are practical because flooded conflict keeps producing consequences after the argument ends. Words spoken in heat require repair. Silence used as punishment creates distance. A door slammed at night may become a craving in the morning. The person who stays too long in the courtroom of right and wrong may leave with no energy for sleep, food, honesty, or support. Conflict does not have to be catastrophic to become costly. A conversation mishandled at nine can still be shaping behaviour at midnight.

The deeper cost is that repeated flooding teaches both people to fear the relationship itself. One person anticipates attack; the other anticipates disappearance. A small disagreement begins to carry the memory of larger ones. The body starts responding to tone, timing, facial expression, and silence as though danger has already arrived. Recovery suffers because the relationship becomes less safe as a place for truth. People hide cravings, resentment, confusion, and needs when they believe every hard sentence may become a storm.

The work begins with recognising flooding as a state, not a command. Rapid speech, tunnel vision, the urge to escape, the need to keep arguing, or the sudden certainty that everything must be solved immediately are not instructions from wisdom; they are signals that capacity is narrowing. From there, the pause must become clean rather than evasive: a time-out with a return point, a purpose, and behaviour during the break that actually lowers risk. Repair then asks for less courtroom and more courage: naming one's part, recognising impact, and agreeing one changed behaviour that makes future conflict safer.

The motif is a red light. It is not an accusation against the driver. It is a signal that continuing at the same speed is unsafe. In conflict, the red light may be the repeated sentence, the rising volume, the hot face, the old urge to wound, the narrowing field of vision, or the thought that if the other person would only admit fault, everything would be fine. A red light does not settle who is right. It prevents collision long enough for direction to matter again.

The unresolved question is whether the next argument will be treated as a courtroom or as a condition to manage. When the body floods, will the conversation keep accelerating because the point feels urgent, or will someone recognise the red light before damage becomes the new subject? Recovery does not require conflict-free relationships. It requires relationships where the hard moments do not repeatedly become the doorway back to harm.

Noticing When You Are Flooded

In 1994, in Seattle, psychologist John Gottman and colleagues published *Why Marriages Succeed or Fail*, bringing wider public attention to the idea that conflict is not only a matter of words exchanged, but of bodies under strain. His laboratory work on couples placed careful attention on physiology: heart rate, stress response, and the way emotional arousal can narrow the capacity to listen, reason, and repair. The useful lesson is plain. In an argument, the body may enter the room before wisdom does.

Flooding often feels like truth because it arrives with force. The voice speeds up. The face grows hot. The chest tightens. The mind starts assembling evidence at alarming speed: every old slight, every unfair tone, every proof that the other person is wrong, unsafe, careless, or impossible. The body wants movement: speak, leave, win, send, prove, slam, disappear. The red light is flashing. The problem is that many people mistake it for a green one.

Emotional flooding is a state of overload in which the capacity for reflection, nuance, and proportion becomes temporarily reduced. It does not mean the feeling is fake. It means the feeling is not fit to govern the whole conversation. A person may be genuinely hurt and still be too flooded to speak well. They may have a legitimate point and still be in no condition to make it safely. They may need distance and still be tempted to use distance as punishment. Flooding does not erase responsibility. It changes the immediate task.

The first sign is often speed. Rapid speech, fast texting, interrupting, repeating the same point, searching for the perfect phrase that will finally force understanding: these are not merely communication habits. They may be signs that the nervous system has begun treating the conversation as threat. The person may believe they are clarifying, but the pace tells another story. When speech accelerates, listening usually contracts. The argument becomes less a dialogue than a vehicle gaining speed downhill.

Tunnel vision is another reliable signal. The other person becomes flattened into one role: attacker, betrayer, obstacle, judge, child, enemy, disappointment. The mind discards inconvenient evidence. It forgets affection, context, fatigue, history, complexity, or its own contribution. The whole relationship is briefly edited through the sentence that hurts most. Tunnel vision can feel morally clean because it removes ambiguity. Yet ambiguity is often where truth lives. When the mind has no room for complexity, the body may be too flooded for repair.

The urge to escape is not always wrong, but it must be read carefully. Sometimes leaving is the safest and wisest action, especially when a conversation has become harmful, threatening, or beyond ordinary regulation. Sometimes, however, the urge to escape is not a boundary but a reflex: vanish before being known, leave before apologising, shut the phone off before hearing impact, drive away before the body has had time to settle. The difference lies in the shape of the exit. A regulated pause has a return point or a safety plan. Flooded escape has fog.

There is also the urge to pursue. Some people flood by leaving; others flood by refusing to let anyone leave. They keep talking, texting, calling, questioning, or demanding resolution because uncertainty feels unbearable. They may call it commitment, honesty, or not going to bed angry. Yet insistence under flooding rarely produces repair. It produces fatigue, resentment, and statements both people later have to carry. The body is not seeking truth then; it is seeking relief from unresolved tension.

Neuroscientist Joseph LeDoux, whose work at New York University in the 1990s examined fear circuitry and the role of the amygdala, helped shape public understanding of how threat responses can operate quickly, before slower reflective processes have fully caught up. Everyday conflict is not the same as acute danger, and the brain should not be reduced to a simplistic slogan. Still, the practical lesson holds: under perceived threat, speed can outrun reflection. The person may feel certain because the body has mobilised, not because the whole situation has been accurately understood.

This distinction matters because flooded certainty can create real damage. A person may send the message that cannot be softened later. They may accuse from old wounds rather than present facts. They may make threats, reveal confidences, resurrect past failures, or use silence as a weapon. They may also turn the conflict inward, deciding they are unbearable, unlovable, or beyond repair, then seek old relief from the shame. In recovery, flooding is not only a relationship issue. It is a risk state.

The red light motif is useful because a red light does not decide the route. It simply says that continuing at the same speed is unsafe. When the body gives red-light signals, the immediate question is not "Who is right?" but "What will reduce harm right now?" This can feel frustrating, especially when the person believes their point is urgent. But urgency is not always accuracy. Sometimes the most responsible action is to protect the conversation from the state in which it is being held.

Flooding signs are personal. One person becomes louder; another becomes icy. One argues in paragraphs; another says nothing but begins planning escape. One feels heat in the face; another feels numbness, distance, or a strange calm that is really shutdown. One starts pacing; another starts cleaning, scrolling, or searching old messages for evidence. Recovery becomes more practical when the person knows their own signature. The question is not whether the sign looks dramatic to others. The question is whether it reliably precedes harm.

The body usually gives several small warnings before the larger one. Jaw tightness, clenched hands, shallow breathing, pressure behind the eyes, a need to stand up, an urge to interrupt, a sudden inability to take in new information, or the feeling that one more sentence must be said immediately. These signs may appear ordinary, but ordinary signs are often the most useful because they arrive early enough to matter. Waiting for full eruption is poor strategy. Earlier pauses prevent later apologies.

The cognitive signs are just as important. Watch for absolutes: always, never, everyone, no one, ruined, pointless, impossible. Watch for mind-reading: "They are doing this on purpose," "They do not care," "They know exactly how much this hurts." Watch for courtroom thinking: collecting evidence, preparing rebuttals, listening only for inconsistencies, treating the other person's feeling as a claim to defeat. These thoughts may contain fragments of truth, but under flooding they become overconfident. The mind is not investigating then. It is prosecuting.

There is a credible limitation in treating flooding as a state to manage. Some conflicts are not merely emotionally intense; they involve coercion, intimidation, abuse, harassment, or danger. In such circumstances, the issue is not simply that one person is flooded and needs a better pause. The issue may be safety, protection, outside support, or leaving the situation altogether. Language about regulation should never be used to minimise harm or pressure someone to remain available to an unsafe person. A red light can mean pause. It can also mean leave and seek help.

The reconciliation is to match the response to the risk. In ordinary conflict, noticing flooding may lead to a time-out, a change of room, a return point, a support message, food, water, movement, or sleep before repair. In unsafe conflict, noticing flooding and threat may require distance, professional guidance, emergency help, or a plan that prioritises safety over continued dialogue. The same skill begins both paths: read the state accurately. Do not let the intensity of the moment pretend to be the whole truth.

A practical flood marker should be specific enough to recognise in real time. "I am upset" is too broad. "I am talking faster, interrupting, and no longer hearing new information" is useful. "I need space" is incomplete. "I want to disappear and not return to this conversation" reveals risk. "I am angry" is ordinary. "I am searching for the cruel sentence that will make them understand" is a red light. Precision gives the person a chance to pause before the argument becomes a larger injury.

The same applies to shutdown. Flooding is not always loud. A person may become quiet because the system has gone past fight into freeze. They may nod while no longer processing, agree to end the discomfort, say "fine" while meaning nothing of the kind, or become so distant that the other person feels abandoned. This is still a state to manage, not a truth to obey. The silence may need protection, but it also needs a return route. Otherwise shutdown becomes another form of harm.

Noticing flooding also requires humility about memory. Arguments held under high arousal are often remembered through emotional emphasis rather than clean sequence. The sentence that hurt most becomes the whole conversation. The tone becomes the fact. The other person's worst moment becomes their entire character. Later repair is easier when the person can say, "I was flooded, so my memory may be narrowed." This does not invalidate their experience. It prevents their experience from becoming the only evidence allowed in the room.

A pause taken early is not avoidance when it has a purpose. The purpose is to restore enough capacity to hear, choose, and speak without creating new damage. The red light is not there to humiliate the driver; it is there because roads are shared. In conflict, the road is shared too. One person's flooded state affects the other person's nervous system, the relationship's safety, and the recovery conditions that follow. Pausing is not a defeat. It is a refusal to let overload write the script.

The person who learns their flooding signs begins to experience conflict differently. Not easily, not perfectly, but with more exits. They can feel the surge and name it. They can hear the speed in their voice. They can notice the courtroom opening in the mind. They can recognise the urge to flee or pursue as information rather than command. They may still be hurt. They may still need repair. But the state no longer has total authority.

The forward test is the next red light. It may appear as heat, speed, silence, certainty, escape, pursuit, or the sudden need to settle everything now. When it appears, will it be treated as proof that the argument must continue, or as evidence that the current state cannot be trusted with the next sentence? The answer may decide whether conflict becomes a doorway to repair, or another corridor back to damage.

Pausing Without Disappearing

On 1 September 1983, Korean Air Lines Flight 007 was shot down after straying into Soviet airspace, a tragedy later discussed in aviation and diplomatic history as a case shaped by pressure, misread signals, and catastrophic escalation. The scale is not comparable to a private argument at a kitchen table, and it should not be treated as though it were. Yet the human lesson is sober: when systems are under strain, continuing at speed can turn confusion into damage. A pause, when used properly, is not weakness. It is a break in acceleration.

Conflict has its own velocity. The first few sentences may still belong to the issue itself: money, timing, trust, tone, responsibility, unmet needs. Then the pace changes. The body heats. The mind begins collecting exhibits. The voice sharpens or disappears. The argument starts feeding on itself. At that point, staying in the conversation can begin to feel morally necessary, as though leaving would be cowardice, avoidance, or defeat. But some conversations are not improved by endurance. They are improved by a clean pause.

A clean pause is different from disappearance. Disappearance leaves the other person with uncertainty: when the conversation will resume, whether the relationship is being punished, whether the issue is being avoided, whether silence is being used as control. A clean pause gives the nervous system room without making the relationship pay for the room. It says, in plain language, "I am too flooded to speak well. I am taking a break, and I will return at a specific time." The sentence matters because it turns absence into structure.

The difference is visible in behaviour. Disappearing looks like leaving mid-argument without a return point, ignoring messages for hours or days, becoming unreachable while the other person grows more anxious, or using silence to make the other person suffer. Pausing looks like naming the state, setting a boundary, giving a return time, and using the break to become more capable of repair. One creates fog. The other creates a bridge. The pause is the bridge.

The first task is to say the pause before the body takes it by force. Many people wait until they are already shouting, crying, stonewalling, or preparing the sentence that will leave a mark. By then, the pause may arrive as a rupture. Earlier is cleaner. "I am getting flooded, and I do not want to make this worse." "I care about this conversation, but I cannot do it well right now." "I need twenty minutes, and I will come back at half past." The language does not need to be poetic. It needs to be usable while the pulse is up.

The return time is not a decorative detail. It is the part that protects the relationship from abandonment and protects recovery from secrecy. A vague "later" can become an escape hatch. A named return point gives the pause a boundary. It also asks the person pausing to remain accountable for re-entry, not simply for exit. If the return time needs to change, that change should be communicated. This is how a pause becomes trustworthy: it does not demand that the other person enjoy the break, but it gives them enough information not to be left in emotional freefall.

The work of John Gottman in Seattle, particularly his public writing in the 1990s on marital conflict and physiological flooding, is relevant here because it helped popularise the idea that some conflict becomes unproductive when arousal is too high. The point is not that every argument can be managed by technique, nor that relationships should avoid difficult truth. The point is more exact: when the body is flooded, the conversation often loses the conditions required for listening, proportion, and repair. A pause restores the conditions before asking the relationship to carry more weight.

What happens during the pause determines whether it is regulation or avoidance. A person who leaves the room and spends the break rehearsing grievances, drafting accusations, scrolling, drinking, driving angrily, contacting a third party to build a case, or replaying the other person's worst sentence may return more activated than before. The body may have left the argument, but the mind has stayed inside it. A good pause changes state. It lowers the heat. It reduces the chance that recovery will seek relief in impulsive coping.

The break should therefore contain actions that make the next conversation safer. The person might walk without composing a speech, drink water, eat if hunger is intensifying the mood, breathe slowly, sit somewhere neutral, write down the specific issue rather than the whole prosecution, contact a support person for accountability rather than ammunition, or move away from triggers that could turn the conflict into a larger setback. The question is not "How do I win the argument when I return?" It is "How do I return as someone capable of hearing and choosing?"

This distinction is especially important for people whose old coping begins after conflict. The pause can become a dangerous corridor if it is unstructured. A person may use the break to seek numbness, secrecy, revenge, compulsive checking, a risky purchase, old contacts, or a behaviour that converts relational pain into private relief. Then the pause has not protected recovery; it has merely moved the risk into another room. A recovery-friendly pause must include reduced access. If the phone is a trigger, it does not belong in the centre of the break. If a route is risky, the break should not travel that route. If isolation fuels the pattern, the pause should include a brief accountability signal.

A clean pause also avoids the courtroom. The purpose is not to prepare a closing argument. Courtroom thinking asks who is right, who started it, who contradicted themselves, which old example proves the larger charge. Repair thinking asks what state the person is in, what impact has already occurred, what the next useful sentence might be, and what one change could reduce harm. The pause should move the mind from courtroom to workshop. The workshop is where something can be fixed.

There is a credible limitation. Pausing is not always safe or sufficient. In relationships involving intimidation, coercive control, threats, stalking, violence, or serious emotional abuse, a "time-out" may be ignored, punished, or used against the person trying to take it. In such situations, the priority may be safety, outside support, professional guidance, or an exit plan rather than continued mutual conversation. It is also possible for someone to misuse "I need a pause" to dodge accountability indefinitely, especially when the same issue is repeatedly postponed and never repaired. A pause is only clean if it returns.

The reconciliation is to judge the pause by its function and follow-through. Does it reduce harm, or does it avoid responsibility? Does it include a return point, or does it create uncertainty? Does the person use the break to regulate, or to gather ammunition? Does the conversation resume with more clarity, or does the pause become another weapon? These questions keep the tool honest. A pause is not good because it is calm-sounding. It is good if it protects the conditions for truth.

The simplest pause scripts have three parts: the state, the break, and the return. "I am flooded. I am taking thirty minutes. I will come back at eight." "I am too angry to speak safely. I am going outside, and I will return after dinner." "I am shutting down and need a pause. I will text you at nine to restart." The exact words can change, but the structure should not vanish under stress. Naming the state reduces blame. Naming the break creates the boundary. Naming the return protects connection.

The pause must be proportionate. A mild irritation may need a breath, not a full evening of silence. A serious escalation may need more time and support. A conversation held late at night may need to resume the next day, especially if sleep deprivation is turning every sentence into a weapon. Proportion matters because overusing long pauses can create distance, while underusing pauses can create damage. The person learns through evidence: what length of break actually makes repair more possible?

Re-entry matters as much as exit. Returning from a pause is not the moment to dump the entire speech that was withheld. It is the moment to restart with a narrower aim. "I can talk now. The main thing I need to say is..." "I am calmer. I can hear your point about..." "I still disagree, but I can speak without shouting now." "My part is..." This kind of re-entry signals that the pause did its work. It also helps the other person trust future pauses because they are not left wondering whether distance means abandonment.

Sometimes the person who requested the pause will return and discover that the other person is still upset. This does not mean the pause failed. A pause is not a device for making another person comfortable on command. It is a way to prevent escalation and restore capacity. The other person may need time, reassurance, or their own regulation. The person returning should not demand gratitude for the break. They should simply keep the promise to return and speak with more care than would have been possible earlier.

Support can help during the pause, but it must be used cleanly. Contacting someone to say, "I am flooded and need help not escalating; please remind me to return at eight," is different from contacting someone to build a case against the other person. The first supports regulation. The second recruits an audience. A recovery-supportive pause may include an accountability text, a brief call with a trusted person, or a grounding action that keeps the person away from impulsive coping. It should not become a side trial.

There is humility in admitting that the pause is necessary. Many people cling to the idea that maturity means staying present at any cost. But presence without regulation can become harm. Mature presence sometimes means leaving briefly so that returning is possible. It means recognising the red light before the crash, not after. It means protecting the relationship from the version of oneself that is about to speak from panic, shame, rage, or exhaustion.

The bridge returns at the edge of the next argument. A bridge has two sides. It is not a place to live forever. The person crosses out of escalation and crosses back into responsibility. If they remain away, it becomes avoidance. If they never leave, it may become damage. The art is in the crossing: clear exit, regulated interval, faithful return. That rhythm can change how conflict feels inside a relationship. Not easy, not painless, but safer.

The forward test is whether the next pause will have a shape. When the voice rises, the mind narrows, and old coping starts to glow in the background, will the person vanish, keep arguing, or build the bridge in real time? The words may be simple: "I am flooded. I am pausing. I will return." The difficulty is not in the grammar. It is in keeping the promise.

Repairing After Arguments

In 1999, in Seattle, psychologists John Gottman and Nan Silver published *The Seven Principles for Making Marriage Work*, bringing the idea of "repair attempts" into wider public language. The term was simple, almost plain enough to be underestimated: a gesture, phrase, pause, apology, or acknowledgement that interrupts negative escalation and helps a relationship return to safer ground. Its importance was not that good relationships avoid conflict. They do not. Its importance was that conflict needs exits.

Arguments become dangerous when they create a closed room. Two people remain trapped with the same accusations, the same injuries, the same evidence, the same need to be vindicated. One person repeats the harm they felt; the other repeats the context they want recognised. The temperature rises. The facts become weapons. Then, after the argument ends, the body still carries the room: tight chest, sharpened memory, shame, resentment, craving, withdrawal, the private urge to find relief elsewhere. The conflict may be over, but the loop is not.

Repair is the act of opening the room after damage has occurred. It does not require pretending the argument was harmless. It does not ask either person to surrender the truth of their experience. It asks for a shift in purpose. The goal is no longer to prove the whole case. The goal is to make the relationship safer than it was at the hottest point of the exchange. Repair says, "Something happened between us, and we need to reduce the chance that it becomes the next trigger."

The first movement is naming one's part. This is not the same as accepting blame for everything. Many people resist repair because they think naming their part means forfeiting the broader issue. It does not. A person can still believe their concern was valid while acknowledging that they interrupted, shouted, mocked, disappeared, exaggerated, sent too many messages, used an old wound as evidence, refused to return after a pause, or kept arguing when the conversation had become flooded. "My concern was real, and my delivery caused harm" is a hard sentence because it refuses the false comfort of total innocence.

The courtroom is the enemy of repair. In the courtroom, every acknowledgement feels dangerous because it may be used as evidence by the other side. The mind becomes strategic: do not admit too much, prove the timeline, expose inconsistency, make the other person concede first. This may produce the satisfaction of winning a point, but it rarely restores safety. Recovery does not benefit from intimate cross-examination. A person can be technically correct and still make the relationship feel unsafe. The question is not only "Was my point defensible?" but "What did my behaviour create in the room?"

John Gottman's work is useful here because it separated conflict from contempt, defensiveness, stonewalling, and criticism as patterns that can corrode relationships over time. The lesson for recovery is not that every couple or family should fit neatly into one research model. The useful point is practical: the style of conflict matters. A hard conversation handled with some respect may leave both people tired but intact. A hard conversation handled with contempt, withdrawal, or pursuit can become a recovery risk because it leaves shame, anger, and isolation behind.

Naming one's part should be specific enough to be believable. "I am sorry for everything" sounds large, but it may be too vague to repair anything. "I kept talking over you after you asked for space" is usable. "I brought up old examples because I wanted to win" is usable. "I left without a return time, and that made the pause feel like punishment" is usable. The language should not become self-erasure. "I am a terrible person" does not help the other person feel safer. It may even ask them to comfort the person who caused the injury. Specific responsibility is cleaner.

The second movement is validating impact. This is where many repairs become fragile because people confuse validation with agreement. To validate impact is not to say the other person's interpretation is perfect, complete, or beyond question. It is to acknowledge that one's behaviour landed in a particular way and that the landing matters. "I can see that when I walked out without saying when I would return, you felt abandoned." "I understand that my tone made it harder for you to hear the apology." "I see that bringing up the past made the conversation feel unsafe." These sentences do not require self-betrayal. They require enough humility to notice the other person's experience.

Impact matters because relationships are lived through effects, not intentions alone. A person may not have meant to intimidate, dismiss, punish, shame, or overwhelm. Yet the other person may still have felt intimidated, dismissed, punished, shamed, or overwhelmed. Repair asks the person to become interested in that gap without instantly defending it. Intention belongs in the conversation, but not as a shield that blocks impact from being named. "That was not my intention" may be true; said too early, it often means, "Please stop telling me what it cost."

The third movement is agreeing one change. Not ten. Not a dramatic reinvention of personality. One change that can be observed the next time pressure rises. "When I need a pause, I will give a return time." "If the conversation happens after ten at night, we will postpone it." "I will not continue if I notice myself repeating the same accusation." "I will send one message, not six." "I will eat before we discuss difficult logistics." "I will ask for support after family conflict instead of carrying it silently." A repair without a behavioural change may soothe the moment while leaving the pattern untouched.

Harriet Lerner's 2017 book *Why Won't You Apologize?,* written from decades of clinical experience, is relevant because it treats apology not as self-abasement but as a disciplined relational act. One of its useful lessons is that genuine apology does not demand immediate forgiveness, nor does it use remorse to control the other person's response. Repair after arguments needs that same discipline. The person repairing cannot require the other person to soften instantly, accept the apology on schedule, or participate in a conversation they are not ready to have. Repair makes an offer; it does not seize the outcome.

The bridge motif fits repair because arguments often leave two people on opposite banks of the same event. Each can see their own side clearly. The bridge is not built from one person abandoning their side. It is built from specific planks: my part, your impact, one change. Without those planks, people shout across the water. With them, movement becomes possible. The bridge may be narrow at first. Trust often returns slowly. Still, a narrow bridge is better than two fortified banks.

There is a credible limitation. Not every argument should be repaired through mutual conversation. In relationships involving coercion, threats, intimidation, persistent manipulation, violence, stalking, or emotional abuse, the priority may be safety, distance, professional support, or legal protection rather than relational repair. The language of "repairing after arguments" should never be used to pressure someone into re-engaging with a person who is unsafe. Nor should it be used to make one person responsible for smoothing over another person's harmful behaviour. Repair is meaningful only where there is enough safety and accountability for it to function.

The reconciliation is to match repair to the relationship's reality. In a generally safe relationship, repair can be direct, collaborative, and spoken. In a strained but workable relationship, repair may require more structure, shorter conversations, support from a therapist or mediator, or written reflection before speech. In an unsafe relationship, repair may mean protecting oneself, documenting facts, seeking help, setting distance, or refusing further engagement. The aim is not perfect harmony. The aim is reduced harm and increased truth.

Avoiding courtroom debates is especially important after the initial repair begins. The person who has named their part may be tempted to add, "But you also..." before the acknowledgement has had time to land. The other person may respond with their own defensiveness. Both may be pulled back into trial mode. A useful repair keeps the first exchange narrow. One part. One impact. One change. Wider issues can be scheduled later, when the nervous system is not still standing among broken glass.

This does not mean one person's perspective disappears. If the argument involved real concerns on both sides, they may need attention. But repair asks for order. Stabilise the relationship enough to discuss the issue. Do not try to solve the issue while the relationship is still bleeding from the way it was discussed. A person may say, "I want to return to the original problem, but I need first to repair how I spoke last night." That sentence protects both truth and connection. It refuses to let process damage swallow content.

Recovery benefits from repair because unresolved conflict often becomes a private trigger. After an argument, the person may feel justified in secrecy, entitled to numbing, too ashamed to check in, too angry to sleep, or too hurt to maintain routines. Repair reduces the emotional residue that old patterns feed on. It does not erase discomfort, but it changes its shape. A repaired argument is less likely to become a long corridor towards craving, withdrawal, compulsive behaviour, or retaliation. Safety in relationship supports safety in behaviour.

The timing of repair matters. Too soon, and the person may still be flooded, defensive, or secretly trying to end their own discomfort. Too late, and silence may harden into distance or resentment. The right time is often after the body has settled enough to speak without making new damage, but before avoidance becomes its own message. This may require a brief statement first: "I want to repair this. I need to calm down so I can do it properly. I will come back after dinner." The promise to return is part of the repair before the repair itself.

A repair attempt may not be received as hoped. The other person may remain hurt, sceptical, tired, or unwilling to talk. That does not automatically mean repair has failed. It may mean the impact was larger than expected, the pattern has repeated too often, or the other person needs evidence over time. A clean repair does not demand that the injured person provide reassurance. It focuses on making the next right behaviour visible. If trust has been damaged by repetition, the change must become repeated too.

There is also the matter of self-repair after conflict. A person who has argued badly may need to speak to themselves in a way that prevents shame from becoming the next trigger. "I handled that poorly; I will repair and reduce risk" is different from "I am impossible." The first sentence leads towards action. The second may lead towards hiding. Self-repair is not self-excuse. It is the inner condition that allows outer repair to happen without collapse, over-apology, or defensive counterattack.

The strongest repairs are often brief. They do not replay the whole argument. They do not require perfect phrasing. They do not seek applause for insight. "I interrupted and raised my voice. I see that made you shut down. Next time I will pause when I hear myself speeding up." This is not the whole relationship. It is one bridge plank laid well. Another may be needed later. The discipline is to lay the plank rather than deliver a speech about architecture.

Repair also changes future conflict by building memory of return. If two people know that arguments can be followed by acknowledgement, impact, and changed behaviour, the relationship becomes less frightening. Difficult topics remain difficult, but they no longer carry the same threat of abandonment, escalation, or shame spiral. Recovery needs that sense of return. A person who trusts that conflict can be repaired is less likely to seek relief in secrecy when conflict happens.

The forward test is what will happen after the next argument, when the courtroom opens and both sides are invited to present their case. Will the person spend the evening proving their innocence, or will they build the bridge where it is most needed? My part. Your impact. One change. The words are simple. The difficulty is letting repair matter more than winning.

Chapter 11
Work, Money Worries, and Busy Seasons

What if the week that looks responsible from the outside is the same week that quietly weakens recovery from the inside? The calendar is full, the inbox keeps refilling, the bill is due, the family expects an answer, the shift pattern has changed, the deadline has moved closer, and the body has begun making bargains in the background. Sleep can wait. Food can be rough. The support call can be skipped once. The evening routine can return when the pressure lifts. Nothing has gone wrong yet. That is the danger.

Pressure has a talent for sounding reasonable. It does not usually announce, "I am about to make harmful coping more attractive." It speaks in practical sentences: this is temporary, this has to be done, people are depending on you, money matters, there is no room for weakness, recovery can be picked up properly next week. The lunch disappears first. Then the walk. Then the honest check-in. Then sleep becomes negotiable. By the time the old relief appears, it can look less like risk and more like compensation for endurance.

Work, money, and busy seasons expose a difficult truth: recovery cannot be built only for spacious days. It has to function when life is cramped, when privacy is limited, when the cost of stopping feels high, and when responsibility itself becomes the pressure point. The aim is not to pretend that pressure excuses harmful coping. It does not. But pressure does change what is realistic, and realism is one of recovery's most protective qualities. A plan that refuses to adjust during high-demand weeks may look principled while becoming useless.

The central tension is between responsibility and self-abandonment. Bills matter. Work matters. Study, caregiving, deadlines, travel, and family obligations matter. Yet recovery also matters, not as a private hobby to be resumed after everything else is handled, but as the condition that makes responsibility sustainable. A person cannot keep drawing from a system they never replenish. The overdraft eventually appears somewhere: in irritability, secrecy, cravings, avoidance, numbness, reckless spending, conflict, or the quiet belief that collapse has been earned.

The stakes are practical because busy seasons create predictable distortions. The person becomes too tired to notice early stress signals, too hurried to ask for support cleanly, too proud to simplify routines, and too anxious to protect boundaries. Money worries add another pressure: they can turn the future into a threat and the present into a place to escape. When the mind is preoccupied with cost, scarcity, unpaid obligations, or professional judgement, quick relief can feel like the only place where control still exists. The ledger is not only financial. It is bodily.

There is also the matter of privacy. Not every workplace, classroom, family system, or extended social circle deserves full access to a person's recovery. Disclosure can be wise in the right setting and costly in the wrong one. Some people need discreet tools: calendar blocks that protect support without explanation, neutral phrases that preserve energy, private check-ins sent between meetings, a prepared exit from a draining event, or a simple food-and-rest plan that no one else needs to understand. Privacy is not the same as secrecy. Secrecy hides risk. Privacy protects dignity while keeping support alive.

The path here begins with planning for pressure before pressure begins editing the rules. It then turns towards keeping recovery solid in places where over-sharing would be unwise or unsafe, without letting privacy become isolation. From there, attention moves to burnout, that flattened state where apathy, irritability, and numbness can make old coping seem less like a choice and more like gravity. The work is not to become endlessly resilient. It is to recognise when the load has changed and adjust before the crash writes the next decision.

The motif is the ledger. Not because recovery is a cold account, but because pressure keeps books whether or not the person reads them. Missed sleep is entered somewhere. Skipped food is entered somewhere. Repeated overextension, unspoken fear, unpaid emotional labour, late-night worry, and private shame all find their columns. Recovery asks for a different kind of accounting: what is being spent, what must be protected, what can be postponed, and what support needs to be moved closer before the balance turns dangerous.

The unresolved question is how the next high-pressure week will be handled before it starts making its own plan. Which routines will be simplified rather than abandoned? Which private supports will remain in place without unnecessary disclosure? Which warning signs will be treated as risk rather than weakness? Work, money, and busy seasons will keep making their claims. The test is whether recovery will remain on the ledger as a non-negotiable cost of staying well, or be treated as the first expense to cut.

Planning for High-Pressure Weeks

What if the week that threatens recovery is already visible on the calendar before it begins? The deadline sits there. The invoice date sits there. The family visit, the exam period, the annual review, the school holiday, the night shifts, the conference, the move, the court appointment, the medical result, the tax return, the double-booked Thursday. None of it is secret. Yet many people treat predictable pressure as though it were an ambush, then blame themselves for reacting like someone under siege.

A high-pressure week changes the terms of the day. It does not erase responsibility. It does not give permission to lie, lash out, disappear, overspend, drink, scroll until dawn, seek old relief, or neglect the people affected by one's choices. But it does change what is realistic. The polished routine may not fit. The long reflection may not happen. The extended social support call may need to become a short check-in. The nourishing meal may need to be simple rather than ideal. The question is not whether the week can be made easy. It cannot. The question is whether the week can be made survivable without letting pressure write the recovery plan.

Pressure makes its case through plausibility. "Just this week" sounds sensible. "I will return to my routine after Friday" sounds disciplined. "I do not have time to check in" sounds efficient. "I deserve something after all this" sounds human. Some of those sentences may contain a portion of truth, which is what makes them dangerous. High-pressure planning exists because the mind under strain is a talented barrister for exception. It can turn every stabilising action into an optional luxury and every risky shortcut into compensation. The ledger begins to tilt.

The first act of planning is to name the crunch times before they are dressed up as surprises. A person may already know that month-end reporting unsettles sleep, that exam weeks loosen food and movement, that family visits lead to late-night conflict, that travel creates anonymity, that financial deadlines sharpen shame, or that busy work seasons make support feel inconvenient. This is not pessimism. It is pattern recognition. A predictable pressure point deserves a prepared response. If the same bridge floods every winter, wisdom does not stand in the rain declaring itself shocked.

The work of Gary Klein, especially his 2007 writing on the "premortem" method in decision-making, offers a useful parallel. In organisational settings, a premortem asks people to imagine that a plan has failed and then identify what likely caused the failure before it happens. Recovery can use the same intellectual honesty without turning life into a corporate exercise. Before the demanding week begins, the person asks: if this week goes badly, where will it probably break? Sleep? Food? Contact? Boundaries? Spending? Secrecy? Late-night phone use? Conflict? The question is not gloomy. It is protective.

A high-pressure plan should simplify routines rather than abandon them. Abandonment says, "The week is too hard, so recovery will wait." Simplification says, "The week is hard, so recovery must be easier to reach." The difference is visible. The full morning routine becomes a five-minute start-up. The long meeting becomes a brief message sent from the car park. The full workout becomes a walk around the block. The carefully cooked dinner becomes prepared food that prevents hunger from turning into grievance. The evening review becomes one sentence: what is the next risk, and what protects it? Minimum is not neglect. It is load management.

The ledger motif matters because high-pressure weeks always spend something. They spend sleep, attention, patience, privacy, money, goodwill, and sometimes the body's basic reserves. A person who refuses to read the ledger may keep making withdrawals until the old coping looks like the only available credit. Planning does not remove the cost. It decides in advance which costs are acceptable and which are too dangerous. Losing some leisure may be unavoidable. Losing all contact may not be. Eating more simply may be realistic. Skipping food altogether may be a known risk. Shorter reflection may be fine. No honesty may not be.

Support should move closer during pressure, not farther away. This is where capable people often make the wrong calculation. They reduce contact because they are busy, embarrassed, or determined not to burden anyone. Then the week grows heavier and help becomes harder to request precisely when it is needed most. Increased support does not have to mean more drama. It may mean a short daily check-in, a planned call after a difficult meeting, an accountability text before the high-risk evening, a practical favour arranged in advance, or a trusted person told that the week carries more risk than usual. The signal can be simple. The timing is the point.

There is a useful lesson in the development of checklist culture after the Boeing Model 299 crash at Wright Field, Ohio, in October 1935. The aircraft was not abandoned because it was too complex; pilots developed checklists so that essential actions did not rely solely on memory under pressure. Recovery during busy seasons deserves the same humility. A person should not depend on remembering every stabiliser when the calendar is already crowded and the mind is full. Essential actions need to be externalised: visible notes, calendar blocks, prepared meals, drafted messages, alarms for shutdown, written limits for spending or availability, and clear decisions about which commitments will not be added.

Pre-deciding protective actions is different from making vague promises. "I will look after myself" is emotionally pleasant and operationally weak. "I will send a check-in before leaving work on Tuesday and Thursday" is clearer. "I will not schedule difficult conversations after nine at night during this week" is clearer. "I will keep the phone outside the bedroom while the deadline is active" is clearer. "I will prepare food before the late shift" is clearer. "I will not make discretionary purchases while anxious about money" is clearer. Specific decisions reduce the amount of negotiation available to pressure.

Money worries need special attention because they can make the future feel both urgent and hopeless. A bill, debt, unstable income, unexpected expense, or fear of professional failure can create a tight internal climate where relief becomes unusually persuasive. The risky behaviour may offer escape, control, status, numbness, or a momentary sense of abundance. Planning around money pressure is not financial advice; it is recovery protection. The person may need to identify what money stress tends to trigger: secrecy, avoidance, compulsive checking, risky spending, conflict, shame, or late-night bargaining. The recovery question is not "How do I solve every financial problem this week?" It is "How do I stop financial pressure from becoming a doorway to further harm?"

High-pressure weeks also create moral camouflage for boundary failures. People can ask more of a person precisely when that person has less to give. Work may ask for extra hours. Family may ask for emotional labour. Friends may ask for flexibility. The person may say yes automatically because the week already feels exceptional. But exceptional weeks require clearer limits, not fewer. "I cannot take that on this week." "I can do ten minutes, not an hour." "I will respond tomorrow." "I am unavailable after this time." Such phrases may feel blunt, but they protect the load-bearing parts of recovery from being quietly dismantled by other people's urgency.

There is a credible limitation. Some high-pressure weeks cannot be simplified enough. A person may be facing bereavement, precarious employment, unsafe housing, health demands, caregiving responsibilities, legal processes, or economic strain that exceeds ordinary planning. In those circumstances, the language of routine and support can sound thin, even insulting, if presented as sufficient. The plan must be scaled to reality. It may need professional help, formal leave, emergency support, material assistance, advocacy, workplace adjustments where appropriate, or the involvement of people who can share the load. A recovery plan should not ask private willpower to do the work of missing resources.

The reconciliation is to keep planning honest about both agency and constraint. Pressure does not excuse harmful coping, but neither should recovery language pretend that all pressure is equally manageable. The person asks what can be changed, what must be endured, what help is available, and what risk must be reduced even if the larger problem remains unsolved. That last part matters. A week can remain difficult and still be made less dangerous. A person can be under strain and still avoid adding secrecy, isolation, sleep loss, or access to known triggers. The plan does not need to solve the storm. It needs to keep the roof from lifting.

A high-pressure plan should identify the most likely rationalisations before they arrive. "I do not have time." "No one will know." "I have earned this." "I can miss one call." "I will sleep properly tomorrow." "It is only because this week is unusual." "I need relief before I can deal with anything." These sentences may appear in different forms, but they are often familiar. Writing them down in calmer time robs them of some of their later authority. When the phrase appears during the crunch, the person can recognise it as a known script rather than a fresh revelation.

The plan should also include a recovery floor for the week. Not the ideal. The floor. Food simple enough to happen. Sleep protected enough to prevent collapse. Movement small enough to remain plausible. Contact brief enough to send under pressure. Reduced access firm enough to matter. Boundaries clear enough not to require a debate. The recovery floor is not glamorous, but it gives the week a lower limit beneath which the person is not willing to sink without calling it risk. A floor prevents the dangerous freedom of having no minimum at all.

Review belongs after the pressure point, but it should be brief and factual. What protected the week? What broke first? Which rationalisation was most persuasive? Which support helped? Which commitment should have been cancelled earlier? Which part of the environment made the old behaviour too easy? This review should not become a trial. Its purpose is to improve the next high-pressure plan. Busy seasons repeat. Financial stress repeats. Family demands repeat. Academic and professional crunches repeat. The person who learns from one pressure cycle enters the next with more honest equipment.

The ledger returns at the end because recovery must remain on the books before the crisis makes cuts. A demanding week will always ask for something. The danger is letting it take from the very accounts that keep the person steady: sleep, food, contact, truth, boundaries, reduced access, and basic care. Planning is the act of deciding, before the pressure starts bargaining, which deposits must still be made. The forward test is simple and severe: when the next busy season appears on the calendar, will recovery be planned as part of the work, or treated as the first thing to be postponed until after the damage is done?

Keeping Recovery Private and Solid

What if the strongest recovery tool in a busy workplace is a calendar block that says nothing revealing at all? The meeting invite reads "personal appointment". The lunch break is protected without explanation. The phone reminder uses neutral wording. The message to a support person is sent from a quiet corridor, brief enough to avoid drama and honest enough to interrupt drift. No announcement is made. No performance occurs. The recovery remains alive, not because everyone has been told, but because the necessary structures have been kept in place.

Privacy is often misunderstood in recovery. Some people hear privacy and think secrecy. Others hear honesty and think exposure. The difference matters. Secrecy hides risk from the people or systems that need to know. Privacy protects dignity, safety, employment, family boundaries, and the right not to turn one's inner life into public property. A person can be private and well-supported. A person can disclose a great deal and still be dangerously alone. The test is not how much is shared. The test is whether the right support exists in the right places without unnecessary self-exposure.

Work and extended family can be complicated theatres for recovery. A manager may be kind but not entitled to the full history. A colleague may be friendly but unsafe with personal information. A relative may love deeply and still respond with panic, judgement, gossip, control, or advice that makes the situation heavier. The person may need time for appointments, check-ins, rest, meals, meetings, or boundaries, but not every setting deserves the story behind them. The ledger is delicate here: oversharing can spend energy that recovery needs elsewhere.

Discreet tools make privacy practical rather than fragile. A calendar block can protect a support call without inviting questions. A neutral phrase can end a conversation without exposing vulnerability: "I have another commitment." "I am not available then." "I need to step away for a few minutes." "I will come back to this tomorrow." A private check-in can happen without ceremony: one sentence naming the state, the risk, and the next action. These tools are not evasions. They are forms of self-respect. They prevent recovery from depending on the permission of people who do not need the whole map.

The boundary between privacy and secrecy is clearest in the after-effect. Privacy leaves the person steadier, more truthful with appropriate support, and less exposed to unnecessary scrutiny. Secrecy leaves the person more isolated, more defended, and more likely to conceal risk from those who could help. Privacy says, "This is not everyone's information." Secrecy says, "No one must know enough to interrupt me." The same action can serve either purpose. A closed office door before a check-in may be privacy. A locked emotional life where no one knows the risk is secrecy. The motive and the support around it decide the difference.

Sociologist Erving Goffman's 1963 book *Stigma: Notes on the Management of Spoiled Identity* remains useful because it gave careful attention to how people manage information about socially sensitive parts of themselves. The relevance is not theoretical decoration. People decide constantly who gets access to which truth, in which context, and at what cost. Recovery can carry stigma in certain workplaces, families, communities, and cultural settings. A mature approach does not demand reckless transparency. It asks for wise information management: enough truth in the right places to protect the person, not so much exposure in the wrong places that recovery becomes harder to sustain.

A calendar block is one of the simplest private structures because it gives time a visible boundary without making the reason visible. The title may be bland. The function is not. It protects the call, the meeting, the walk, the appointment, the meal, the shutdown ritual, the time needed after a difficult conversation, or the pause between work and home. The calendar becomes a quiet fence around a stabilising behaviour. Without that fence, recovery may be crowded out by the next request that looks urgent because nothing else has been named as unavailable.

There is a particular discipline in using neutral boundary phrases at work. Many people over-explain because they fear seeming unhelpful. They say more than is needed, then feel exposed and resentful. A neutral phrase keeps the boundary clean: "I cannot stay late tonight." "I can respond in the morning." "I have a prior commitment." "That deadline is not workable without moving something else." "I need ten minutes before I return to this." Such phrases do not reveal recovery, but they protect the conditions recovery requires. The sentence is ordinary. The purpose is serious.

Extended family often requires a different kind of privacy because the pressure may be emotional rather than procedural. A relative may ask why the person no longer stays late, drinks, lends money, answers every call, joins every argument, or attends every gathering. The temptation is to justify the change until everyone approves it. But approval is a poor foundation for recovery. A steadier phrase may be shorter: "I am keeping my evenings quieter." "That does not work for me now." "I am taking better care of my routines." "I am not discussing this tonight." The words need not persuade everyone. They need to protect the gate.

Private check-ins are the hidden wiring of this approach. The person does not need to announce to the office, family table, or group chat that pressure is rising. They do need a way to tell the right person before pressure becomes secrecy. A discreet message can be enough: "Long day, risk is higher, I am eating before I go home." "Family visit is getting sharp; I will leave before dinner if it escalates." "Money stress is making me want to avoid everything; please check in later." The message keeps recovery connected while keeping disclosure contained.

The motif here is the locked drawer. A locked drawer is not a lie. It holds what does not belong on every surface. But if the only copy of the safety plan is hidden there and never used, the drawer becomes a problem. Privacy should function like a well-kept drawer: accessible to the person, opened for the right purpose, closed to the wrong audience. The point is not to hide recovery from support. It is to keep recovery from being handled by every passer-by.

There is a credible limitation. Some workplaces, educational settings, or family contexts may require more direct disclosure for practical, medical, legal, safeguarding, or safety reasons. Some people may need formal accommodations, clinical letters, leave arrangements, emergency contacts, or trusted workplace allies. Others may be in environments where disclosure would create risk, discrimination, gossip, retaliation, or pressure. No single rule can decide this for every life. The safer principle is proportionality: share what is necessary with those who need it, and seek appropriate guidance when the stakes are formal or serious.

The reconciliation is to separate privacy from isolation. Isolation says, "I will handle this alone because disclosure is risky." Privacy says, "I will choose carefully who knows what, so I am not alone and not overexposed." That difference is practical. A person may keep recovery private at work while maintaining daily support elsewhere. They may avoid discussing recovery with extended family while having a therapist, peer group, sponsor, trusted friend, or other support contact who does know the relevant truth. The private life is not unsupported. It is selectively supported.

Energy is also part of the calculation. Explaining recovery repeatedly can be exhausting. It can invite debate, advice, curiosity, pity, admiration, or surveillance. Even positive reactions may become tiring if they require the person to manage another person's feelings about the disclosure. Protecting energy is not coldness. It is recovery maintenance. The person does not owe everyone a narrative just because they have made changes. Sometimes the cleanest answer is simply, "I am not available for that."

Discreet recovery also requires planning for visible changes. If someone stops attending certain events, leaves earlier, declines drinks, protects mornings, blocks time, or avoids specific conversations, others may notice. The person does not need to improvise a new explanation each time. Improvisation under social pressure often leads to oversharing or vague excuses that create further questions. Prepared language keeps the change ordinary: "I am keeping a different routine now." "Early mornings work better for me." "I am not drinking tonight." "I have plans after this." "I am heading off before I get too tired." These are complete sentences. They do not require a confession attached.

Workplace recovery tools should be especially boring. Boring is useful. The lunch break should happen before hunger sharpens judgement. The walk after a difficult meeting should be framed as a reset, not a revelation. The appointment should sit on the calendar like any other commitment. The private check-in should be sent before the commute becomes a craving corridor. The phone boundary should protect sleep without needing a speech about why sleep matters. The less theatrical the tool, the more likely it is to survive ordinary professional pressure.

Money worries complicate privacy because they often generate both shame and exposure. A person may not want colleagues, relatives, or friends to know the details of financial stress, yet the stress may be affecting sleep, mood, concentration, and old coping. Private and solid recovery does not require disclosing the figures to everyone. It may require telling one appropriate support person, using neutral boundaries around spending, avoiding risky financial decisions while flooded, and protecting routines when anxiety about money rises. The private truth still needs a route out of isolation.

The locked drawer returns as a test of access. Who has the key? If no one does, privacy may be hardening into secrecy. If everyone does, the person may be overexposed. The right people need enough information to help: a support person who knows the risk hours, a professional who knows the relevant history, a trusted friend who can ask direct questions, a peer who understands the pattern. The wrong people may receive only the boundary, not the backstory. This is not deception. It is stewardship.

For thoughtful professionals and students, there may be a fear that privacy looks inauthentic. The culture of disclosure can make restraint seem dishonest, as though every significant truth must be publicly named to be real. But authenticity is not the same as unrestricted access. A person can be authentic in action: keeping commitments, telling the truth where it matters, setting clean limits, asking for help from safe people, and not pretending to be available when they are not. Recovery can be deeply real without being widely discussed.

There is also a risk in making recovery too private within close relationships that genuinely need transparency. A partner, household member, or trusted support person may not need every thought, but they may need enough information to understand changes, risks, boundaries, or repair. "I am keeping this private" should not become a shield against accountability. Where one's behaviour affects others, privacy must be balanced with their legitimate need for honesty. A recovery life can have closed doors, but it should not contain hidden rooms where harm is stored.

The strongest private systems are quiet but testable. Did the calendar block hold? Did the check-in happen? Did the boundary phrase prevent overexposure? Did the person eat, pause, leave, rest, or contact support before the risky hour? Did privacy leave them more connected to the right people? These are the measures. Privacy is not successful because no one noticed anything. Privacy is successful when recovery remains protected without unnecessary disclosure.

The forward test is not whether every setting can be made understanding. Some will not be. The test is whether recovery can remain solid where disclosure is limited. When work presses, family asks, money worries tighten, or old shame suggests that privacy must mean handling everything alone, will the person keep the drawer locked to the wrong audience and open to the right support? Privacy and support can coexist, but only if both are designed rather than left to fear.

Preventing Burnout-Driven Slips

In May 2019, the World Health Organization included burnout in the eleventh revision of the *International Classification of*

Diseases as an occupational phenomenon, not as a medical diagnosis. The distinction matters. Burnout was described in relation to chronic workplace stress that has not been successfully managed, with features including exhaustion, mental distance or cynicism towards work, and reduced professional efficacy. The language is formal, but the lived experience is blunt: the person does not feel dramatic. They feel used up.

Burnout often enters recovery through a side door. It does not always announce itself as crisis, craving, or collapse. It may look like apathy: the message unanswered, the meal skipped, the meeting missed because nothing seems to matter enough. It may look like irritability: small requests landing like insults, ordinary delays feeling personal, the body braced against everyone. It may look like numbness: the person going through the motions with a blank interior, neither well nor obviously unwell, simply absent from themselves. The lights are on. Nobody is home.

That absence is dangerous because burnout can remove the emotional resistance that usually protects recovery. When a person is rested enough to care, they may remember consequences, relationships, values, and the effort already invested in steadiness. When they are depleted, those same truths can feel faint, abstract, almost embarrassing. The old relief does not need to sound persuasive in a grand way. It only needs to sound easier than caring. Burnout turns "I should not" into "I cannot be bothered not to."

The first task is to treat burnout as a risk factor rather than a moral failure. A burnt-out person may appear lazy to themselves because they no longer move with their usual force. They may appear selfish because they have less patience. They may appear unreliable because routines are slipping. But moralising depletion rarely restores capacity. It more often adds shame to exhaustion. The more useful question is not "What is wrong with me?" but "What has been spent, what is still being demanded, and what must be restored before I make the next week worse?"

The ledger returns here with unusual force. Burnout is what happens when withdrawals become a way of life and deposits are treated as optional. Sleep is borrowed from, then borrowed from again. Meals become irregular. Movement disappears. Enjoyment becomes vague. Support is postponed because there is no energy to explain. Work, caregiving, worry, study, financial strain, family obligations, and emotional labour keep presenting invoices. At first the person pays with effort. Then with irritation. Then with numbness. Eventually, old coping starts looking less like a choice and more like debt relief.

Christina Maslach, whose work on burnout became influential from the 1970s onward, helped shape the understanding of burnout as more than ordinary tiredness. Her research distinguished exhaustion, depersonalisation or cynicism, and reduced personal accomplishment as key dimensions of the burnout experience. The relevance for recovery is not academic decoration. It is practical. Burnout changes how people interpret themselves and others. Exhaustion says, "I have nothing left." Cynicism says, "None of this matters." Reduced efficacy says, "Nothing I do works anyway." Each sentence can weaken recovery if treated as truth rather than as a symptom of overload.

Apathy is one of the most overlooked warning signs because it can feel calm. Unlike anxiety or anger, it does not always demand attention. The person simply stops initiating. They no longer make the call. They no longer prepare food. They no longer care whether the room is chaotic, whether sleep is protected, whether the old app is back on the phone, whether the risky route is avoided. The danger of apathy is not noise; it is drift. It lets stabilisers fall away without the drama that might have triggered intervention.

Irritability is louder but often misread. The person believes the world has become more irritating, when their capacity has actually shrunk. A question feels like pressure. A colleague's delay feels like disrespect. A partner's need feels like an accusation. A child's noise, a friend's message, a family expectation, a bill, a small mistake: each lands on a nervous system already running on credit. Irritability under burnout is not an excuse for harm, but it is a signal. If read early, it can prompt rest, simplification, food, sleep, apology, reduced commitments, or a boundary. If defended, it becomes conflict, shame, and another reason to seek relief.

Numbness may be the most deceptive form because it appears to reduce pain. The person is no longer sharply distressed. They may even function better for a while, moving through tasks without much feeling. But numbness is not the same as regulation. It often blunts both warning and care. The person may take risks they would normally avoid because the internal alarm is muted. They may say yes to more because no clear no rises in the body. They may act out because consequence feels distant, as if it belongs to someone else. A numb state should not be trusted with high-risk decisions.

Responding early begins with rest, but rest must be understood honestly. Rest is not always a spa-like interval or a beautifully arranged evening. Sometimes it is cancelling the optional thing, leaving work on time where possible, not starting the argument, eating before answering messages, going to bed without solving the whole problem, declining a favour, sitting in silence, or allowing the body to stop being useful for a while. Rest can feel irresponsible to people who have built identity around endurance. Yet without rest, responsibility begins to degrade. The person still acts, but from a poorer and poorer state.

Reducing commitments is often the most direct intervention and the hardest to accept. Burnout thrives when every obligation insists on being essential. The person must therefore sort with unusual severity. What truly must be done? What can be delayed? What can be simplified? What can be delegated? What can be declined without catastrophe? What has been kept alive only because guilt keeps feeding it? The recovery question is not whether the person can force themselves through everything. They may be able to, briefly. The question is what they will become, and what they will reach for, after doing so.

Restoring basics is not a sentimental return to simplicity; it is risk management. Food, sleep, hydration, movement, daylight, contact, and reduced access to old coping are not glamorous, but burnout makes them load-bearing. A person who tries to solve burnout with insight while still skipping meals and sleeping badly is asking thought to do the work of physiology. A person who delays all support until they feel articulate enough to explain burnout may never make the call. The basics come first because they make higher-order responsibility possible.

Herbert Freudenberger's 1974 article "Staff Burn-Out" gave early professional language to the exhaustion and depletion seen among people in helping roles. Its context was specific, but the pattern has wider resonance: people who give, perform, care, strive, or endure beyond replenishment may eventually lose contact with the very values that animated their effort. Recovery must take this seriously. Burnout does not always mean a person does not care. It can mean they have cared, worked, worried, adapted, and tolerated beyond the point where caring can still feel like itself.

There is a credible limitation. Burnout is not always solvable through better personal habits. A person may be depleted because the workload is exploitative, the money is not enough, caregiving is relentless, housing is unstable, discrimination is present, management is unreasonable, or the household has no true rest built into it. Telling such a person merely to breathe, stretch, or sleep earlier can become a form of insult.

Individual recovery tools cannot substitute for safer conditions, fairer workloads, material support, medical care, advocacy, or structural change where those are needed.

The reconciliation is to work on two levels at once. The immediate level asks, "What reduces risk today?" Eat. Sleep as well as possible. Cancel what can be cancelled. Contact someone. Remove access to known triggers. Do not make big decisions from depletion. The larger level asks, "What keeps creating this depletion?" Work hours, money stress, emotional labour, lack of childcare, conflict, isolation, perfectionism, a role that no longer fits, or a system that benefits from the person's silence. The first level prevents further damage. The second level prevents the first from becoming a permanent emergency response.

Burnout-driven slips often happen when the person mistakes collapse for permission. "I have worked so hard." "I cannot care any more." "One night will not matter." "I need something." "Nobody sees how tired I am." These sentences deserve compassion, but they should not be allowed to run the evening. Beneath them is often a legitimate need for relief, recognition, rest, or support. The danger is choosing a form of relief that deepens the deficit. A recovery-friendly response asks what kind of relief will leave the person less damaged afterwards, not merely less conscious of pain for an hour.

The warning signs should be mapped before the crash. Some people know burnout has arrived when they stop replying to safe people. Others notice it when their room becomes chaotic, when they stop cooking, when they resent every request, when they lose interest in things that normally restore them, when their humour becomes cruel, when they spend money impulsively, when sleep becomes revenge rather than rest, or when they begin fantasising about disappearance. These are not quirks. They are dashboard lights. The person who has named them in advance can act before the engine smokes.

Shorter recoveries depend on earlier thresholds. Instead of waiting until everything has collapsed, the person can create a rule of response: when two or three burnout signals appear together, the routine moves to minimum mode. Not forever. Not as defeat. Minimum mode protects the basics while capacity is low. Fewer commitments. Simpler food. More sleep protection. Earlier support. Less exposure to risk. No optional arguments. Reduced access to behaviours that become tempting under numbness. The standard changes because the conditions have changed.

Support during burnout needs a different tone from support during acute panic. Panic may need containment. Burnout may need help reducing load. A useful message might say, "I am not in crisis, but I am depleted and starting to stop caring. Can you check that I eat and log off tonight?" Or: "I need help choosing what to cancel this week." Or: "I am too tired to explain fully, but I need accountability not to use burnout as an excuse for old behaviour." These requests are not dramatic. They are preventive.

Privacy may still matter. A person does not have to announce burnout at work or to extended family in order to protect recovery. They may use neutral boundaries: "I cannot take that on this week." "I need to move this to tomorrow." "I am at capacity." "I have a prior commitment." "I will respond after I have reviewed my workload." Such phrases can protect recovery without exposing private history. The point is not to make everyone understand. The point is to stop the ledger from being drained further by explanations that are not owed.

The recovery plan also has to watch for rebound behaviour after the pressure lifts. Many slips happen not in the middle of the busiest stretch, but immediately afterwards. The deadline passes. The guests leave. The shift run ends. The bill is paid or postponed. The body finally releases, and the mind searches for reward, numbness, intensity, or escape. This is a known danger point. The post-pressure window should be planned as deliberately as the pressure itself: food, sleep, low-risk relief, contact, and reduced access before celebration or collapse chooses the menu.

There is a quiet grief in recognising burnout early because it often reveals that the person cannot keep living at the pace they have normalised. Something may need to be reduced, renegotiated, delayed, shared, or refused. The person may have to disappoint someone, spend money differently, change expectations, seek help, speak to a manager, alter study habits, ask family to carry more, or admit that endurance has been mistaken for stability. This grief is not failure. It is the cost of returning to truth.

The ledger appears again at the point of decision. What is being spent that cannot keep being spent? What deposit is missing? Which commitment is quietly taking from sleep, food, contact, or honesty? Which old coping behaviour is presenting itself as compensation? Which crash could be shortened by acting while the signs are still mild? These are practical questions, but they have moral weight because they protect the person from becoming careless with themselves and others under the cover of exhaustion.

The forward test is whether burnout will be allowed to masquerade as character. When apathy says nothing matters, irritability says everyone is the problem, and numbness says old relief has no real cost, will the person believe those voices or read them as risk signals? The next slip may not begin with desire. It may begin with depletion. The task is to respond before the crash: rest, reduce, restore, reconnect, and keep recovery on the ledger even when the body claims it is too tired to care.

Chapter 12
Keeping It Steady Over Time

What if the real test of recovery is not whether it can save a hard day, but whether it can keep fitting a life that keeps changing? The tools that once felt essential may begin to feel awkward in the hand. A support routine that worked during an early fragile season may become too heavy for a fuller life. A boundary script that once protected a strained relationship may need to soften, sharpen, or move elsewhere. A plan built for one job, one home, one grief, one risk pattern, one version of the self, cannot be expected to remain perfect by loyalty alone.

There is a particular quiet danger in outgrowing a tool without noticing. The person keeps the old routine because it once helped, even as the shape of the day has changed around it. The meeting time no longer fits. The check-in has become automatic rather than honest. The craving plan still names a route no longer taken, while a new risk has appeared in a different hour. The notebook fills with the same phrases but less truth. Nothing dramatic has failed. The hinge simply needs oil.

Steadiness over time requires a different maturity from early recovery. At the beginning, urgency may do some of the organising. The danger is clear, the need for change is sharp, and the tools feel close to survival. Later, life may become calmer, larger, or more complex. Work changes. Relationships deepen or end. Money pressure rises or recedes. Health shifts. Confidence returns. Boredom appears. Meaning becomes possible again. The task is no longer only to prevent collapse, but to keep the recovery structure alive without letting it become either a museum or a prison.

The central tension is between consistency and adaptation. Too much change, and the plan becomes another form of impulsiveness: always being redesigned, never being trusted.

Too little change, and the plan becomes stale, unable to meet the actual life being lived. A steady recovery is not rigid. It is maintained. It has parts that remain load-bearing and parts that can be adjusted without drama. It asks for review rather than reinvention, small repairs rather than theatrical overhauls.

The stakes are high because neglect often disguises itself as confidence. The person feels better, so the check-ins loosen. The relationship improves, so boundaries become vague. The busy season passes, so support is allowed to drift. The old craving seems distant, so access is left unexamined. Progress is real, but progress can make risk harder to see. The danger is not that recovery has failed; the danger is that success can invite carelessness if it is not accompanied by maintenance.

There is also a deeper risk in letting recovery become the whole identity. A life built only around avoiding harm can become narrow, even if it is safer than before. Stability needs more than vigilance. It needs friendship, skill, humour, usefulness, rest, creativity, service, curiosity, and the ordinary pleasures that make quick relief less powerful. Recovery should protect the person's life, not replace it. A fuller self has more reasons to pause before returning to an old pattern, and more places to go when discomfort arrives.

The path now turns towards upkeep rather than rescue. The tools need regular review so that what is working can stay, what is fraying can be repaired, and what no longer fits can be retired without shame. Beyond the tools, the person has to become more than a recovery project, cultivating roles and sources of meaning that make steadiness worth protecting. Then the hard day protocol gathers the book's practical work into one repeatable sequence: minimum routines, craving responses, boundary language, and support contact held close enough to use when the mind is least inventive.

The motif is the house key. It is small, ordinary, and easy to misplace, but it gives access to the place where one can return. Recovery over time needs such keys: the question that opens an honest review, the routine that still works under pressure, the person who can be contacted before secrecy forms, the phrase that keeps a boundary from collapsing, the plan that can be run when the day is not noble. The key does not make life easy. It keeps return possible.

The unresolved question is whether the recovery system is still current enough to be trusted. Which tools have become ceremonial? Which supports have drifted out of use? Which parts of life are asking for more meaning, not more control? Which hard day is predictable enough that being surprised by it has become its own risk? Steadiness is not a finish line. It is the ongoing practice of keeping the key where the tired self can still find it.

Reviewing and Updating Your Tools

In 1986, at Bell Laboratories in New Jersey, statistician W. Edwards Deming published *Out of the Crisis*, a book that helped bring wider attention to continual improvement in systems, work, and quality. Its world was manufacturing, management, and measurement, not personal recovery. Yet one of its enduring lessons travels well: a system does not stay reliable because it was once designed with care. It stays reliable because someone keeps noticing what is working, what is drifting, and what needs adjustment before failure becomes the teacher.

Recovery tools deserve the same sober respect. A craving plan that saved an early evening six months ago may not fit a new job, a changed commute, a different relationship, a new money pressure, or a body that has begun asking for rest in another way. A support map may still contain the right names but the wrong roles. A boundary script may have worked with one person and become too blunt, too soft, or too exposed with another. A minimum viable day may have become either too ambitious for the life now being lived or too small for the strength now available. The key still exists, but the lock has changed.

The danger is not only neglect. It is loyalty to a version of recovery that no longer matches the day. People often keep old tools because they are grateful to them, ashamed to change them, or afraid that adjustment means regression. But a tool does not need to remain unchanged in order to remain honoured. The question is not whether it once mattered. The question is whether it still helps the tired self choose better when pressure rises. If it does, keep it close. If it does not, revise it without ceremony.

A monthly review is useful because it is frequent enough to catch drift and modest enough to avoid drama. It does not require a personal reinvention. It asks for a clear look at the working parts of the system: the check-ins, the food and sleep routines, the craving responses, the boundary phrases, the support contacts, the environmental barriers, the repair habits, the stress resets, the privacy tools, and the high-pressure week plan. The aim is maintenance, not confession. The person is not standing in court. They are standing in a workshop.

The workshop is the motif here because recovery over time is less like building a monument and more like maintaining something used every day. Hinges loosen. Handles stick. Shelves sag under a new weight. A tool that was once sharp becomes dull. None of this is scandalous. It is what happens to anything that serves a real life. The disciplined person does not curse the chair because a screw needs tightening. They fetch the right tool and make the small repair.

"What is working?" is the first question because recovery review should not begin with failure. Beginning only with what is wrong trains the mind to equate attention with accusation. What is working might be visible in small evidence: fewer late-night messages, earlier support contact, more reliable food, shorter arguments, quicker repair after slips, reduced secrecy around cravings, a phone boundary that actually protects sleep, a support person who asks direct questions without shaming, a calendar block that keeps recovery private and solid. These are not decorative successes. They are parts of the structure carrying weight.

"What is fraying?" is the second question, and it requires unusual honesty. Fraying is not the same as collapse. It is the early loosening that appears before a full failure. A check-in becomes automatic and less truthful. A support call keeps being postponed. A boundary phrase is still spoken, but with too much explanation afterwards. A minimum routine has begun collecting extra expectations until it no longer feels minimum. A private recovery tool has become secretive rather than discreet. A stress reset has drifted into a vague intention. Fraying is valuable because it gives warning without requiring catastrophe.

"What needs adjusting?" is the third question, and the answer should be deliberately small. Shame loves dramatic overhauls. So does excitement. Both can produce plans that are too elaborate to survive ordinary fatigue. A good adjustment changes one variable close to the problem. If evening cravings have returned, the adjustment may be moving the support text earlier, changing the route home, or removing access before the vulnerable hour. If arguments keep escalating, the adjustment may be a shorter pause script with a return time. If burnout signals are rising, the adjustment may be cancelling one recurring commitment rather than redesigning the whole life.

The history of aviation maintenance offers a useful parallel. Commercial aviation relies on scheduled inspection, not because aircraft are assumed to be failing constantly, but because wear is expected in complex systems that must remain safe. The lesson for recovery is not mechanical coldness. It is humility. Anything that carries load should be inspected before it breaks. A person who waits until every tool has failed before reviewing the plan has placed too much trust in crisis. Maintenance is quieter than rescue. It is also kinder.

There is a credible limitation. Some people can turn review into surveillance. They begin checking their recovery plan with such intensity that every ordinary fluctuation becomes evidence of danger. They revise too often, judge too quickly, and mistake anxiety for vigilance. The review becomes another way to stay preoccupied with recovery rather than living. This is not steadiness. It is a new form of pressure. A useful review should leave the person clearer and more capable, not more trapped inside analysis.

The reconciliation lies in proportion. The monthly review should be brief enough to complete without dread and practical enough to change behaviour. It should not ask for a full emotional autobiography. It should ask what evidence has appeared since the last review. Which tool was actually used under pressure? Which tool looked good on paper but stayed untouched? Which support contact helped? Which situation became riskier than expected? Which part of life has changed enough that the old plan no longer fits? Evidence keeps review from becoming mood-based judgement.

Life changes are the main reason tools need updating. A new job may alter the dangerous hour. A relationship may change the boundary problem. Recovery progress may make some supports less urgent and others more important. Parenthood, study, grief, illness, travel, money pressure, ageing, a move, a break-up, success, loneliness, or a new friendship can all change the shape of risk. Even good changes require review. A promotion can increase stress. A new relationship can unsettle routines. A calmer season can tempt the person to abandon tools too quickly. Stability does not remove the need for attention; it changes what attention should watch.

The review should treat success as information, not as permission to dismantle the system. When life has been steady for a while, it is tempting to assume the tools are no longer needed. Sometimes that is partly true. Some tools can be reduced, simplified, or retired. But the question should be tested carefully: is the person stable because the tool is unnecessary, or stable because the tool is working? Removing a load-bearing support too early can create the very wobble that later looks mysterious. The workshop asks the practical question: what happens if this piece is loosened?

Retiring a tool can be healthy when it is done honestly. A person may no longer need daily check-ins but may still need them during busy seasons. A craving plan may no longer need certain details but should still include a high-risk travel version. A support person may move from crisis contact to ordinary friend. A boundary may no longer need to be sharp in one relationship because trust has improved, while another relationship now needs clearer limits. Retirement should not mean erasure. It may mean moving the tool from daily use to the shelf marked "hard days".

Updating support requires particular care because people change too. A friend who was once available may now be overwhelmed. A partner may have become more skilled at listening. A recovery peer may no longer be the right person for accountability. A professional support arrangement may need review. A family member may remain loving but unreliable for certain kinds of truth. The map should be revised without melodrama. The purpose is not to rank people's worth. It is to match need with realistic function.

The same applies to language. Scripts can go stale. A phrase that once sounded firm may begin to sound rehearsed and defensive. Another may no longer fit because the relationship has matured. The monthly review can test phrases against recent use. Did "I need space" include a return point, or did it become disappearance? Did "I cannot take that on" hold, or did over-explanation reopen the gate? Did apology language name impact and change, or did shame turn it into self-erasure? Language is a tool. It needs sharpening.

A review should also examine the environment because surroundings quietly mutate. Apps return. Notifications creep back. The phone migrates to the bedside table. Cash becomes more available in a risky context. The kitchen stops supporting food. The commute changes. The calendar fills with commitments that leave no room for recovery. These changes may not feel like major decisions, but they alter the path of least resistance. Environment is often where recovery drifts before the person's values have changed at all.

Small updates protect continuity because they avoid the drama of starting over. Starting over can feel intoxicating after a scare: new notebook, new rules, new identity, new promises. But repeated starting over can become its own instability. Maintenance is less exciting and more trustworthy. It says, "The plan is mostly sound; this part needs repair." That sentence builds confidence. It teaches the person that fraying does not require collapse, and adjustment does not require shame.

There are times, however, when a larger overhaul is necessary. A pattern has become unsafe. A support system has failed repeatedly. A living situation has changed. A relapse or serious setback has revealed that the current structure cannot carry the load. In those moments, a small adjustment may be too polite. The person may need more formal support, stronger boundaries, a different environment, professional help, or a new level of accountability. The wisdom is in matching the scale of response to the evidence. Small repairs for ordinary wear. Larger redesign when the structure itself is no longer safe.

The monthly review should end with one chosen update, not a pile of intentions. One change is easier to remember and easier to test. Move the check-in. Shorten the evening routine. Add a backup support contact. Prepare food before the high-risk day. Remove an app again. Clarify a boundary phrase. Schedule a private appointment block. Change the post-conflict pause. Set a review of money stress before it becomes avoidance. A single update made well is more powerful than ten vows made in a rush.

The workshop returns at the close because the person maintaining recovery over time must become less afraid of tools needing care. A loose hinge is not a failed house. A dull blade is not a failed craft. A support plan that needs revision is not proof that recovery is weak. It is proof that recovery belongs to a living person, and living persons change. The work is to keep the system current enough that it can still be found by the tired self.

The forward test is whether review will happen before the next breakdown forces it. What is working now? What is fraying quietly? What needs one small adjustment before pressure finds the gap? The answers may be ordinary, even dull. That is their value. Steady recovery is often preserved not by dramatic recommitment, but by the modest act of tightening what has loosened before the whole structure complains.

Building Identity Beyond Recovery

In 1946, in Vienna, neurologist and psychiatrist Viktor Frankl published *Man's Search for Meaning*, a work shaped by extreme human suffering and by his conviction that people can endure more when life still contains purpose. Recovery is not the same as Frankl's historical context, and it should not borrow suffering that does not belong to it. Yet one insight travels carefully: a person needs more than restraint to stay alive to their own life. They need reasons to return.

A life organised only around avoiding harm can become safer and still remain too narrow. The person has routines, check-ins, scripts, plans, support contacts, and strategies for cravings, conflict, shame, stress, and setbacks. These matter. They may have saved days that once would have collapsed. But if recovery becomes the only story, every hour can start to feel like a risk assessment. The person becomes excellent at not falling, yet unsure what they are standing for. Stability needs a wider room.

This is the quiet danger of making recovery the whole identity. At first, the focus is necessary. The old pattern has to be interrupted. Safety has to be protected. Relationships may need repair. The body needs steadier care. The environment has to be rearranged. But over time, a person who is only "in recovery" may begin to feel trapped inside vigilance. They may know every danger sign and still feel unclaimed by ordinary joy. They may be technically safe and emotionally underfed.

Identity beyond recovery does not mean recovery becomes less important. It means recovery is allowed to do its proper work: protecting the conditions under which a fuller life can be built. A person is not only someone who avoids relapse, manages urges, repairs arguments, and maintains boundaries. They may also be a friend, parent, sibling, student, worker, artist, neighbour, gardener, reader, mentor, volunteer, craftsperson, athlete, cook, believer, sceptic, citizen, learner, or quiet keeper of a small private pleasure. These roles are not decorations. They give the self more places to live.

Friendship is one of the first places where identity can widen. Recovery relationships are important because they speak the language of risk and repair, but a person also needs relationships where the conversation is not always about recovery. A walk with a friend, a shared meal, a regular game, a book discussed badly and with affection, a message about nothing urgent: these ordinary forms of contact remind the person that they are not merely a problem under management. They are company. They can laugh without performing wellness. They can belong without making a disclosure.

Skills offer another form of expansion because they restore agency without demanding drama. Learning an instrument, cooking properly, repairing a bicycle, practising a language, swimming, writing, drawing, coding, growing herbs, joining a choir, taking photographs, studying local history, building furniture, or returning to a neglected craft all create a relationship with progress that is not moralised in the same way recovery can become. A skill allows for clumsiness. It measures attention, practice, patience, and curiosity. It gives the hands something to do besides reach for old relief.

Creativity matters for similar reasons, though it should not be romanticised. Not everyone wants to paint, write poems, compose music, or call themselves creative. Creativity can be as simple as arranging a room with care, making a meal from what is available, telling a story to a child, planting a window box, solving a practical problem, or noticing a sentence worth keeping. The value lies in making rather than consuming, shaping rather than merely escaping. Quick relief often narrows the world to one need. Creativity widens it by asking, "What can be made here?"

Service can be stabilising when it is grounded rather than compulsive. Helping others can give a person dignity, perspective, and connection. It can remind them that their experience, once handled with humility, may become useful. But service has a shadow. It can become over-giving, people-pleasing, avoidance of one's own pain, or a way to earn worth through exhaustion. Recovery-friendly service has boundaries. It does not require secrecy, sleep loss, resentment, or neglect of the basics. It is chosen, limited, and honest. It gives without disappearing.

Rest deserves to be named as part of identity, not merely as a recovery tool. Many capable people treat rest as an emergency repair, something used only after depletion has become undeniable. But a fuller life includes rest as a legitimate human role: the person who sits in the garden without producing anything, who reads without extracting a lesson, who sleeps because the body is not a machine, who takes quiet seriously. Rest softens the tyranny of usefulness. It teaches the nervous system that stillness need not be a prelude to danger or collapse.

The work of psychiatrist Robert Butler, who coined the term "life review" in the 1960s while studying ageing and meaning, offers a useful lens here. Human beings do not experience themselves only through present habits; they live through stories about what has mattered, what has been lost, what has been repaired, and what remains possible. Recovery, if it becomes too narrow, can trap the person in a story of risk. A wider identity restores narrative range. The person is not only the one who fell, struggled, stopped, repaired, or returned. They are also the one who learns, contributes, enjoys, creates, loves, rests, and begins again in forms that are not always dramatic.

Meaning reduces the pull of quick relief because it gives discomfort competition. This does not mean a meaningful life eliminates cravings, stress, grief, boredom, anger, loneliness, or shame. It does not. But when life contains roles and joys worth protecting, old relief has to argue against more evidence. The urge must speak in a room where friendship, skill, service, sleep, humour, trust, and future plans are also present. A thin life makes quick relief look larger. A fuller life restores proportion.

The house key returns here as a practical symbol. Recovery tools are keys back to steadiness, but identity beyond recovery is the house itself: the rooms where a person studies, cooks, rests, forgives, practises, fails at a hobby, keeps a promise, listens to music, visits a friend, tends a plant, writes a letter, or watches the evening without needing to alter it. The key matters because return matters. But a person does not live in the key. They live in the place it opens.

There is a credible limitation. A person should not be rushed towards meaning as if meaning were a cure for early instability, acute risk, grief, trauma, unsafe conditions, or serious mental distress. "Build a fuller life" can become cruel if the person first needs safety, treatment, housing, sleep, protection, or basic material support. Some seasons are survival seasons. In those seasons, the task may be to keep the floor underfoot, not to cultivate a rich identity. Meaning cannot be forced like a productivity target.

The reconciliation is to let identity widen at the pace of capacity. A fuller life does not have to be built through grand gestures. It may begin with one recurring friendship, one skill practised badly, one small act of service, one place where the person is not required to explain recovery, one form of rest that is not secretly another task. The expansion should support stability rather than compete with it. If the new activity causes secrecy, exhaustion, financial strain, resentment, or exposure to known triggers, it needs adjustment. Meaning should make recovery more liveable, not more precarious.

There is also the danger of replacing one consuming identity with another. A person may leave behind the identity of crisis and adopt the identity of relentless self-improvement. They become the disciplined one, the healed one, the inspirational one, the person with a perfect morning routine and flawless boundaries. This can look healthier while still being narrow. A real life includes inconsistency, boredom, awkwardness, humour, ordinary errands, mixed motives, and days that do not turn into lessons. Identity beyond recovery should make the person more human, not more polished.

A fuller identity also changes how setbacks are held. When recovery is the entire self, a setback can feel like annihilation. If the only identity is "someone who is doing recovery well," then a slip, argument, craving, or boundary collapse seems to destroy the whole person. But if the self has many rooms, the event remains serious without becoming total. The person is still accountable, but not erased. They are still a friend, learner, worker, neighbour, parent, reader, musician, cook, or volunteer. The wider life helps prevent one hard moment from swallowing the whole identity.

The work should include joy that is not merely relief from distress. Relief says, "The pressure has stopped." Joy says, "Something in life is worth being present for." The difference is subtle but important. A person can seek relief endlessly and still feel undernourished. Joy may be quieter: the satisfaction of improving at a skill, the warmth of being expected by a friend, the pleasure of a clean room, the absurdity of a shared joke, the calm of a familiar walk, the dignity of helping without rescuing, the deep permission of rest. Joy does not need to be spectacular to be protective.

Meaning also introduces time. Quick relief collapses time into now. It says the next ten minutes are all that matter. A fuller life stretches time again. The person remembers the class they want to attend, the friend they promised to meet, the craft they are improving, the person they want to be trustworthy for, the morning they do not want to poison, the body they are trying to treat with less contempt. Future does not have to be grand to matter. It only has to be real enough to interrupt the spell of immediacy.

The social dimension is crucial. Identity beyond recovery should not become another solitary project. Many people in recovery already know how to monitor themselves. They may be less practised at being ordinary with others. A community that knows them only through struggle may be necessary but incomplete. A community that knows them through shared interest, contribution, play, learning, or service gives the self different mirrors. It becomes possible to be recognised for more than survival.

There is a kind of humility in allowing recovery to become less central without becoming less respected. The person still keeps the tools current. They still review risk, maintain support, protect sleep, reduce access, and tell the truth early. But the tools serve a life that has grown larger than the toolkit. The aim is not to graduate into invulnerability. It is to live with enough meaning that coping is no longer the main event.

The forward test is not whether recovery can be left behind. That question is too simple. The sharper question is whether recovery is protecting a life broad enough to make steadiness worth the effort. What roles, joys, skills, friendships, services, and forms of rest are asking to be cultivated? Which part of the self has been waiting outside the recovery room, not because recovery is unimportant, but because it has done enough good work to open the door?

Planning for the Next Hard Day

On 15 January 2009, after US Airways Flight 1549 lost engine power over New York, Captain Chesley Sullenberger and First Officer Jeffrey Skiles did not have time to become different people. They had time to run what training had made available under pressure: aviate, decide, communicate, act. The event belongs to aviation, not private recovery, and the scale should not be confused. Yet the principle is exact: when the hard moment arrives, the usable plan is the one close enough to reach before panic begins writing its own.

A hard day in recovery rarely arrives with theatrical warning. It may begin with poor sleep, a curt message, a skipped meal, a money worry, a difficult conversation, a craving that rises in the wrong hour, or the sudden sense that everything is too much and not enough at once. The mind becomes persuasive.

It argues for postponing support, loosening boundaries, delaying food, answering while angry, walking the risky route, keeping the phone close, or treating the old relief as a private exception. The day has its own weather. Carry a key.

The aim is not to predict every challenge. That ambition belongs to anxiety, not wisdom. A hard day protocol exists because difficulty has patterns even when details vary. The names may change, the setting may shift, the trigger may wear different clothes, but the first tasks remain familiar: keep the body regulated enough to think, reduce access to old behaviour, use a short craving response, speak boundaries before resentment takes command, contact support before secrecy forms, and choose repair over drama if damage occurs. The plan is not a cage. It is a route home.

The first movement of a hard day protocol is recognition. The person must know when the plan has been activated. Without an activation point, the protocol remains a good idea waiting politely in the background while the old pattern moves quickly. The signal might be a combination of signs: poor sleep, irritability, isolation, craving, skipped food, shame, conflict, financial panic, secrecy, numbness, or the phrase "I do not care" appearing with unusual force. One sign may be ordinary. Several together deserve respect. The red light does not settle the whole matter. It says the day needs a different operating mode.

That operating mode begins with the minimum routine. Minimum does not mean careless; it means stripped to the behaviours most likely to prevent further drift. Eat something steady. Drink water. Move the body briefly. Protect the next sleep opportunity. Check the immediate environment for risk. Do not make dramatic decisions from depletion. These actions may sound too small for an intelligent person's distress, but distress does not become safer because the analysis is sophisticated. A body that has not eaten and a mind that has not slept will often produce conclusions that feel profound while being mostly exhausted.

The craving response belongs near the beginning because hard days often make quick relief seem rational. The plan should not require a deep internal debate. Delay the decision. Change location. Do one competing action. Reduce access. Send the prepared message. The old behaviour gains power from speed, privacy, and proximity; the protocol interrupts all three. A ten-minute delay, a walk outside, a glass of water, a moved phone, a blocked app, a different route, a support text: none is heroic. Each makes the harmful action less automatic. The wave may still rise, but it no longer receives a clear road.

Alan Marlatt's relapse prevention work at the University of Washington in the late twentieth century remains useful because it treated high-risk situations as patterns with antecedents, expectations, coping responses, and aftermaths. The practical lesson is not to analyse endlessly while in danger. It is to recognise that a hard day has structure. If the structure is known, another structure can be placed in its path. The person does not need to wait until they feel brave. They need a sequence that can begin while they are tired, ashamed, angry, lonely, or unconvinced.

Boundaries are part of the hard day protocol because many difficult days become worse through contact that should have been limited earlier. A hard day is not the time for circular arguments, late-night emotional trials, heroic rescuing, over-explaining, or saying yes from guilt. The person may need short phrases ready before the pressure arrives: "I cannot discuss this tonight." "I need a pause and will return tomorrow." "I am not available for that." "I will not continue while we are shouting." Such phrases protect recovery from being negotiated away in the name of keeping peace. A boundary is often the difference between a hard day and a damaging night.

Support contact should also be pre-decided. On a hard day, the question "Who should I tell?" can be enough to delay the telling until secrecy has settled in. The protocol names the person or line for listening, the person for accountability, the person for practical help, and the route for serious risk. It also names the message. "This is a hard day. I am not in immediate danger, but my risk is higher. I am eating, reducing access, and need a check-in later." Or: "I am craving and near access. Please ask me in ten minutes whether I have moved away." Specific support turns distress into a task another person can understand.

There is a credible limitation. Some hard days exceed ordinary self-management. If the person is unsafe, being threatened, at risk of immediate serious harm, or unable to reduce danger through the usual plan, the protocol must move beyond private tools into appropriate urgent support. A hard day plan should not flatter self-sufficiency when the situation requires help. The purpose is steadiness, not pride. A wise plan knows when it has reached the edge of its own usefulness.

The reconciliation is to build a protocol with levels. The ordinary hard day calls for minimum routine, craving response, boundary language, support contact, and reduced access. The severe hard day calls for stronger outside help, more distance from risk, and fewer optional demands. The post-slip hard day calls for stabilisation before analysis: safety, food, water, rest, contact, and a return point for repair. The person should not have to invent the level while flooded. The plan should already say what changes when the risk changes.

A hard day protocol should include what to cancel. This is where recovery becomes practical rather than ornamental. Optional arguments can be cancelled. Non-essential errands can be moved. Draining social plans can be shortened. Risky routes can be avoided. Unnecessary spending decisions can wait. Late-night messages can be left until morning. The person may still have duties that cannot be abandoned:

children, work, medical appointments, caregiving, study, bills, urgent responsibilities. But even then, the day can be simplified. The question is not "How do I escape life?" It is "What can be removed so recovery does not have to carry avoidable weight?"

The house key returns as the image of the plan. A key is not impressive. It does not explain the house, decorate the doorway, or prove virtue. It simply opens what must be opened when the person is standing outside, tired and wanting entry. The hard day protocol should be like that: small enough to carry, familiar enough to use without ceremony, and reliable enough that the tired self does not have to bargain for shelter. If the plan is too elaborate, it will be admired and abandoned. If it is too vague, it will fail at the door.

The protocol also needs a closing rhythm. A hard day should not simply dissolve into sleep or secrecy. Before the day ends, the person can ask a few factual questions: Did I eat? Did I reduce access? Did I send the message? Did I avoid the riskiest conversation or pause it cleanly? Did I protect sleep? Did I repair what needed immediate repair, or set a return point? Did I keep one event from becoming a week? This is not a moral trial. It is a handover note to tomorrow.

There will be imperfect hard days. The plan may be started late. A support person may not answer. The boundary may be clumsy. The craving response may reduce harm without preventing every slip. The minimum routine may be thinner than hoped. This does not make the protocol useless. A plan that shortens a spiral has done serious work. A plan that prevents one lie, one late-night escalation, one risky route, one missed meal, one isolated craving, or one week of collapse has changed the future in a modest but real way.

The final test is not whether life can be made free of hard days. It cannot. The test is whether the next hard day will still be allowed to act like a surprise. When the signs gather, will the person wait for motivation, clarity, or crisis, or will they reach for the key: minimum routine, delay and reduce access, use the boundary sentence, contact support, cancel what worsens risk, protect sleep, repair without drama? The hard day will make its argument. The question is whether the plan will already be in the hand.

About the Author

Priya Dhanvel writes for people who are trying to change without turning their lives into a spectacle. Her work is grounded in the everyday reality that recovery is rarely a straight line: it is shaped by fatigue, relationships, work demands, and the private stories we tell ourselves when no one is watching. She is interested in the small, repeatable choices that make stability more likely, especially on ordinary days that do not feel inspirational.

With a practical, compassionate editorial voice, Priya focuses on tools that are simple enough to use under stress: brief check-ins, clear boundaries, and repair after setbacks. She is drawn to approaches that reduce shame and increase responsibility at the same time, because both are needed for change that lasts. Her aim is to help readers build supportive systems rather than rely on mood, motivation, or perfect circumstances.

A recurring thread in her perspective is how communities have always passed down steadying practices in hard times: shared meals, daily rituals, and the kind of plainspoken encouragement that keeps people moving. In an era that often rewards extremes and public reinvention, Priya advocates for quieter strength: doing the next right thing, telling the truth sooner, and returning to your plan without drama.

www.ingramcontent.com/pod-product-compliance
Lightning Source LLC
LaVergne TN
LVHW100727061126
851857LV00011B/425
* 9 7 8 9 3 0 9 3 3 3 0 1 9 *